American Ideologies

American Ideologies

The Competing Political Beliefs of the 1970s

SECOND EDITION

KENNETH M. DOLBEARE
and
PATRICIA DOLBEARE
with
JANE HADLEY

a MARKHAM book from
Rand McNally College Publishing Company / Chicago

MARKHAM POLITICAL SCIENCE SERIES
Aaron Wildavsky, Editor

Current printing   (last digit)
15   14   13   12   11   10   9   8   7   6   5   4   3

Acknowledgments

This brief analysis is intended for the college-level introductory course in American politics or American social problems. We think it is past time for today's contending ideologies—particularly those change-seeking ideologies that have injected such a new and dangerous dynamic into American politics—to be taken seriously as subjects for analysis in such courses. Each of us has sought to do so in our respective political science and sociology courses, but have found original materials inefficient for classroom use and existing secondary sources lacking in depth and comprehensiveness. Nevertheless, both the idea and the impetus for this book came from John Applegath of Markham Publishing Company. If it does serve a useful purpose for teachers and students, despite its brevity, his perceptive capitalism may be credited.

In a more basic sense, our interest in the characteristics of American political ideas is the product of several years' exchange with students and other friends at the University of Wisconsin and the University of Washington. They are too numerous to name, but we owe this book primarily to them, and we are both glad and anxious to acknowledge our debt to them. Several experienced teachers read the first edition of this manuscript and contributed significantly to its improvement. We are grateful to Mark Greenside of Merritt College, Oakland, California; to Harvey M. Karlen of Wright Junior College, Chicago; Thomas Morrison of California State College, Hayward; and Jon Schiller of the University of California, Berkeley, for their many helpful comments. Perhaps necessarily, a brief analysis of complex ideologies cannot completely satisfy anyone, and we must take full responsibility for defects in our presentation. We invite reactions from readers who want to take issue with us or suggest further extensions and implications of our analysis. Many useful suggestions in regard to the first edition resulted in substantial reconstruction and major additions to the chapters in Part 2. We hope it is a much improved book.

Contents

1

The Role of Ideology
in the United States

Not long ago, American social scientists and journalists were proclaiming the "end of ideology" and the broad consensus of all Americans. In their view, all basic needs had been satisfied, conflicts were readily compromised, and challenges to the character of the American social, economic, and political systems had ceased. Two important lessons may be drawn from their mistake. First and obvious, they must have been looking in the wrong place, at the wrong things, with the wrong kinds of antenna. Fundamental economic and social problems, where they exist, must sooner or later manifest themselves—frequently in the form of the social fragmentation, conflict, and sometimes desperate solution-seeking that we are experiencing in the United States today.

The second lesson may be even more important. A dominant ideology may be so pervasive, so all-encompassing, that it is not even perceived by observers and analysts. Or the observers and analysts may be more or less willing parties to the routine task of using that ideology for social control purposes—in this case, for the purpose of persuading others that the structures, policies, and practices (and the results thereof) of ruling elites were inevitable, desirable, and widely accepted by all strata of the population.

We shall try to use these lessons to avoid the mistakes of the "end of ideology" thesis as well as of its antithesis—overestimation of the significance of ideological conflict in a nation's history. In retrospect, it seems clear that fundamental economic and social problems were gathering in the post-World War II years. Central among these are the most basic economic issues on both a national and a world scale: growth, stability, employment, equity of distribution, and the like—issues that experience has taught us have *not* been solved. Related and closely secondary problems include war and the threat of war, race relations, bureaucracy-technology developments, ecology crises, and general dissatisfaction with the quality of life. These problems are still escalating, and fast-changing world conditions can only exacerbate—never moderate—them. American ideologies today must be examined entirely in the context of these problems and as manifestations of peoples' responses to these problems.

Most important, the character and development of ideologies must be studied from an impartial perspective. This will not be easy. The depth and subtlety of society's dominant ideology (essentially capitalism-liberalism as later analyzed) make it very difficult for us to wrench ourselves free of its grip and see it anew in all its dimensions. Moreover, many (if not most) of those who are looking for solutions to problems through the conscious development of other ideologies will not be able to withdraw themselves fully from the dominant ideology. Because they have been imbued with capitalism-liberalism doctrine and because they live in a social system that reflects that ideology in both rhetoric and practice, they may not have stepped very far out of the basic American ideological pattern. This is an issue to which we will return from time to time.

For the moment, it is sufficient to note that the first three years of the 1970s have been rife with intense ideological conflict in the United States. The civil rights, antiwar, and student movements of the 1960s were relatively superficial responses to deeper problems that are still spawning conflict. Their heirs and successors —other minority movements, women's liberation and ecology movements, anarchist, countercultural, and populist tendencies, and various socialist approaches—are rapidly adding to the ideological tension. In reaction, defenders of the status quo are also seeking rationalization and justification of particular practices—both present and contemplated. For their own sakes, citizens must understand the many contemporary ideologies. American politics of the 1970s are portentous and dangerous, and an understanding of this ideological conflict is crucial to a citizen's capacity to cope with his or her most vital concerns. We shall clarify some basic terms before we map out an approach to the analysis of ideologies that now contend for our support.

The Nature and Sources of Ideology

Politics, and much of social life, involves the use of power to achieve goals amidst changing circumstances. Central to this process are beliefs about the present nature of the world and the hopes one has for its future. Such beliefs and hopes, when integrated into a more or less coherent picture of (1) how the present social, economic, and political order operates, (2) why this is so, and whether it is good or bad, and (3) what should be done about it, if anything, may be termed an "ideology." Ideology, of course, plays a varied part in different times and places. Contrasting beliefs and hopes may be the driving force behind bitter conflicts. They may mobilize millions in massive movements or they may be the principal resource enabling a small but dedicated band of people to defy great nations. Or, in other settings, the dominance of one set of beliefs may be so encompassing that new ideas not only are doggedly resisted, but their advocates are either ignored or punished. Thus, whether realistic or not, assumptions and aspirations move people alternately to action and to acceptance.

We shall make no effort here to identify the number of believers in any particular ideology or to characterize the part that such ideologies play in their lives or in the process of politics generally. Our focus is on the substance—the specific principles—of the various ideologies that now contend for political impact in the United States. For our purposes, it is enough that an ideology is held by some segment of politically active people and that it has the potential of gathering support and affecting American politics. When we speak of ideologies, therefore, it is in terms of their content and not in terms of their breadth of support or their function as a source of social movements.

In spite of such a focus, some of our assumptions about the

nature and sources of ideologies or political belief systems are relevant to the way in which we will analyze them. The *nature* of ideology, as we shall use the term, is suggested by the definition just given: it is a system of related beliefs about how the political world does and should operate. In part, it is a series of images that seem to describe and *interpret* what happens in politics from day to day. Those who hold an ideology have, in effect, a series of expectations or a map in their mind, orienting them and telling them how things work. Thus, one knows where to fit facts perceived and how to understand their significance. It is also a series of cues for evaluation of what one sees. Such "facts" are good or bad, or things *should* be done in certain ways because of the standards or imperatives of the ideology to which one consciously or unconsciously subscribes. An ideology may be held with varying degrees of specificity and intensity. For some, it may be comprehensive, detailed, and integrated—that is, interconnected explanations and interpretations already exist in their minds for nearly everything that they see or feel about politics. For others, it may be fragmented and/or not strongly felt.

Obviously, an ideology may serve important political purposes for those who hold to it. An ideology provides not only cues for understanding and evaluating public affairs, but also serves as a guide to action, as a means of self-expression, and/or as a means of relating to other people. Ideology may thus become integrated with an individual's personality. This is neither unusual nor undesirable, either for the individual or for the political system as a whole. Quite naturally, all people develop images of the world around them; they cannot help but see things in terms of their life experience, values, and aspirations. Some political activists disparage ideology as the antithesis of reason, but this may be merely because they hold a *different* ideology. All established political systems generate ideologies that explain, justify, and mobilize support for their practices. Divergent ideologies may be necessary means of enabling people to see their own individual interests more clearly. Thus, ideology may, in effect, serve as a way of developing representation for segments of the population whose real values and interests are not reflected in the preferences of those who manage the system.

The *sources* of ideology are many. People acquire their political belief systems through a complex and little-understood process in which parts are played by the individual's own personality and values, his social setting and life experiences, the effects of the education he has undergone, and the way in which he understands the events that occur in the world around him. Family and school are leading early sources of political beliefs. As young children, most people acquire from their families the basic elements of political loyalties, an image of the political world, and a sense of right and wrong in politics. These are usually reinforced by the public school system, which teaches the propriety, inevitability, and utility of American institutions and practices.

For some children, however, the everyday facts of their surroundings so challenge the idealized interpretations offered in school that they mature with conflicting commitments. This may happen if their families are among the relatively few who hold decisive views that do not conform with dominant ideologies. Still others may begin life imbued with the usual benevolent concepts and, through a process of shedding orthodox assumptions and expectations, emerge with a whole new set of beliefs about what is and should be in American politics. Or a single dramatic condition or policy such as racism or the Vietnam war might so detach people from their previous convictions that they may seek and find new explanations and aspirations for their political system.

Like other concepts and interpretive images that people carry in their minds, ideology tends to resist change. Many people retain a static view of the world in terms of assumptions and values long after forces and events have changed things. The individual clings to the familiar because a whole web of other beliefs and commitments may depend on such orientations; his own identity or the meaning he sees in life itself may be involved. The ideology itself also tends to resist change. It reaffirms its basic principles strongly, adapting to new conditions and problems only marginally, in patchwork fashion. In part, this is because a network of social and economic interests, institutions, and practices is supported and justified by the ideology.

Thus, at different levels, there are bulwarks against change in ideologies. This raises important questions for analysis: under what circumstances do individuals change their political ideologies? To the extent that such an act is rational and deliberate, what criteria should they employ in this process? And, how do ideologies themselves adapt to changing conditions and these changes among individuals? Some aspects of these questions are beyond the scope of this book, but we shall comment on others in Chapter 10. The fact is, of course, that many individuals *do* experience changes in their ideologies, and new patterns of beliefs and values *do* arise to challenge orthodox ideologies. The political system may suddenly be confronted with new (and, to some, unintelligible) demands. This is why it seems to us essential to focus first on the beliefs and principles currently held by each major ideology. When their makeup is known, their prospective impact and attraction may be better understood.

The Substance of American Ideology: A Framework for Analysis

What kind of approach will provide understanding of the content of contemporary American ideologies? Naturally, the questions to be asked depend on the purposes to be served by this inquiry. Our primary purpose is to *describe* the beliefs and hopes that move people in the United States today. Secondarily, we want to *analyze* ideologies, to see what they share, and where they diverge; we must therefore compare them with each other in regard to some key components. Ultimately, we hope in this way to contribute to explanation of contemporary political behavior and to understanding of the roots of current conflicts. Readers, of course, may well seize the opportunity to go farther. By looking objectively into the belief system of others on an alternative basis, they will at least decisively widen their own frame of reference with regard to politics. They will empathize with the perspectives and actions of others and gain a new sense of the range of possibility in politics. By raising both factual and ethical questions, they will move closer to the day when they have personal political convictions. Thus, there are also *evaluative* purposes involved in this investigation: to give citizens confidence in their own political beliefs and actions.

The central questions to be applied to each ideology must therefore include descriptive, analytical, and evaluative dimensions. In order to provide understanding of political behavior, basic beliefs must be exposed, fundamental assumptions must be related to underlying values, and both must be connected to resulting commitments to action. No other approach can link premises and perceptions to an understanding of *why* such views are held and *what they imply* in terms of efforts to bring about change. At the same time, we must explore the values and aspirations of each ideology for their own sakes so that citizens may not only see the range of beliefs people have but also reach sophisticated ethical judgments about the propriety or desirability of particular goals and tactics.

We shall use three distinct categories to describe and analyze each ideology: (1) the *world view,*[1] or general perspective on how the American economic and political systems work today, for whom, and why; (2) the *values* that are central to the ideology and the *goals* that it holds out as most desirable for the United States; and (3) the image of the process of *social change* to which it subscribes and the *tactics* that it deems appropriate in the light of its world view, values and goals, and image of change. Let us explain each of these organizing questions in turn.

(1) WORLD VIEW

Ideologies are integrated systems of belief in which definitions of reality bear a relation to a goal and methods of achieving it. First in logical sequence, though not necessarily in order of formulation, is the nature of one's understanding of what is happening in the world around one and why. What is the nature of the social order? Is it egalitarian, or is it stratified so that some have more of the things that are valued (status, wealth, and the like) in the society? Did this pattern in society evolve because of inherent differences in the talents or capabilities of men, or is it the result of some other factors? Here we shall touch upon the extent to which the ideology sees the society divided into contending social classes (segmented by wealth, prestige, and power, for example). If society is so divided, are people aware of the divisions? What part does or might this consciousness play in politics? How is the economy run, and

---

[1] We employ the term "world view" here in spite of its long history and much more complex usage elsewhere in the social sciences because we are unable to frame an equally expressive and felicitous term. We mean it synonomously with "image of social reality" or "image of power and process," and we trust no unnecessary confusion will be caused by our usage.

who benefits from such a system of organization? How is power distributed and what sustains such patterns? A distinct set of perceptions about these questions characterizes each ideology, evoking a decisively different reaction.

In some respects at least, the accuracy of such beliefs is open to empirical investigation. It is possible to define the pattern of distribution of wealth in the United States, for example, or the extent of racial discrimination in various aspects of life. Such factual descriptions can be produced, tested, and checked by research. Even then, however, differences of perspective appear: some attach great concern to the fact of inequality, while others see it as a natural manifestation of inherent differences among people or as a condition undergoing steady improvement. Looking at the same facts, some see problems, while others see progress. These differences may be due not to disagreement about the facts, but to their meaning in the context of other facts. Our understanding of the nature and significance of facts themselves reflects assumptions and preferences about the political world. In many cases, of course, no agreed "facts" are available, and we have only assumptions or outright guesses to go on. In all cases, all our perceptions (assumptions *and* facts) must be correlated in some coherent, interpretive way before they can have full significance for us. All along the line, ideology tells us what significance to see in facts, how to supplement fact with assumption, what relationship each fact has to others, and what they all add up to. This explanation of our surroundings is what we mean by the term *world view. What* people believe, after all, not whether or not it is accurate, is crucial for understanding their behavior.

From time to time, however, the issue of the accuracy of an ideology's world view may become important. Occasionally, readers may find that the world view held by a particular ideology seems wholly at odds with the facts as they understand them. This may force or induce them to seek to resolve the factual issue and/or revise their own perceptions about their world. Regardless of the extent of convergence between his own world view and that of the ideology under examination, however, specification of that world view offers a concrete point of comparison with all other ideologies. Some of them are bound to be closer to the "reality" described by the empirical evidence—or adhered to by the reader—and all can be efficiently contrasted as to the major components of their world views. Analysis of world views thus serves both the descriptive and the evaluative purposes that we have in mind.

(2) VALUES AND GOALS

As we dig deeper into the first principles of the ideology, its fundamental commitments become apparent and a coherent relationship between its perceptions of the world and its priorities and aspirations should begin to emerge. Each ideology is attached to some values, such as equality or justice, in preference to others. The crucial questions are *the way in which such values are understood or defined* by the ideology, and *how they are ranked in priority* when they conflict with each other. Equality, for example, may be defined in exclusively formalistic legal and political terms (that is, the right to vote), or in terms of the tangible social and economic conditions of a person's existence. It may be given high status in rhetoric but low status in practice or when it conflicts (as is often the case) wiith property rights or commitments to established procedures. Similarly, "due process" or "law and order" may mean different things to different ideologies, and our analysis must seek to specify carefully the precise meanings intended.

The goals of each ideology reflect its perception of the *distance* between the conditions of the society today (as understood in its world view) and the values to which it subscribes. In general, ideologies seek to attain the conditions, institutions, and policies that will permit realization of their values. In some cases, this may mean defending the status quo in every respect. In others, it may require drastic changes and the development of a series of interim goals. Out of the interplay of world view, values, and goals emerges a conception of the *scope* and *direction* of social change that will be necessary to achieve the ends to which the ideology is committed.

We will try to distinguish the meaning of reform and revolution used by different ideologies. The distinction lies partly in the realm of values and partly in the area of social change and tactics. In regard to values, we will see that the values and goals of some ideologies are modest extensions or reaffirmations of the basic values already dominant within the political system. For other ideologies, contemporary values must be drastically reshaped or replaced. The former often is seen as reform, the latter as revolution. In regard to images of the process of change and the tactics necessary to bring about a desired change, a similar distinction will be apparent. Some ideologies adhere to the established procedures of politics. Some are prepared to undertake extra-legal methods, now or at some future time, because they see no other way to achieve their goals. Again, the former represents reform, the latter revolution.

(3) THE PROCESS OF SOCIAL CHANGE AND THE TACTICS AND
METHODS OF ACHIEVING CHANGE

Each ideology develops an image of the process by which desired change can best be achieved. This sense of what is needed to accomplish change is based on its world view and its understanding of the scope and direction of change that is necessary. A given ideology's world view may posit only one or two historical determinants of change or a specific dynamic that must be followed. Thus, in spite of a strong desire for fundamental change, adherents of such an ideology would be constrained to wait until conditions were perceived as right for them to gain their ends. In other words, the *process* by which change is to be sought is not controlled by the *scope* of change sought; it depends also on the ideology's world view definition of present circumstances and power distribution within the society.

Tactics and methods of change may differ over time as well as between ideologies. Ordinarily, they are designed to conform with the requirements of the current stage in the long-term process of change as understood by the particular ideology. Thus, almost no ideology has an absolute commitment to *employ* or *not to employ* physical violence, and the presence or absence of violence is not a sound way to characterize an ideology. Both reform and revolutionary ideologies may advocate violence under particular conditions, and either may feel that circumstances require peaceful means throughout the process. The point is that the use of violence must be understood in context, as a tactic that an ideology sees as appropriate under certain defined conditions and for specific reasons, not as a universally applicable (and therefore inevitably characterizing) aspect of its system of beliefs and practices.

To be sure, there are individuals who feel that violence is abhorrent and morally condemnable; ethical pacifism has a long established and well-respected place in American thought. But for most political ideologies, violence is a relative matter. The current social reality is neither neutral nor perfectly equitable. Nevertheless, some people see that reality as highly desirable and a good approximation of justice. Normally, they see war or other violence in defense of the established order as entirely legitimate. Others, however, may see existing social reality as unjust, corrupt, and destructive, and they may therefore see violence as a necessary means of achieving essential change. It is unlikely that society's existing political procedures or power distribution will help the "change-seekers" achieve their goals. It is much more likely that those in power will use violence to force obedience to the rules that sustain the existing order. Thus, official censure of violence may be self-serving or even hypocritical. To view all nonofficial violence as evil, no matter what the provocation or the consequences, is to fall into the world view of those in power. Normally, then, violence would not be used as a basis for ethical judgment within a suitably wide frame of reference in analysis. Because violence is neither "good" nor "bad" of itself, judgment must depend on the purposes, manner, and consequences of its use in any given situation.

Each ideology subscribes to a wide variety of tactics and methods, of course, and we shall be examining more than merely the extent of willingness to employ violence. Although in most cases, tactics flow consistently from world view perceptions, values, and goals, there may be occasions on which commitments to particular tactics are so strong that they amount to one of the major values of the ideology. Or, for a variety of possible reasons, an ideology may be quite without prescriptions for the means by which change is to be secured. In these and other situations, we shall gain further insight into the nature of the ideology itself—its internal contradictions and characteristics—by comparing its tactics with its world view and its values and goals.

Some Problems in This Approach

Almost inevitably, there are substantial problems in approaching ideologies with this sort of analytical perspective and intent.

Some of these are linked to the specific approach we undertake here, and others are more closely related to the more general problem of understanding ideologies as such. Let us touch on some of these problems as they are involved in our analysis.

It will not always be possible for us to follow the three-stage analytical framework just outlined. In some cases, we will supplement extensively or employ several subcategories in order efficiently to portray reality. But our general approach will always proceed in accordance with this scheme. Any standardized approach will result in some oversimplification, and our analysis is no exception. The remedy for this is further reading in the original works of major representatives of an ideology. For this purpose, we have appended annotated bibliographies at the close of each chapter. We have also slighted the historical origins of the systems of thought presented. Each has a rich past, and many thinkers have contributed to the evolution of each ideology. But our focus on the contemporary character and impact of these ideologies has obliged us to curtail discussion of their origins and development. In the case of the established ideologies, we have included some preliminary paragraphs appropriate to setting a historical frame. The change-seeking ideologies, for the most part, may be seen as generated out of established ideologies, and works that explore the antecedents and evolution of both are included in the bibliographies.

We are acutely aware of another problem in presenting a synthesized interpretation of political ideologies in this fashion. How can we give each a fair hearing without abdicating our professional analytical responsibilities? Only a detailed reading of several original works and documents can give citizens a truly full understanding of the beliefs and aspirations of the various ideologies, and anything short of that is an accommodation that poses the threat of being biased by the interpreter's selections and manner of presentation. It is our specific function here to provide a comparative analysis that will enable citizens to see some crucial features of each ideology and to better understand their politics. We cannot avoid intruding between the ideology and the citizen. Under the circumstances, perhaps the best we can do is to urge the citizen to be alert and view our contributions with skepticism. We can also briefly describe some of the ways in which our views may intrude into this analysis.

In general, we have tried to allow each ideology to speak for itself as much as possible. We have used the most sophisticated spokesmen on behalf of each and tried to let their perspectives shape our presentation. We think this course assures that there will be no "straw men" erected at any point. Each ideology seems to us to have been presented by its most persuasive advocates. Nevertheless, we have felt obliged to comment from time to time about possible internal inconsistencies, lack of clarity on some points, or failure to deal with some vital questions. Moreover, we have had to make several choices in presenting each ideology, which may affect the reader's view of the ideology's viability. For example, we have selected representative authors for inclusion and quotation, extracted particular points from their works and termed these principles of the ideology, rearranged component beliefs to fit our framework, and characterized ideologies on the basis of evidence that is slim in some cases. *We* think this has been done fairly, responsibly, and objectively—but we do not expect all to agree with us on this point.

We are aware of three significant biases that have quite consciously structured our presentation. One is the conviction that it is time to take contemporary American ideologies seriously as important political forces in their own right and to cease viewing them as symptoms of psychological maladjustment, emotional immaturity, or antitechnological romanticism. In our view, people see problems and seek their solutions principally because there *are* problems —problems that are inherent to American social, economic, and political structures—and not chiefly for sociopsychological reasons. Second, we think that citizens must strive to become critical, independent thinkers capable of analyzing and evaluating their political ideas and the alternatives that face the United States within the widest possible frame of reference. This means, in our eyes, that they must free themselves of the accumulated stereotypes and assumptions with which they may have become encumbered in the elementary and secondary school systems and learn to think for themselves. Finally, we believe that the focus of their critical analysis should be on problems of change—whether changes in the principles, policies, and practices of American politics *should* be made and, if so, *what kind* and *by what means*. Fast-changing circumstances simply will not permit the United States to remain fixed politically. The problem (in our eyes) is one of determining which institutions are worthy of retention and what must be changed and selecting new forms. The sooner and more perceptively Americans take up this task, the better their chances for controlling their destinies.

We expect that the alternative ideologies presented here will raise substantial and perhaps frustrating problems of analysis and choice for readers. At some points, it may appear that there are six or seven plausible interpretations of what exists in the world and what should be done about it. The reader may begin to long for evidence capable of resolving some of the wide divergences in world views that characterize various ideologies. To an extent, such needs may be satisfied by further inquiry or research or by purposeful use of other courses about the United States. But in another sense, a political system has no true nature *except* in terms of one's values and goals. It is what it is because we see it against a background of our own hopes and fears. In other words, ideology transcends facts, gives them meaning, and motivates us toward goal-seeking action. To understand the behavior of others and to gain a clear sense of our own commitments, we must learn to identify and analyze ideology's role with the utmost care.

This is the point at which the question raised earlier reappears with profound import. Suppose we are all so entrapped within the dominant American ideology that we are unable to understand that all the "ideological conflict" we see is just a competition among variations of the orthodoxy—capitalism-liberalism in various shades and forms—and never rises to the level of fundamental challenge to the basic elements of that system of thought at all? Only an analysis of the various "competing" ideologies and an exploration of their contrast with the more fundamental process of underlying consciousness change can begin to address that question. We shall undertake the former task as the main body of this book and reserve the latter for the last part. Organization of the subject into three major parts reflects the importance of this question for the full understanding of the role of ideologies in American politics.

American Ideologies: An Overview

We have chosen to present eight major ideologies, each in a separate chapter. Four of these are included in Part I, *The Main-*

stream of the Capitalist-Liberal System: Capitalism, Liberalism, Reform Liberalism, and Conservatism. Four others make up Part II, *Challenges of the 1970s: Reform or Reconstruction?* They are Minority Liberation, Women's Liberation, The New Left, and Socialism. In our concluding part, we shall ask important questions about the implications of these ideologies and about the kinds of change they appear to seek. In every case, we shall follow our analytical framework insofar as it fits the nature of the ideology involved, but often, we shall end up with an exploration of the various tendencies and variants that appear to be evolving out of the ideologies as they are now shaped. In this way, we hope to set into developmental context such current manifestations as anarchism and anarcho-syndicalism, counterculturism, fascism, and so forth.

Our reasons for this approach are grounded in the characteristics of the ideologies themselves and in the nature of the American ideological scene. We have already discussed our combined analytical and evaluative purposes, in fulfillment of which we must take up each ideology as a separate belief system. But we must indulge in some general analysis of the nature and substance of American ideologies in order to justify the selection and order of presentation of ideologies in the chapters that follow.

First, some political postures that might be termed ideologies under some definitions are not included. Variants of American fascism have not been considered, for example, nor has any single-issue movement. We have deliberately excluded doctrines so little developed or seldom expressly put forward as to have little chance of generating significant political impact. No political party position is represented as such, partly because each position incorporates superficial aspects of several ideologies that are better analyzed separately and at a deeper level. Single-issue movements have been excluded because they lack comprehensiveness.

In other words, our definition of ideology as a more or less integrated belief system with a world view, values and goals, and an image of the correct process and tactics of change operates to exclude many political moods, groups, and movements. This is *not* to say that they are unimportant or unworthy of understanding. For some people, the status quo is its own justification and needs no rationale. For others, reaction or economic interest may be the sole or leading basis of political action. And it is certainly possible that the strongest and most likely to succeed thrust toward change in the American political system today comes from the reaction of the powerholders and their supporters against the claims and pressures of one or more of the change-seeking ideologies. Our purpose is not to analyze all the determinants of action in politics or even most of them, but to try to understand those ideologies that are comprehensive in nature, explain the political world, and justify particular forms of change. Thus, we focus exclusively on those comprehensive patterns of belief that offer a full and considered rationale for a particular relationship of institutions, policies, and practices in the United States.

Second, we see a continuing intimacy between economic and political thinking in the United States that defies their separation. One cannot develop a political ideology without making some assumptions about the present and proper nature of the economic order or about the social structure to which it gives rise. To think about power, which is the central focus of politics, is to speculate about its sources and distribution. That leads immediately to wealth, status, and other resources of power, many of which have their origins in the nation's economic order—the organization of the economy and the patterns of distribution and social class structure that it establishes in the society. We have dealt with this intertwining of economic and political thinking by seeing political ideologies as including an economic strand and seeking explicitly to define the nature of each ideology's economic assumptions. At the outset of our presentation, capitalism has been abstracted from liberalism as fully as possible and each is presented separately—recognizing, of course, that they are complementary.

Finally, we have first presented ideologies that we characterize as "mainstream ideologies"—ideologies that are established, enduring, and "orthodox" and have dominated the thinking of American political and other leaders throughout the twentieth century. On occasion, clashes among these ideologies have been of such magnitude and bitterness as to suggest that they have conflicting premises or goals. Nevertheless, once they are understood within a wide frame of reference, it is clear that they do not. Their antagonisms are exaggerated by an active mass media and viewed out of proportion by many observers because they see only the midpoints of the spectrum and miss the poles. In fact, mainstream ideologies share fundamental values and assumptions that make deep-seated conflict among them unlikely.

Shared elements of the mainstream ideologies. The basic perspective of mainstream ideologies toward the American system is one of acquiescence and approval. They take the existing class structure and the contemporary economic order of the United States as fixed or "given" and they raise no fundamental challenge to the characteristics, principles, or practices of either. They share an image of the American political process as "pluralist"—a bargaining, compromising process among many legitimate interests in which accommodations reached are in the interest of the people as a whole. Needless to say, such benevolent images are not shared by all ideologies outside the mainstream.

Those who advocate the established ideologies insist that existing rules and procedures must be followed precisely because only in this manner can legitimate ends be attained. Their argument that bargaining and negotiation are the only proper means to an end and that there is room for all to work through existing institutions is compatible with the pluralist assumptions. This image of the efficacy of existing institutions similarly is not shared by the other ideologies.

Perhaps most important, capitalism and liberalism share basic values. Both emphasize individualism and the "natural" rights of the individual to serve his own needs as he sees fit. They see the economic marketplace as the chief instrument through which individual self-seeking will lead to the greatest good for the greatest number. A network of legal rules supports these commercial processes and limits interference from the state or other outside sources. This insistence on the market and on the materialist values that accompany it has provoked some to reject and challenge the capitalist and liberal ideologies. They deny that the market is operable today and contend that the values associated with it are not only outmoded but destructive of the good life, properly conceived.

Capitalism and liberalism parallel and complement each other so completely and their overlapping effects suffuse American thinking so thoroughly that to separate them is a difficult and somewhat arbitrary act. But there are two strands—one economic, the other social and political—and major American theorists tend to focus chiefly on one or the other. Thus, the effort to treat them separately may yield greater understanding of each. *Capitalism* is an ideology that is concerned with how and why the economy should be organized. As the economy is never divorced from the state or the society, the principles of capitalism relate to the manner in which the state should be organized and conducted, and these principles overlap substantially with liberalism. *Liberalism* is an ideology that concerns how and in the service of which values the polity should be organized and operated. But because the polity's organization and activity must be based on some assumptions about how the economy does and should operate, liberalism substantially overlaps capitalism. Capitalism and liberalism are interdependent. Both proceed from some shared assumptions about the nature of man, the nature of society, motivational forces in the world, progress, and the like and two ideologies grew up together (each influencing the other) in the same historical era. In the United States, the two ideologies have dominated two hundred years of development, and they are intricately intertwined. This complementary relationship will become clearer as we examine each in turn.

The margins of the mainstream: Reform liberalism and conservatism. Neither of these ideologies has come close to enjoying the status and dominance accorded capitalism and liberalism. But each has been recognized as worthy of a hearing, as having potent advocates, and as being semi-legitimate expressions of the viewpoint of a significant segment of opinion. Occasionally, each has been put into practice as the guiding principle behind a statute or a program of the national government. Frequently, through their proponents, both are given a voice in the institutions of government through which they continue to promulgate laws that reflect their views—again, in the semi-legitimate manner of an authorized court gadfly. But their expression and achievement always occur within the general context formed by the congruence of capitalism and liberalism, and they have learned to operate within that frame of reference.

Reform liberalism is a term intended to include those thinkers who hold essentially the same premises as do other liberals but seek somewhat greater emphasis on equality and a somewhat reduced role for property rights, materialism, and individual self-interest. Many of the so-called "old left" of the 1930s are included in this category, thinkers who recoiled in revulsion at communism, adjusted to the incrementalism of the system in pragmatic fashion, and set their sights at defending freedom of speech against men such as Senator Joseph McCarthy. Also included are some of the early democratic socialists whose program consisted of several social insurance plans that have been implemented in the last thirty years. Reform liberalism accepts the basic outlines of the American economic and social systems, including their emphasis on individualism and legalism. Its adherents are distinguishable from orthodox liberals by their willingness to try new programs for social improvement, by their somewhat greater concern for equality in the tangible socioeconomic (rather than merely formal or legalistic) sense, and by their distaste for merely materialistic standards.

Conservatism is more than the opposite of reform liberalism. It consists of two quite distinguishable strands, the second of which amounts to a truly distinctive set of ideas in the American context. The first strand, individualist conservatism, is equivalent to nineteenth century liberalism, with its insistence on a completely free market and a strict policy of laissez-faire on the part of government. This ideology, stemming from the classical economist's belief that a totally free market would ultimately be self-regulating and provide the greatest good for the greatest number, holds that individuals and corporations should be free to do whatever they wish with the power flowing from their economic possessions without government interference. In this version of liberalism, property rights are given complete ascendancy over equality—which is seen as formal, political equality only (equality of opportunity to take part in the quest for economic success). Senator Barry Goldwater and other "rugged individualists" who believe in a firm American posture against the encroachment of communism fall within this category. As it is used in newspaper headlines, the term "conservative" usually refers to this set of nineteenth century liberal ideas.

The second strand of conservatism is tied closely with classical conservatism, a type of ideology only rarely expressed in the United States. Classical conservatism proceeds from the view that the needs of society are superior to those of individuals, that the society is a continuing organism independent of the individuals who comprise it at any time, and that government should be conducted by an elite of talent who take the masses' wishes into account but actually decide matters on the basis of what is right and proper for the society's advancement. This is a distinctive mode of thought (not subject to some of the characterizations made earlier) that we shall investigate in detail later. For the moment, it is enough to point out that, in practice, both forms of conservatism espouse the validity and preferability of older values and ways of doing things. Both forms are antimajoritarian and grudging about the use of government for social purposes, and both value property over equality in distinctive fashion. As a result, they become associated in many causes and may be seen together for the sake of efficiency.

The Challenge of the 1970s: Reform or Reconstruction?

Minority liberation, women's liberation, the new left, and socialism represent the major thrusts toward change in the 1970s. They do not share the benevolent view of the American system as open, inclusive, and capable of flexibly delivering all legitimate goals to those who take part in it. Instead, they see a more or less closed system that is run by and for the benefit of a relative few and is committed to racist, sexist, and exploitative standards and policies. An integrated arrangement of rules, rhetoric, and repression operates to prevent modification of the system's basic priorities, which center on the material achievements of the American economy, particularly perpetuation of the present pattern of distribution of benefits. Advocates of these ideologies, defining equality and justice in broad social and economic terms, find such values denied at every turn by American institutions and practices. In their eyes, individualism and market values must be replaced by emphasis on community and cooperation.

Apparently, the scope of change necessary is great, reaching to the fundamentals of the economic and social order as well as to the basic distribution of power in the political process. The means by which such changes are to be secured, however, are the subject of considerable and continuing disagreement. To some, persuasion and traditional politics, spiced with occasional protests and demonstrations, seem the only route to success. Others see no alternative to full-scale upheaval, but disagree as to the timing, tactics, and alliances necessary to its achievement.

These four major change-seeking ideologies and the evolving tendencies we shall describe provide much of the dynamics of American politics today. Their proponents are raising questions and challenges not heard with such force, depth, or comprehensiveness for decades, perhaps at any time. Even if they should lose some of their current impetus or support, their impact may be dramatic. For one thing, they create a situation in which more moderate change-seeking ideologies may acquire new support and influence over public policies. For another, they raise the immediate prospect of generating a reaction which, in defending the status quo with an increasingly rigid determination, may effect a fundamental change in the character of the American system.

In Part III, the question that is perhaps the most important will have to be answered: to what extent have these "competing" ideologies provided any real alternatives to the dominant capitalist-liberal system? To what extent are they all merely variants of the same basic (capitalist-liberal) consciousness, and thus actually more confining than liberating? In coming to grips with these questions, we shall first have to face issues pertaining to the implications of the ideologies examined. In important ways, we can best understand ideologies in terms of their consequences; thus, determining where these ideologies *lead* can be a vital clue to their real character. If they lead back to capitalism-liberalism in only slightly revised form, for example, they could hardly be called *conflicting* ideologies. We may well ask whether what appears to be different actually is different in real terms. Undoubtedly, in the process, we shall learn much about the nature and role of ideology (including our own personal version).

Annotated Bibliography

Bell, Daniel. *The End of Ideology*. Glencoe, Ill.: Free Press, 1960. The classic argument about ideology's demise as a fighting force capable of moving modern men.

Boorstin, Daniel. *The Genius of American Politics*. Chicago: University of Chicago Press, 1953. Argues that the American experience is so unique that no philosophy has been developed, nor is one necessary.

Chamberlain, John. *Farewell to Reform*. Gloucester, Mass.: Day, 1932. Progressivism and liberalism in the early twentieth century.

Commager, Henry. *The American Mind*. New Haven, Conn.: Yale University Press, 1959. History of political ideas in the nineteenth and twentieth centuries.

Grimes, Alan P. *American Political Thought*. New York: Holt, Rinehart and Winston, 1960. A good standard source on the evolution of American political ideas.

Hartz, Louis. *The Liberal Tradition in America*. New York: Harcourt, Brace & World, 1955. A major argument concerning the lack of conservative *and* radical traditions, resulting from dominance of liberalism.

Hofstadter, Richard. *The American Political Tradition*. New York: Knopf, 1948. Critical analysis of twelve major figures in American political development and of the ideas that motivated them.

Lynd, Staughton. *Intellectual Origins of American Radicalism*. New York: Vintage Books, 1969. Good revisionist account of the early radical ideas and their submergence/surfacing processes since.

Minar, David W. *Ideas and Politics*. Homewood, Ill.: Dorsey Press, 1964. Good standard account of the evolution of ideas.

Parenti, Michael J. *The Anti-Communist Impulse*. New York: Random House, 1969. An analysis that finds the roots of American foreign policy in anti-Communist ideology.

Schumpeter, Joseph. *Capitalism, Socialism, and Democracy*. New York: Harper & Row, 1942. A major study of the relationship between social and economic change and the role of economic ideologies and/or systems.

PART I

The Mainstream of the Capitalist-Liberal System

2

Capitalism

Capitalism is the private ownership of the means of production and allocation of the resources, goods, and services of the society through the mechanism of prices set by competitive markets. No doubt, many people understand capitalism essentially as a term descriptive of the American economy. But capitalism is much more than a descriptive term for most Americans. It is an ideology, because those Americans who subscribe to capitalism make value-based assumptions about the nature of man and the desirability of certain procedures and their expected results. Such a network of assumptions about man, about ways to reach particular goals, and about the desirability of those goals converts capitalism from a descriptive term to a prescriptive and justifying ideology.

Modern capitalism may be dated from a comprehensive statement of the principles of economics by eighteenth century economists Adam Smith,[1] David Ricardo,[2] and Thomas Malthus.[3] They

---

[1] Adam Smith (1723–1790) was both a moralist and economist. His major work, *The Wealth of Nations,* is available in a variety of editions and still serves as a major source of basic capitalist ideology.

[2] David Ricardo (1772–1823) followed Smith's principles, applying them particularly to the value of land as a key factor of production. See *Works and Correspondence of David Ricardo,* Sraffa, ed. (Cambridge: University Press, 1951).

[3] Thomas Malthus (1766–1834) is well known for his *Essay on Population* which, like Smith's work, has been reprinted in many editions. His major theme is that population increase is a drag on wages and leads to cyclical starvation.

saw a nation's economy as dependent upon three "factors of production": land, labor, and capital. Land is vital for the production of food, for the development of various natural resources, and as the geographic site of other productive facilities such as factories. Labor is needed to work in factories, till the land, and provide other services. Capital, money or its equivalent, is essential for investment in machines and other implements of production. When supply of these factors is matched by demand for their use, they argued, profits, wages, and rents are produced, and the economy is more fully able to meet demands upon it.

These classical economists believed that the various factors of production would be kept in balance by means of the economic market. We shall explore contemporary assumptions about the market in detail shortly, but its basic nature and purpose should be familiar to all. Smith felt that if all individuals sought to serve their own self-interest, an impersonal process of equating supply with demand would result. This would lead to maximum use of all factors of production and maximum possible distribution of the best possible products at the lowest possible cost. In short, the market was the instrument whereby the greatest good for the greatest number was to be realized. All men were to have an equal right to take part, to pursue their own self-interests as they saw them, and the result would be socially beneficial. The best men, of course, were those individuals who were better suited for (or more diligent and self-disciplined at) the competitive practices of the marketplace —for these were the men who made the greatest good for the greatest number possible.

Smith and the others saw capital as the essential ingredient for making profits, providing employment opportunities, and achieving progress. They acknowledged, however, that these results would lead to a rise in the value of land and the rent derived from its use, and, in turn, reduce profits, lower wages, and produce food shortages. In this system, income could not for very long rise above the minimum level necessary for the physical survival of an ever-expanding population, and the wage rate absorbed the burden of the "squeeze." In contrast, the landlord and the capitalist would be left sufficiently well off to begin a new cycle from a somewhat more advanced position—that is, to achieve progress. The grim pessimism of this version of economic life led to the famous characterization of economics as "the dismal science."

In spite of repeated swings from boom to depression, the American economic experience has been interpreted in much more optimistic terms. In this chapter, we will first set forth the basic framework of assumptions and beliefs that characterize the American capitalist ideology. Next, we will describe three major dilemmas faced by capitalist ideologists in the twentieth century and explore the major modifications that have arisen in response to them. Finally, we will try to see how capitalist ideology has evolved as a result of these modifications.

World View

(1) THE BASIC ASSUMPTIONS

Capitalism is based on the premise that man's needs for food, shelter, and protection against environmental dangers, and the like are primarily *individual* rather than community needs. The individual is seen as seeking to serve his personal needs first, and he becomes the unit around which subsequent analyses and assumptions are built. Man is acquisitive by nature; he first tries to fulfill his minimum current needs and then aspires to assure against future hardship or privation. The unending nature of the quest for greater and greater security against want and danger provides the dynamic force behind social life. In economic terms, it translates itself into the profit motive: individuals seek to maximize their personal returns—their net reward—from all transactions in which they engage.

The profit motive is an essential component of capitalism; it is the basis of all subsequent assertions and the prospect of attaining desirable goals. Every man, whether destitute or millionaire, must seek to gain the highest possible net return from every transaction to which he is a party. If he does not, the market will not work effectively as a regulator of supply and demand, and there will be neither efficiency in the allocation of goods and services nor progress for the society as a whole.

Second only to the profit motive, and also proceeding from the individualist focus, is the principle that man is by nature competitive. He is attentive to the behavior of others and aspires to excel in a variety of attainments. In the economic world, this means that producers will find it natural to vie with each other for customers, and no man will be content with even a high level of achievement. The combination of competitiveness and profit motivation assures constant individual self-seeking, which will ultimately mean progress for the entire society. Those who are unsuccessful in the competitive race may even be viewed as somehow unfit or unsuited for the natural rigors and demands of the real world.

The chief economic and social problem with which a capitalist society must contend is that of regulating the supply and demand for the various factors of production. Adherents of capitalism assume that there is a natural harmony among these factors and that they tend to regulate themselves. But either too much or too little of any one factor may upset their natural harmony and prevent realization of a profitable production level with stable and full employment. An oversupply of labor, for example, will drive wages below the level necessary to provide the resources with which to purchase the products of the economy, and perhaps even below that needed to sustain life. Too little capital will mean the absence of investment necessary to provide employment opportunities and perhaps an excessively high price of products. Too much capital will mean an unprofitable investment situation and, perhaps, unserved needs on the part of consumers.

(2) THE CRUCIAL ROLE OF THE MARKET

The chief regulative instrument of supply and demand, and ultimately of the factors of production themselves, was and is the free and competitive market. From Adam Smith to the present, assumptions about such a market have been fundamental. The market's proper operation depends upon prices being determined independently—solely by the individual decisions of producers and purchasers, with both groups competing. There must be many sellers, each aware of the others' practices and each seeking competitively to undersell the other and still make a profit. At the same time, there must be many purchasers, each with knowledge of the others' bidding and of the quality and prices of the sellers' products. No seller or buyer can be large enough to exercise an appreciable influence on prices. In this way, nobody controls prices, and everybody must adapt to them. This leads to the impersonal and nearly perfect equilibrium that is consistent with the natural harmony of the various factors.

Much capitalist writing centers on the utility of the market for these purposes. Perhaps none has summarized the principle as succinctly as the United States Department of Commerce did in its 1965 pamphlet entitled "Profits and the American Economy":

> Price is the mechanical arbitrator in our market system.
>
> In our capitalistic economy, we adhere to the belief—indeed we have established safeguards to insure—that the pricing process is completely impersonal. This means that normally the free play of demand and supply produces a price on which the buyer and seller agree, and a bargain is struck. To the extent that a price is reached by means that are *not* impersonal—to the extent that either the buyer or the seller can dictate or influence the setting of the price—to that extent our system of controlling the efficient use of resources is not working properly.[4]

Many desirable results flow almost automatically from the proper working of the free market system. First, maximum efficiency in allocation of scarce resources is realized. Capital is directed toward profitable uses. Thus, all available capital is put to work in the most productive way possible, and all relevant natural resources are used. Such widespread productive activity means employment for the maximum possible number of workers which, in turn, means that they earn the wages necessary to buy the economy's products. The resources of the society, in other words, are in full use in the most productive way. They are producing what the community wants, and competition induces continued efforts to improve products, lower costs, and attract new buyers. This makes for economic change and progress that is always maximally efficient. When consumer desire for one product slackens and causes a reduction in both price and production levels, the employer reduces his labor costs by discharging some workers and leveling off at a new but profitable balance of costs and prices. Discharged workers do not suffer because other employers who are experiencing a rising con-

---

[4] U.S. Department of Commerce, "Profits and the American Economy" (Washington, D.C.: U.S. Government Printing Office, 1965), p. 13.

sumer demand for their products need labor to produce larger quantities. Or the labor rate can be reduced to a level that the employer can afford, just as the employer, on occasion, was forced to reduce his prices to his purchasers.

A second result is a high degree of stability or equilibrium at this efficient level. The aggregate of demand always equals the aggregate of supply, except for marginal adjustments from time to time as consumer demand shifts from one product to another or the ratio of savings to consumer expenditure shifts. As we have just seen, the former case is a characteristic of progress and temporary dislocations are quickly cured. The latter case is dealt with by the natural forces of the market in much the same way. When capital is needed to produce new products, potential consumers are induced to save (and ultimately invest) by the offer of high interest rates. When the need for capital drops, interest rates go down, and the consumer is likely to shift again and use all of his earnings in consumption. Thus, consumer demand has been interrupted only temporarily by the thrifty tendency toward savings, and the long-run effect is beneficial because the savings were used to finance the manufacture of new products. As long as consumer demand keeps up, there can be no major depression. Indeed, capitalism does not consider that a serious prospect as long as the natural forces of the market are at work. Only when "artificial" forces (unions or government regulation of prices, wages, and trade) enter is the market inadequate as a natural regulator of the economy.

Third, the market achieves a kind of consumer sovereignty. Demand is the key, and because it shapes supply, the consumer is enabled to get what he wants by "voting" with his purchase money for the products of his choice. Thus, not only are all the factors of production used fully and most efficiently, but at the same time, the consumer is enabled to specify what will be produced. This "sovereignty" of the consumer is also celebrated in the Department of Commerce's characterization:

> The dollars you spend in the marketplace for your needs, your wants, and your preferences are, in a very real sense, your "votes" for allocation of our resources to the production and distribution of the goods and services you buy. These votes are a *demand* and they dictate to producers what they must *supply*. If a producer interprets these votes

correctly, he earns profits. If a producer does not interpret these votes correctly and produces too much or too little, or at a price that is too high or too low, or at a level of quality uncalled for or inadequate, he will soon realize his mistake, thanks to the absence of profits.[5]

Finally, this whole process takes place exclusively through private decision-making and with an irreducible minimum of coercive requirements. Nobody is forced to do anything if he is normally endowed with competitiveness and the profit motive and his wants are roughly similar to those of others in the society. If he is highly unusual in either of these categories, he might be economically coerced—that is, unemployed or unable to obtain particular kinds of goods. But there would be no government coercion applied to structure his behavior, and he would never face the prospect of losing his liberty or being physically coerced concerning his choices. Indeed, one of the highest achievements of the market arrangement is the elimination of government involvement. Assuming that the market is in operation, the government's role is that of complete laissez-faire, except for such necessary supports as defense of the society from enemies, enforcement of contracts, collection of debts, break-up of monopolies, provision of public education, and maintenance of general domestic order. Intrusion by governments would not only apply coercive power to individuals, but also would upset the natural workings of the market and destroy its achievements.

The achievements of the free market and of the capitalist system itself are perceived as very great. Indeed, everything desirable about the American standard of living and/or way of life is often attributed to the nature of the capitalist system. This too is well illustrated in the official words of the United States Department of Commerce:

> As American citizens, we are convinced that the sum total of these private decisions not only proves profitable to those who make the decisions but also brings great benefit to the entire national economy. . . .
> Our country has only 6% of the world's population, occupies only 7% of the world's land area, and yet produces

---

[5] *Ibid.,* p. 11.

and consumes something over 40% of the free world's goods and services.

Finally, we would do well to remember that our private enterprise system is the world's mightiest economic engine. It has generated the highest profits, wages, and family income in man's history. It has achieved a broadly based distribution of goods and services with many benefits to our citizens. It has given the United States of America the highest standard of living the world has ever known.[6]

Admittedly, this review of the basic world view of capitalism is oversimplified and, as we shall see in subsequent sections, outdated in the minds of some twentieth century advocates. Nevertheless, it represents the core of the thinking of many Americans and can be seen in a variety of sources. A group of Harvard economists, for example, made an exhaustive study of the ideology of American business, drawing on advertising, speeches, publications, official testimony of business leaders, and trade association pamphlets. Their detailed findings as to the essential beliefs closely resemble the representation presented here in distilled form.[7] Robert Heilbroner, a leading economist, employed the addresses given by the presidents of leading American corporations to develop the same basic characterization.[8]

Values and Goals

Just as capitalism's world view proceeded from a focus on the individual, so does its value system place paramount emphasis upon *individualism.* This individualism stresses the moral responsibility and opportunity of each person to serve his own needs as he sees fit. It is his responsibility to act purposefully in his own behalf; he should not be concerned for others, nor should he expect others to serve his needs for him. Of course, he is accountable for his actions

---

[6] *Ibid.,* pp. 40–41.

[7] Francis X. Sutton, Seymour E. Harris, Carl Kaysen, and James Tobin, *The American Business Creed* (Cambridge: Harvard University Press, 1956).

[8] Robert Heilbroner, *The Limits of American Capitalism* (New York: Harper & Row, 1966).

and will experience their consequences, whether good or bad. The other dimension of individualism is the insistence upon full opportunity for individual choices and action. Autonomy, self-reliance, and private self-seeking must be given full play: this is the meaning and substance of freedom. To the extent that there are restrictions on individual choice, whether that of businessman or consumer, freedom has been diminished.

Individualism carries with it a special set of emphases concerning the relationship of the individual to the society. Because the good society is synonymous with the most prosperous, and can be attained only through a determined pursuit of private interests by each and every member of the society, that pursuit constitutes the individual's sole obligation to his society. Thus, because of the exclusive moral duty to serve one's own private needs and the conviction that such a course is the way to progress for all, questions of the justice of social or economic arrangements either do not arise or are deflected. The sum total of many such private decisions, and only such action, will carry the society inevitably to its next higher stage. No moral or ethical distinctions are made between types of production, types of services rendered, or particular forms of consumption; all are equally worthy if they return a profit and are chosen freely by the individual.

The emphasis placed on individualism in this form is closely related to one of the major values of capitalism: individual self-fulfillment seen as material self-interest and accumulation. Only through the growth and development achieved by successful competition and by the satisfaction of having achieved one's goals in spite of difficulties does an individual reach a sense of fulfillment. His character has been molded, tempered, and uplifted by the struggle he has been through, and he emerges a far better man morally *and* materially. In addition, the fact that the moral and material progress of society also is enhanced should not be overlooked. The society in which many such men are produced is indeed fortunate, for the talents they have applied and the strength of character they have developed are the basic fibre of that society and assure its continued improvement.

A second major value, again closely related to individualism, is *materialism*. It is the dominant (and sometimes the only) standard by which the achievements of individuals or of the economic system as a whole are to be measured. The emphasis in American capitalism on a high standard of living, defined as the possession of specific material goods for private consumption purposes, is indicative of the extent to which this value has become its chief measuring standard. Materialism is sometimes expressed as an emphasis on productivity, which in turn becomes one of the highest virtues to which a system may aspire. Capitalism makes few, if any, distinctions about the types of material goods or the nature of the productivity that is valued. It is enough that individuals be able to serve their wants by amassing material goods of their choice and that total productivity (presumably of the kinds of goods that individuals demand) be high—high enough to fill all wants.

Several other values combine with materialism and individualism to fill out the capitalist value system. For the individual, an active life based on a practical grasp of the "realities" of the economic world is in order. The good man will have confidence in the economic system and in his capacity to make it work in his behalf. He will take risks, seek new opportunities, and look pragmatically to the future. If he does, he will be rewarded exactly in proportion to the quality of his foresight, the nature of his talents, and the extent of hard work he invests in his own cause. For the society, steadily increasing productivity and utter freedom for individuals to serve their own interests in this manner will amount to progress. *Progress,* defined as increasing levels of goods and services, is both a value and a goal. It is good, and must continue. Channels of opportunity should be kept open so that all or most individuals may feel the values of capitalism and act accordingly. In this way, the underlying dynamic that makes for broad societal progress will be kept at work.

Behind this constellation of values, and vital to giving them meaning, is the concept of *private property.* The idea that an individual can "own" something to the extent of being absolutely entitled to exclude others from its enjoyment is fundamental to capitalism. This exclusive entitlement to land or moveable goods is what makes individual self-satisfaction and achievement possible; it permits others to compare one individual with another and judge their relative talents, and it enables an individual to provide for not only his own wants, but for those of his family. Unless man can realize something tangible from his labor, he will have little incentive to work. The opportunity to acquire private property, which can then be used either to acquire more or to achieve other goals, is the crucial inducement that makes the individual's self-seeking a rational act.

Social Change and Tactics

Capitalism envisions its goals of individual self-fulfillment and general material progress of the society as being attainable automatically, through the "natural" operation of private forces. The principal mechanism is the free and competitive market, in which profit-maximizing individuals seek their private ends. The simple beauty of this arrangement is that all men, merely by doing what comes most naturally to them (seeking material satisfactions), will advance the society as a whole through steady stages of progress. Transformation of technological advances, changes in values, and world developments into market forces will inspire and suggest responsive behavior by all participants in the nation's economic and social life.

Because operation of the market is crucial to the process by which social change occurs, it must be protected from external and "artificial" forces. This means that government should observe a strict laissez-faire policy, avoiding all "interference" with the operation of the market. Government has, of course, the important task of enforcing the contractual and other arrangements with which the business of the society is carried on. In discharging these necessary functions, government should take care that its revenue matches its expenditures lest it influence the market by creating an unbalanced or "artificial" excess of demand.

In addition, it is the government's task to defend the integrity of the market against challenges from domestic or foreign enemies. We will explore these aspects of the state's role more fully when we examine liberalism's commitment to particular economic practices, but it should be noted here that property rights are one of the most fundamental constitutional rights. The state is obligated to defend each individual's possessions against not only the claims of other individuals, but also against the claims of majorities. The people are powerless to change the status of property rights except under very limited circumstances. Furthermore, if the market is to be effective, it must extend throughout the society. Advocates of other, noncapitalist economic systems must be persuaded, educated, legally required, or, if necessary, coerced by whatever means are required to conform with the capitalist practices. The same principles apply wherever the effective power of the state reaches: it is always preferable to have capitalist economies in foreign countries, regardless of the cost to national well-being in those countries or the level of force required to maintain such practices.

When these principles are operating, capitalism is essentially self-regulating and its method is no more than the free and unrestricted activity of many individuals in pursuit of profit. Those individuals who are not yet persuaded of the propriety of this form of economic organization have either not been offered an opportunity to see how it will benefit them or are in the grip of some false alternative ideology from which they should be rescued. Wherever possible, they should be firmly confronted with the merits of the capitalist system. Both rhetorically and militarily, capitalism acts upon its vision in messianic ways.

Three Dilemmas of Mid-twentieth Century Capitalism

The basic framework of an ideology might sometimes be oversimplified or outdated without actually affecting the adherence of its advocates. But the challenges aimed at American capitalism in the mid-twentieth century led many sincerely devoted adherents of capitalism to reexamine and revise some of their beliefs. In the United States, these challenges stemmed from inescapably obvious facts and events that had widespread social consequences. It is not surprising that for some people, orthodox capitalist ideology has been bent in new directions. But many people, including the leaders of business and government, have adhered firmly to the basic framework that we have just reviewed. A summary of three of the major challenges to capitalism in the United States will give us an idea of the scope and depth of the problem. We will consider, first, how the Great Depression of the 1930s and the apparent failure of the market affected capitalist ideology; second, the effects of new concentrations of power resulting from the rise of the new economy based on supercorporations, vast governmental expenditures, and the apparent nonexistence of the market; and third, the more recent problem of "stagflation" and wage-price controls.

(1) DEPRESSION AND APPARENT FAILURE OF THE MARKET

After the Depression, neither economists nor ideologists could continue to talk exclusively in terms of "normal" conditions of high, stable prices and full employment. Nor was it enough to posit cycles or the rhythmic rise and fall of business activity in which the economy would be self-correcting if left alone. The stark social fact was that several million newly unemployed persons were desperate; they were facing hardship and even death from starvation. In the face of this kind of reality, business, labor, and farmers exerted heavy pressure to force the government to "do something" to get the economic engine going again. Capitalist ideology offered no solution, of course, because it held that the economy would correct itself and that government involvement was bad. As the New Deal went ahead with its "pragmatic" and "problem-solving" approach to economic recovery, it found itself using industrywide agreements to prevent ruinous competition and permit the return to profitable prices at one stage and to promote competition and prevent domination of product areas by one or a small number of producers at another stage. No principles seemed to emerge as to *how* government should act, but the basic conclusion that government had the responsibility to do *something* under conditions of hardship was firmly established.

The Depression had the further effect of peremptorily calling attention to a social fact that was often ignored or dismissed in American capitalist ideology—that of sharp inequality in the distribution of economic rewards in the United States. At the time when the great industrial machinery of the United States was being developed, substantial segments of the American population were living on the margin of subsistence. From the Civil War on, the plight of such people had moved reformers to seek government assistance of some kind to supplement the private philanthropies that clearly were no longer able to carry the burden, if indeed they ever had been. Advocates of strict laissez-faire capitalism responded to the threat generated by this social concern with the famous doctrine of "Social Darwinism." This doctrine held that those who were low in economic attainments were economically unfit and therefore should be allowed to starve or die in the interest of improving the moral character and competitive quality of the population. Nevertheless, the reformers succeeded in getting some social legislation passed in the early decades of the twentieth century. But their successful uses of governmental powers (such as to require minimum wages or to prevent excessive prices where sellers had a monopoly) were not reflected in capitalist ideology, which continued to assert the virtue of laissez-faire and the inevitability of widespread distribution of wealth to all. With the reality of the Depression, however, it was no longer possible to insist that poverty was attributable to the failure of individual poor people or that there were only marginal differences in the level of material wealth possessed by the working and middle classes.

Both the fact of the Depression and the extent of inequality to which it called special attention drastically undermined confidence in the free and competitive market as an allocative device. Of course, the Depression might be attributed to excessive government interference with the market (as some at first sought to do). But the more usual reaction was a gnawing uncertainty about the market's capacity: apparently, it could no longer be relied upon to do its assigned job. In fact, beginning in the latter part of the nineteenth century, economic groups increasingly and successfully had sought to *protect* themselves from the vicissitudes of the market. As a result, the market simply was not fully operative in many areas of economic life. Nevertheless, people generally believed that the market performed all of the functions that Adam Smith and other exponents of capitalism said it did. With the advent of the Depression, however, many of the old doctrines were called into question, including that of the market. Further, the market apparently had not actually spread income and wealth as widely as it should have during sustained periods of prosperity. If depressions and poverty were unavoidable and inevitable under market economy conditions, one of two results seemed to follow. Either economic life was going to be full of hardships and have a high potential for social unrest or some new way of supporting the market and preventing drastic cycles would have to be found.

(2) NEW CONCENTRATIONS OF POWER

The facts of American economic life also challenged the orthodox capitalist ideology from another perspective. Publication in 1932 of Adolf Berle and Gardiner Means, *The Modern Corporation and Private Property*[9] ultimately had a profound impact on perceptions of the nature of the American economy. Drawing on stockholders' reports, sales and assets figures, government calculations, and other empirical data, the authors argued that there were really two very different economies in operation in the United States. One was made up of millions of sole proprietorships, partnerships, and small corporations and functioned much in accordance with the assumptions of the marketplace. The other, by far the most significant because it included most of the major industries, was composed of a relative handful of giant corporations. These supercorporations dominated the economy in terms of assets, sales, and profits, dwarfing other forms of business entirely. Berle and Means showed, for example, that in 1930, 130 companies trading on the New York Stock Exchange had gross assets of more than one hundred million dollars, but together, these companies held 82 percent of all the corporate assets traded on the exchange.[10] The 200 largest nonbanking corporations received 43 percent of all income earned in 1929 by all nonbanking corporations.[11] Further, the authors argued, since this concentration was proceeding steadily, the economy would soon be completely dominated by concentrations of power of this magnitude.

The second major point in the Berle and Means presentation was that the size of these corporations—and the resultant large number of stockholders—none of whom owned a substantial proportion of stock—made it impossible for stockholders to exercise control over the corporation's policies. They showed that all but a handful of the large corporations had wide diffusion of stock ownership, with voting rights spread among tens of thousands of people in some cases. Under such circumstances, stockholders' meetings

---

[9] Adolf A. Berle and Gardiner C. Means, *The Modern Corporation and Private Property* (New York: Macmillan, 1932).

[10] *Ibid.*, p. 29.

[11] *Ibid.*, p. 30.

could be little more than ceremonies in which uninformed laymen ratified the actions and choices of the company's management. Most people would simply return proxy votes supporting the management's slate of nominations for the Board of Directors; their relationship to the company became reduced to that of cashing dividend checks. All the decisions involved in actually running the company would be left in the hands of the officers and directors.

The implications of these two major findings were very serious for capitalist ideology. The existence of giant corporations that dominated major industries meant that the giants could, and often did, establish prices at which they would buy materials or sell products. Where one or two companies account for a very large share of a particular type of product, such as in the automobile industry, they can dictate the sales price. Tacit agreements among producers to refrain from long and destructive competitive price-cutting minimizes the risk of losing gigantic investments in plants and machinery that characterize the industry and eliminates competition. The size of the investment behind these giant corporations also prevents potential competitors from entering the field. A similar advantage accrues to the large corporation in regard to acquiring materials: it can set suppliers' prices effectively because of the sheer size of its purchases, because it is often the only buyer, or because it can threaten to go into the supply business itself.

The giant corporation thus foreclosed the possibility of a free and competitive market. It failed to respond to impersonally determined reflections of supply and demand and instead set prices. It neither competed with other producers through pricing nor responded to consumer demands. Indeed, it could hardly be expected to respond to consumer demands when the complexity of many products required years of research and design in addition to careful advance planning of material acquisition, production, and marketing arrangements. If necessary, the giant corporation was more likely to rely on the power of advertising to create "artificial" consumer demands in the image of the product it found to be practical and profitable to manufacture. Under such circumstances, the "market" lost much, if not all, of its relevance and function.

The implications of diverging the ownership of stock from the capacity to control the corporation were equally fundamental. Supposedly, the owners of invested capital would seek to maximize profits—and thereby do their part to keep the market operating properly. But if the corporate management were actually in control, not being owners, they might respond to a wholly different set of priorities. They might be more interested in maintaining themselves in power or in doing any of a number of other things than in maximizing profits. If they were, of course, the market would be undermined from this direction too. There also would be substantial units of power loose in the economy, acting on essentially arbitrary bases and threatening unpredictable consequences.

The concerns expressed by Berle and Means as a result of their analyses made headway chiefly among economists, in government, and in a few leading business circles in the 1930s. Then, during the 1940s and 1950s, the nature of the supercorporation became apparent and the business community joined in the concern. Popular expressions of this concern can be found in the works of John Kenneth Galbraith, Harvard economist-politician. In *The Affluent Society*,[12] for example, he stresses the dangers emanating from the unrecognized power of the large corporation. An exclusive insistence upon production of material goods, he argued, was merged with corporate manipulation of consumer "wants" through advertising. This led, in his eyes, to a kind of "social imbalance" in which no attention is paid to more general, nonconsumable public needs such as schools, hospitals, and recreation facilities.

At the same time as the giant corporations were creating the new economy that Berle and Means (and ultimately others) described, a second development threatened to turn capitalist ideology on its head in the form of huge expenditures by the United States government to prosecute World War II. Vast stores of food, equipment, and supplies had to be produced and transported overseas. The national government became a giant revenue-raising engine and an even greater engine of economic recovery. At one point, the national government absorbed nearly half of the gross national product in furtherance of the war effort. These vast purchases not only restored the American economy, but put many businessmen on notice that sales to the government could be highly profitable. In the postwar decade, some defense suppliers and contractors

---

[12] John Kenneth Galbraith, *The Affluent Society* (Boston: Houghton Mifflin, 1957).

found that this could also be a *steady* source of demand for their products. The point is that government has acquired a major role as a taxing agent for the purpose of purchasing the products of a particular segment of the economy—almost a complete reversal of the traditional capitalist ideology. It also serves to maintain the general level of demand, so that profits remain high. In short, events have forced at least some adherents of the ideology to revise the image of capitalism to incorporate a variety of permanent government expenditures.

(3) "STAGFLATION" AND WAGE-PRICE CONTROLS

Early in the Kennedy Administration, the government proposed a tax cut by which it hoped to stimulate the stagnating economy. This policy represented the first conscious application of Keynesian fiscal principles, and it was held to have been relatively successful in its results. Nevertheless, as escalation of the war in Vietnam increased, inflation began to pose a serious problem. During the middle and late 1960s, many economists had predicted that a policy of wage-price controls ultimately would be unavoidable. But politicians were loathe to initiate such controls and instead employed such halfway measures as wage-price "guidelines."

Then, in August of 1971, President Nixon reversed this trend by instituting a system of wage-price controls that amounted to a further major revision of capitalist principles. This policy was especially striking because it was initiated by a President who not long before contemptuously had described such controls as unnecessary and destructive of freedom. However, the President had been faced with the problem of simultaneous inflation and persistent and climbing unemployment. This new dilemma that confronted the capitalist system was labeled "stagflation" to indicate the heretofore unusual *combination* of stagnation and inflation in the economy. Clearly, the economy faced another crisis, as indicated by the President's appointment of a succession of economists representing several different schools.

President Nixon said he hoped the wage-price control policy would be only temporary, but it seems that capitalist ideology is on the brink of accepting yet another important modification. The operation of the market has been qualified even further, and the government has acquired a new and important role: controlling wages and prices.

Modernizing the Ideology: Capitalism in the 1970s

At the start of this chapter, we pointed out that our concern is with capitalism as an ideology, not as a purported description of actual practice. We are analyzing beliefs, not activities. But the facts of the real world, if salient enough, may affect beliefs. That is what seems to have occurred in the case of capitalist ideology. Evidence of the great divergence of reality from the orthodox capitalist model has forced various modifications. Two problems stand out: (1) the free and competitive market, having been exposed as either inoperative or undesirable, must be replaced by some device that promises to assure wage and price stability, growth and full employment; and (2) government, having been found a vital source of economic stability and profit, must be integrated into the new scheme.

Not all adherents of capitalism make such adjustments, of course; the grip of an established ideology is not released so readily. But over the last two or three decades, the ideology has been sufficiently revised to warrant substantial exploration. We will examine two major directions of the revision: (a) Keynesianism and a permanent supportive role for government, and (b) "People's capitalism" and the "managerial ethic." These are not mutually exclusive, but are rather closely related themes in the modification of capitalist ideology. The first deals principally with a new role for government, the second with changes in relationships between people and other economic entities such as corporations. Both are current in the United States and, together, they serve as overlapping or alternative justifications of American capitalism today.

(1) KEYNESIANISM AND A PERMANENT SUPPORTIVE ROLE FOR GOVERNMENT

In 1936, the British economist John Maynard Keynes published an analysis and prescription concerning depressions that gradually became adopted (in simplified form) by many Americans as a new rationale for the role of government in the economy.[13] In the course of a complex and abstract economic argument, Keynes made two crucial points. First, he denied that depressions were abnormal and that the "natural" condition of the economy was an equilibrium of high productivity, full employment, and stable prices. He saw alternative periods of depression and inflation as the natural order and held that the economy *could* stabilize at a *low* level of productivity and a *high* level of unemployment.

Second, through an analysis too complex to recount here, Keynes concluded that an excess of savings was the key to depressions and that savings were not subject to the demand-and-supply workings of the free market. The danger he saw was that people might hold their money out of consumption, causing a drop in actual purchasing power and ultimately a drop in prices, production, and eventually employment. He contended that employment and overall consumer demand would remain high if savings were fully used, either in purchasing goods and services or in investment.

At this point, government entered Keynes' prescriptions. By exercising its powers to tax, borrow, and spend, government could tap income that would otherwise become unproductive savings or release income to bolster purchasing power. Or it could borrow or otherwise spend to supplement private investment and maintain productivity and employment. In simpler terms, when the economy is heading downward toward recession or depression, the government should decrease taxes, incur a deficit between revenues and expenditures, and invest in public works or other employment-generating activities. When the economy is heading upward toward inflation, it should increase taxes, run a surplus, and cut back its own expenditures and investments. Over the long range, assuming that there are alternating deflationary and inflationary trends, the government's budget would be in rough balance.

Although Keynes' arguments were not heeded during the Depression, capitalism came to adopt them in both ideology and practice. The reversal in the role of government—from an implacable enemy to an indispensable ally—did not sit well with some business-

---

[13] John Maynard Keynes, *General Theory of Employment* (New York: Macmillan, 1936).

men. But for many, the essentials of private decision-making in the economy seemed to have been preserved, while new assurances about stability and full employment had been gained. Although many Americans may be either unfamiliar with or hostile toward Keynesian ideas, only the most rigidly orthodox exponents of capitalism doubt that the government has the legitimate role of managing the economy and assuring its stability.

The modification of capitalist ideology that acquiesced in a Keynesian definition of government responsibility has also come to terms with other means of promoting economic security. The Depression-initiated web of social security legislation, beginning with unemployment compensation and retirement insurance and continuing with aid to families with dependent children and medical care for the aged, has achieved a legitimacy of sorts. It is rationalized as a means of reducing or eliminating individual hardships. Other forms of government assistance that fall into the general category of "welfare" are also legitimated as either necessary to prevent excessive individual suffering or desirable as a means of providing opportunity for all to take part in the competitive economy.

American capitalism has not enthusiastically embraced the new role of government in either of these two forms. But it has come to terms with them on the grounds that the excesses or inadequacies of the market should be moderated. Perhaps another basis for this adaptation is the fear that failure to accept government participation on a limited scale can lead only to its participation on an even larger scale. Both of these grounds are illustrated in passages from an address by President Thomas B. Watson of I.B.M.:

> Much as we may dislike it, I think we've got to realize that in our kind of society there are times when government has to step in and help people with some of their more difficult problems. Programs which assist Americans by reducing the hazards of a free market system without damaging the system itself are necessary, I believe, to its survival. . . .
>
> To be sure, the rights and guarantees that the average man believes in and insists upon may interfere, to some degree, with our ability to manage our enterprises with complete freedom of action. As a result, there are businessmen who either ignore or deny these claims. They then jus-

tify their views by contending that if we were to recognize or grant them, the whole system of free enterprise would be endangered.

This, it would seem to me, amounts to an open invitation to exactly the kind of government intervention that businessmen are seeking to avoid. For if we businessmen insist that free enterprise permits us to be indifferent to those things on which people put high value, then the people will quite naturally assume that free enterprise has too much freedom.[14]

However, regardless of the reason, American capitalism is coming to accept the government's active role. Perhaps this is best illustrated by the fact that businessmen—especially where large corporations and establishments are concerned—have not appeared hesitant to accept President Nixon's wage-price controls program and have not interpreted such controls as inconsonant with capitalist principles.

In addition to the substantial, if reluctant, incorporation of the market-supplement role of government into capitalist ideology, this new principle occasionally has been celebrated under the label of "welfare capitalism." In effect, by making a virtue and an achievement out of what began as necessity, this argument holds that the harshness of market economy has been so fully contained by government assistance and assurances that capitalism has become a mass-oriented system. In other words, the economic system not only spreads material affluence widely, but also provides revenue for the government. This revenue is then applied to the use of the people through various forms of social and economic improvement programs. It is said that "cradle to the grave" security is provided by government and real poverty has been eliminated for all but a handful of untrainable or unmotivated persons. In part, the vast sums annually expended by government are seen as confirmation of its "welfare" role, even though the major share of such expenditures is in the form of purchases from business or salaries to employees.

Within the framework provided by the new role of government, of course, it is assumed that many of the established practices of orthodox capitalism will take place. Indeed, the part played by gov-

---

[14] Cited in Heilbroner, *op. cit.*, p. 34.

ernment is not intended to replace the basic freedom and independent choice of individuals within the system; rather, it is designed to make these rights more effective. In some respects, the government may be seen as a detached referee whose function it is to promote the fairness of the contest taking place. Galbraith is responsible for the famous image of "countervailing powers" which sums up the primary role of private forces as regulators of the economy.[15] Galbraith believed that, when applied, every economic force would attract or create a counterforce to contain it. Therefore, there ordinarily would be no uncontrolled power loose at any time. Confrontation of labor and management provided a convenient illustration, and he generalized from this to other areas. Most important, private forces were capable of exerting a preeminent self-regulating control in most instances. This meant that the regulatory role of government should be limited to those special cases where, for some reason, the private system did not generate the necessary countervailing forces or where inflation made them less effective. When rationally applied, as Galbraith found it had been since the 1930s, this principle had the effect of assuring widespread prosperity for all amid stable economic conditions.

The breakthrough accomplished by Keynesianism was its provision of an *economic* (as opposed to a social, moral, or political) rationale for the use of government. The types of activity in which Keynes believed the government should engage were not, after all, very different from the kind of activity in which governments typically do engage—that is, taxing, borrowing, and spending. The specific purposes for which these acts of state were now to be designed and the scale on which they were to be applied were distinctive. And the consequences, in terms of reliance upon the same government that had heretofore been exclusively the source of intervention or interference, were profound. Among other things, as we have seen, Keynesianism brought with it an umbrella that legitimated several other forms of government assistance to individuals. It also legitimated public works in economic terms and blunted the attacks that characterize them as mere unwise spending. The net result was to place the government squarely within the revised principles of

---

[15] John Kenneth Galbraith, *American Capitalism* (Boston: Houghton Mifflin, 1952).

capitalist ideology. This left as the major question only the *nature* of the relationship between the government and the economy (particularly, which was to dominate the other), not whether there should be any contact between the two centers of power.

(2) PEOPLE'S CAPITALISM AND THE MANAGERIAL ETHIC

The second theme in the modification of capitalist ideology concerns the emergence of new forms of private relationships within the economy as opposed to the new role of government that was the subject of the last theme. It is composed of two main strands. One is the argument that new forms of ownership and control of economic power have developed and, as a result, the giant corporation is not the threat it once seemed to be. The other is the argument that the managers of the great corporations have developed a special type of professionalism and public spiritedness that makes them relatively benign and socially responsible entities.

A. A. Berle's *The American Economic Republic*[16] illustrates both of these. Faced with his own landmark finding that the managers of large corporations apparently were free of stockholders' control, Berle concluded that such managers were restrained by the force of public opinion. This principle also assumed, of course, that public opinion occasionally would manifest itself—and make real its threat to corporate autonomy—through regulatory action on the part of government. The overall effect would be to render the corporation approximately as socially responsible as any other person in the society. In time, corporate managers would develop a kind of "conscience" and employ their powers moderately and without danger to the rest of the economy or society.

Berle finally integrated this principle of managerial behavior into a more comprehensive image of the new "economic republic." He added the vital dimension of active popular involvement and control—ultimately a kind of "people's capitalism." He argued that the people really had assumed control of the corporate economy through a number of means and that the economy therefore was obliged to (and did) respond to public preference. This control was

---

[16] Adolf A. Berle, *The American Economic Republic* (New York: Harcourt, Brace & World, 1963).

exercised through a wide diffusion of stock ownership. This diffusion did not give rise to direct control over specific corporations (which would have been contrary to his own prior analysis) but assured that managers would not be directed by a few wealthy persons and would be free to act subject to their own socially responsible inclinations. The people also shared widely in the wealth produced by this corporate economy, both by virtue of the spread of ownership (and dividends) and through the general level of affluence that it created. Reduced inequality would contribute to increased political awareness and capability, and an attentive public would use its political power through the vehicle of the government to impose restraints upon corporate activities of which it disapproved. Only occasional exercises of such power would be necessary to keep managers tuned carefully to the trends of public opinion.

For Berle, this prospect of socially responsible managers seeking avidly to conform their behavior to the principles and preferences of an attentive public is the key to the progress and the ongoing democratization of the American economy. He terms this "the transcendental margin," declaring that it is the means whereby standards of justice, equality, and morality are being integrated steadily into the American economy. In his eyes, individual self-interest no longer is the sole motivation that animates the economy. Instead, popularly shared communitarian and humanitarian values are operative; the economic system becomes a means to ends that are both material and transcendental—morally and spiritually ennobling and uplifting.

This glowing image has not found its way into capitalist ideology in its entirety, but the ideology has endorsed a substantial part of it. Certainly, the idea of a "people's capitalism," in which ownership and control are spread democratically and highly professional managers respond to popular preferences expressed in public consensus or government action, has achieved widespread acceptance in the United States. So has the belief that this economy has generated *and distributed on an essentially egalitarian basis* an affluence unimagined elsewhere in the world. Only a handful of the unmotivated or the wilfully ignorant, it is assumed, can have failed to enjoy a share in this unique productivity. In this view, American capitalism has modernized itself naturally and taken on the forms that are most profitable for, and most desired by, the American people.

Berle's emphasis on popular controls over the economy is less frequently echoed than are his assertions about the socially responsible character of the new professional managers. Many writers have detailed the ways in which the new business ethics have diverged from the old standards.[17] This "managerial ideology" is an important new strand in mid-twentieth century capitalist ideology.[18] It is associated with the larger corporations and the business community surrounding them, rather than with the myriad smaller businesses where the traditional capitalist ideology is more current (and more likely to be confirmed in market and other economic conditions). It holds that the American economy has been through a vast transformation, that it is now indeed a new economy, that its technological sophistication mandates large size, and that the economy today is really a collective effort in which everyone is working for the common good. The problems it sees are exclusively technical. In other words, we all want to achieve maximum affluence for the largest number and are dedicated to that end. Only some technical questions about how best to achieve that goal, rather than deep, value-based issues of who should get how much or who should control the economy, remain to be solved.

Summary: Capitalism in the Late Twentieth Century

These two types of modifications of capitalist ideology have thus added new elements concerning the role of government and the nature of private relationships and motivations. What is new and different is a change from the view of government as almost exclusively a threat. Capitalism has not come full circle to the point of viewing government as a fully legitimate participant in the economy. But it has acknowledged that there are stabilizing purposes for which government can and should be used and that government expenditures and other policies provide a means for the advancement of business enterprise. Obviously, government's new role is not without constant controversy: there is ample room for disagreement about the propriety of any particular use of government, about its timing, sufficiency, and so on. There are also divergences within

---

[17] For three major illustrations, see James Burnham, *The Managerial Revolution* (New York: Doubleday, 1956).

[18] A full account may be found in Sutton et al., *op. cit.*

capitalist ideology about the extent to which government and the economy should be seen as antagonists or partners. Nevertheless, the main thrust of the ideology today acknowledges government in a way that was unknown prior to the New Deal.

Another addition to capitalist ideology is the aura of benignity and egalitarianism that now forms part of the image of the American economy. Its new size and concentration involve not threat, but opportunity; monopoly, oligopoly, technology, impersonality—all are for the best. Depressions are no longer real possibilities because government is managing and stabilizing the business cycle. Productivity is higher than ever and affluence is well distributed throughout the population. Individual security and opportunity are assured by government-sponsored programs of various kinds. Wide agreement as to the purpose of economic activity assures socially desirable behavior by the big corporations, which are subject to popular control in a variety of ways in any event. Together, welfare capitalism, people's capitalism, and the new business ethic of the professional managers have produced the prospect of ever-expanding affluence and individual satisfactions in the United States.

These two modifications have come to full flower in the post-World War II years. They represent much greater optimism and pride in achievement than did the prewar version of the ideology. But for the most part, they remain merely a gloss upon the basic world view, values, and goals of capitalism. What is *not* different, or at least only marginally changed, are the broad assumptions about man as a competitive, profit-seeking individual and the need to allow full freedom in the economy and society. The values of individualism, materialism, and the rights and prerogatives of private property are unchanged or only marginally affected. The free and competitive market is still taken to be the standard, from which deviations are to be accepted only after a showing of special need and circumstances. Individuals perform their social duty by serving their own self-interest. Those who do not succeed in the competition bear the primary responsibility and should suffer the consequences and, through the limited assistance properly made available to them, should seek to prepare themselves for productive roles in the system as soon as possible. Conversely, those who do well have earned their rewards and should not be expected to share their achievements with others.

This amalgam of economic beliefs, with the new interpretations engrafted upon the established principles, makes up the economic half of the mainstream of American ideology. It is closely integrated with the political half, which we shall describe in the next chapter. Indeed, the congeniality between the two segments of the mainstream of American ideology is so great that they are frequently blurred together. Nevertheless, a strict analysis reveals that one set of assumptions and beliefs deals chiefly with economic matters and the other with political arrangements. The two are mutually supportive belief systems, however, for each makes sometimes unstated assumptions about the other. For example, capitalism assumes a government of limited powers which practices laissez-faire policies. Liberalism constructs such a government because it assumes the effective working of the capitalist economic system, particularly the free and competitive market. Both ideologies rest on the same basic values—individualism, materialism, private property, and individual self-seeking as a primary element in the definition of freedom.

Annotated Bibliography

Anderson, James E. *Politics and the Economy*. Boston: Little, Brown, 1966. Good survey of the national government's role in the contemporary American economy.

Barber, Richard J. *The American Corporation: Its Power, Its Money, Its Politics*. New York: Dutton, 1970. A thorough current analysis of the role of supercorporations and the economy they dominate.

Baritz, Loren. *The Servants of Power*. New York: Wiley, 1965. A study of American industry's use of and dependence upon the skills of social science expertise. The leading example is industrial psychology.

Berle, Adolf A. *The American Economic Republic*. New York: Harcourt, Brace & World, 1963. A recent summary of Berle's thought, emphasizing the themes of peoples' capitalism and managerial ethic.

Berle, Adolf A., and Gardiner C. Means. *The Modern Corporation and Private Property*. New York: Macmillan, 1932. The classic study of concentration and control in the corporate economy. Reissued in paperback and updated by the authors in 1967 by Harcourt, Brace & World.

Burnham, James. *The Managerial Revolution*. New York: Doubleday, 1956. A classic study of the trend toward control by corporate managers and their standards of operation. Subsequent writings develop a generally conservative view of capitalist evolution.

Drucker, Peter. *The Concept of the Corporation*. New York: Day, 1946. One of several thoughtful works, again from a conservative perspective.

Edwards, Richard, Michael Reich, and Thomas Weisskopf, eds. *The Capitalist System*. Englewood Cliffs, N.J.: Prentice-Hall, 1972. A large collection of articles, essays, and excerpts concerning the problems, structure, and functioning of capitalism, with a focus on the United States. Also a section dealing with alternatives to the capitalist system.

Galbraith, John Kenneth. *The Affluent Society*. Boston: Houghton Mifflin, 1957. A summary of the views of the celebrated liberal economist prior to his government service and subsequent move to stronger reformist analysis.

Heilbroner, Robert. *The Limits of American Capitalism*. New York: Harper & Row, 1966. A brief argument by a prolific liberal economist concerning the basic values and scope of capacity of American capitalism.

Miliband, Ralph. *The State in Capitalist Society*. New York: Basic Books, 1969. An analysis of the role of the state in advanced capitalist societies from the perspective of a Marxist.

Moynihan, Daniel P. *Capitalism and Democracy: Schumpeter Revisited*. New York: New York University Press, 1972. Although Moynihan shares many of Schumpeter's views, he believes that capitalism can survive along with democracy if corporations respect the public interest and act responsibly.

Reagan, Michael D. *The Managed Economy*. New York: Oxford University Press, 1963. One of the best short analyses combining business ideology with evidence about government activities regarding the economy. Contains an excellent bibliography.

Shonfield, Andrew. *Modern Capitalism*. New York: Oxford University Press, 1965. An excellent comparative analysis of trends in public-private power relationships in Britain, France, Germany, and the United States.

Stein, Herbert. *The Fiscal Revolution in America*. Chicago: University of Chicago Press, 1969. An in-depth study of the gradual emergence and development of what is popularly known as the "New Economics": that is, the government's imperative role as "economy-manager" in achieving goals of economic prosperity, growth and stability.

Sutton, Francis X., Seymour E. Harris, Carl Kaysen, and James Tobin. *The American Business Creed*. Cambridge: Harvard University Press, 1956. An exhaustive but highly readable analysis of the beliefs of American businessmen.

United States Department of Commerce. *Profits and the American Economy*. Washington, D.C.: U.S. Department of Commerce, 1965. A government pamphlet intended for popular consumption giving the capitalist explanation of the role of profits in a "free-enterprise" system.

3

Liberalism

Decades of highly varied use, both as justification and as denunciation, have robbed "liberalism" of much of its specific meaning. In its early classic usage, liberalism—much like capitalism, its sibling—implied primacy for the individual and strict limitations upon governments to ensure full freedom for the individual to serve his needs as he saw fit. In the twentieth century, growing concern that changing economic and social conditions made it impossible for many individuals to do so led to a near reversal in liberalism's attitude toward the use of government. Given such flexibility and such a course of evolution, it is not surprising that the term liberalism carries many meanings for different people. A brief survey of the origins and evolution of liberalism will provide a setting for understanding the contemporary version and the challenges it faces.

Liberalism's individualist beginnings may be traced to an earlier time, but its emergence as a comprehensive set of political principles usually is associated with John Locke, a seventeenth century Englishman. Although it was written much earlier, Locke published his major work, *A Second Treatise of Government,*[1] in 1690, shortly after the English Parliament had asserted its authority and replaced one line of kings with another in the Glorious Revolution of 1688. Locke's perspective was that of the mercantilist financier and busi-

---

[1] John Locke, *A Second Treatise of Civil Government.* Citations here are to the Hafner Library of Classics edition, Thomas I. Cook, ed. (New York: Hafner Publishing Co., 1947).

nessman, caught in the middle between lords and peasants. No such social group had existed under the social and economic conditions of feudalism, and legitimating and protecting the right of such financiers and merchants to do business seemed a heavy task.

The central theme of Locke's ideas was the right of individuals to be secure in their property—which in turn required strict limitations on the potentially threatening power of government, then dominated by nobles and the king. Locke defined property as that body of goods, land, and rights to which individuals gained title through mixing their labor with unimproved resources and producing something that had greater value than it had in its original state. The sole purpose of government was to protect these natural rights of individuals. It had no broader social functions and was limited by the individuals who created it through a contract that spelled out the authority of officeholders and the limits on the scope of their powers. Locke summed up the individual-government relationship in these words:

> The reason why men enter into society is the preservation of their property; and the end why they choose and authorize a legislative is that there may be laws made and rules set as guards and fences to the properties of all members of the society to limit the power and moderate the dominion of every part and member of the society; for it can never be supposed to be the will of the society that the legislative should have a power to destroy that which everyone designs to secure by entering into society, and for which the people submitted themselves to legislators of their own making.[2]

As capitalism became more prominent, liberalism also evolved, in effect, applying capitalist principles to the organization and operation of government. Liberalism emphasized individualism and saw economic self-interest as the principal motivational force in social life. Moreover, the free and competitive market was the vital means —and the only means—to the good life. Government was a danger, constantly threatening to interfere with the natural processes of the market. In general, economic life was central and politics was strictly a secondary sphere. All individuals were concerned primarily with

---

[2] *Ibid.,* p. 233.

their economic needs and goals. Men who succeeded in the economic world could bring great benefits to society; those in politics could serve best by doing nothing or by heeding the instructions of the economy.

With industrialization, urbanization, and rapid population increase, both the needs and the consequences of economic life began to impose new demands upon the state. Business and industry began to secure government subsidies, supports, and protections of various kinds. Segments of the public sought regulation of some of the activities of business and protection for individuals against some of the economic hardships that resulted from the new conditions. Liberalism responded to these changing economic circumstances, much as did capitalism, by developing a rationale for occasional government actions, ostensibly to support and promote the workings of the market. Thus we come to the middle and late twentieth century.

The World View of American Liberalism

(1) THE DOMESTIC SCENE

When liberals look at the United States, they see a mixed but essentially capitalist economy, which they accept unquestioningly as the major achievement of American social life. Capitalism, operating through the market as supplemented and aided by government, has succeeded in creating a unique affluence that has, in turn, been spread broadly throughout the society. By alert use of the economy-managing tools, government can both maintain stability and growth in the economy and help to steadily reduce the number of poor people in the society. A generally middle-class social structure in which agreement on fundamental policies and practices is widely shared is the result.

Liberalism's world view not only assumes that the political system's task is to support and promote the operating capitalist economic sytem, but it views the political process itself through capitalist economic concepts. Politics is seen as a free market for the exchange of demands, support, and public policies. Each individual has his specific wants and equivalent purchasing power—one vote. He "buys" the policies and candidates of his choice in the competitive market on election day. If the products he seeks are not available, the demand will soon create the supply. Officeholders act as brokers, adjusting government policy products to the wants of the number of consumers necessary to obtain the votes of a majority. In this fashion, participating individuals control major government policies, which in turn may be understood as flexibly responding to changing popular preferences *and* representing the public interest. In realistic and modern language, this is democracy.

In a complex industrial society such as the United States, special conditions must be maintained to keep this market truly free and competitive. By and large, however, these conditions have been met. In particular, three combined legal and social processes assure their fulfillment. First, opportunity for all individuals to voice their wants and demands is maintained through adherence to the civil rights of freedom of speech, freedom of press, and freedom of association. Constitutional protection of these rights enjoys the support of most leaders and is guaranteed in practice by the courts. The judicial process effectively and neutrally balances the needs of the society for self-preservation against its simultaneous interest in maintaining open political processes.

Second, competing political parties offer voters choices representing the realistic alternatives that a potential majority of the population might actually want. This is made possible by regular elections of party officials and delegates, by the natural desire of politicians to win office, and by a necessary internal process of compromise between extremes of popular preference within the party. This electoral system is consistent with the social heterogeneity of the population, the diversity of their interests, and the varying levels of participation in politics that are natural to them. At the close of a major study of voting behavior, for example, the research team concluded that classical democratic theory placed too much emphasis on the participation of all citizens and allowed the achievements of the system as a whole too little weight:

> We need some people who are active in a certain respect, others in the middle, and still others passive. . . . Low interest provides maneuvering room for political shifts necessary for a complex society in a period of rapid change. Compromise might be based upon sophisticated awareness of

costs and returns—perhaps impossible to demand of a mass society—but it is more often induced by indifference. Some people are and should be highly interested in politics, but not everyone is or needs to be. Only the doctrinaire would deprecate the moderate indifference that facilitates compromise.[3]

Finally, an elaborate network of voluntary associations (or interest groups) provides supplementary representation for many individuals. These groups reflect the social reality and diversity of ethnic, religious, occupational, economic, and regional interests within the nation, and their interaction is the principal dynamic of between-elections politics. A leading political scientist characterized the importance of interest group activities in this way:

> At bottom, group interests are the animating forces in the political process. . . . Whatever the bases of group interest may be, the study of politics must rest on an analysis of the objectives and composition of the interest groups within a society. . . . The chief vehicles for the expression of group interest are political parties and pressure groups. Through these formal mechanisms groups of people with like interests make themselves felt in the balancing of political forces.[4]

Liberalism sees this interest group activity as the leading characteristic of American politics, the means whereby the contemporary political "market" is kept open and responsive to popular preferences. Liberalism's image of politics in the United States is sometimes labeled "pluralism" [5] or "pluralist democracy" [6] by its spokesmen. Americans are seen as such joiners that every significant inter-

---

[3] Bernard R. Berelson, Paul F. Lazarsfeld, and William N. McPhee, *Voting* (Chicago: University of Chicago Press, 1954), pp. 314–315.

[4] V. O. Key, Jr., *Politics, Parties, and Pressure Groups* (New York: Knopf, 1942), pp. 23–24; cited in Daniel Bell, "The Adequacy of Our Concepts," in Bertram Gross, ed., *A Great Society?* (New York: Basic Books, 1966).

[5] See, for example, Theodore Lowi, *The End of Liberalism* (New York: Norton, 1969), or William Kornhauser, *The Politics of Mass Society* (Glencoe, Ill.: Free Press, 1959).

[6] Robert A. Dahl, *Pluralist Democracy in the United States: Conflict and Consensus* (Chicago: Rand McNally, 1967).

est is represented by one or more groups that press their claims upon each other and upon the government. The political arena is a vast array of competing groups engaged in a continuing process of building alliances, appealing for popular support, bargaining, pressuring, and negotiating. Finally, officeholders weigh the conflicting claims, mediate compromises, and produce policy. Then the scene shifts again to implementing agencies, the courts, and the electoral realm and goes on in slightly revised form. The structure of power in the institutions of American government is highly conducive to the impact of interest groups, for the many committees, agencies, levels of government, and the like assure that every group has access at some point and thus a chance to make itself felt at some stage of decision-making. Again, this process amounts to a definition of democracy. Another leading political scientist says:

> It is a markedly decentralized system. Decisions are made by endless bargaining; perhaps in no other national political system in the world is bargaining so basic a component of the political process. . . . With all its defects, it does nonetheless provide a high probability that any active and legitimate group will make itself heard effectively at some stage in the process of decision. This is no mean thing in a political system.[7]

Interest-group politics produces some vital returns for the American political system. Participants feel included in the system, and they learn to become politically effective and tolerant of each other's views. Those who rise to group leadership become particularly committed to protecting the rights of others because they realize that their own future opportunities to be heard may be at stake. Groups balance each other and individuals within them feel conflicting pressures, keeping the whole political system closer to the middle of the road. Thus, stability is enhanced, democratic values are promoted, and representation is provided—all at the same time and through an entirely natural American process.[8]

This is not to say that advocates of liberalism believe all problems have been solved, for they see the ideology as acutely tuned to

---

[7] Robert A. Dahl, *Preface to Democratic Theory* (Chicago: University of Chicago Press, 1963), p. 150.

[8] For a full statement, see David B. Truman, *The Governmental Process* (New York: Knopf, 1951).

unserved needs in many dimensions—from broader sharing of
wealth and opportunity among the poor to provision of more public
goods, such as hospitals and roads, to greater sensitivity to the needs
of the human spirit. But the key to solving these problems is a productive, stable economy. When such unserved needs are seen against
the background of the past and in terms of the practical problems of
achievement amid many other demands and needs, the American
political system must be understood to be highly responsive and to
have delivered effectively in recent decades.

(2) THE INTERNATIONAL SCENE

American liberals see the United States as uniquely favored
among the nations of the world. No other country has approached
the standard of living generated by the productivity of the American
economy. Nor do other peoples exhibit the political maturity of the
American people or enjoy the broad scope of democratic freedoms
and popular government control that is characteristic of the United
States. However, these American achievements both impose responsibilities upon the national government and cause it difficulties in its
relations with the rest of the world. The power of the United States
can be a great force for good in the world, as can the example of our
political institutions and processes. Our sole interest in the rest of
the world is continued peace, stability, and opportunity for American business to trade with, and invest in, other countries. But hostile
forces prevent the realization of these altruistic goals.

Communism is the principal obstacle to world peace and orderly development. The form of government actually created by
those who profess to endorse the disarmingly attractive goals of
communism is a totalitarian dictatorship that denies free expression,
eliminates democratic choice in elections, and manages the lives of
its citizens. These self-perpetuating elites are compelled by their
ideology and self-maintenance needs to seek expansion of their
domination and to try to undermine the United States. Writing in
1969, Arthur Schlesinger, Jr., characterized the roots of communist
behavior from the cold war to the present as follows:

> Marxism-Leninism gave the Russian leaders a view of
> the world according to which all societies were inexorably
> destined to proceed along appointed roads by appointed

stages until they achieved the classless nirvana. Moreover, given the resistance of the capitalists to this development, the existence of any noncommunist state was *by definition* a threat to the Soviet Union. . . . So long as the United States remained a capitalist democracy, no American policy, given Moscow's theology, could hope to win basic Soviet confidence. . . . So long as the Soviet Union remained a messianic state, ideology compelled a steady expansion of communist power. (Italics in original.) [9]

The disillusionment of some older American liberals with communism as it evolved in Stalin's Soviet Union has had an important influence on liberalism generally. What results is a specially rigid posture or "hard line" against the evils of communism and, in particular, against Soviet or Chinese expansionism. Communist nations' actions generally have been perceived as united and controlled by a single central source. Similarly, Third World social reform movements are perceived as Communist where, in fact, they may be nationalist, socialist, or merely opportunistic independence movements. In the late 1960s, some liberals began to see separate centers of power within the communist world and to treat them independently. But nearly all shared the view that the only way in which American security could be assured was to be ready at all times to employ massive military power to hold back Communist expansion. The form of the continuing conflict with communism might vary, from the chiefly ideological, to the small war over Third World territory, to the brink of nuclear confrontation. But only American firmness and military readiness can dissuade Communist adventurism and permit the competition to remain a "cold war" that takes the form of a battle for men's minds, in which the allegiance of the Third World nations is the prize. During the time purchased thereby, space exploits, military assistance, and economic aid will help to maintain American predominance. With the open door for American business thus maintained, the Third World may be enabled to develop in a stable and perhaps capitalist fashion.

Occasionally, either indigenous or Communist-inspired local movements arise to threaten the status quo. The United States re-

---

[9] Arthur Schlesinger, Jr., *The Crisis of Confidence: Ideas, Power and Violence in America* (Boston: Houghton Mifflin, 1969), p. 136.

peatedly has been obliged to defend established governments against such encroachments, either economically or militarily. This necessity of defending the non-Communist ("free") world has led to some actions that probably are not desirable for their own sakes. Vietnam is one of these. But experience teaches that peace and stability sometimes can be obtained only at the risk and cost of small wars. Remembering Munich and other pre-World War II appeasements of Hitler's Germany, liberalism sees the avoidance of ultimate nuclear war as requiring a firm military posture today. The major flaw in Vietnam, in this view, was error in calculating the chances and means of achieving a desirable result. In reviewing what went wrong in Vietnam, Arthur Schlesinger, Jr., declares:

> The tragedy of Vietnam is the tragedy of the catastrophic over-extension and misapplication of valid principles. . . . I do not see that our original involvement in Vietnam was *per se* immoral. What was immoral was the employment of means of destruction out of all proportion to rational purposes. The wreckage we wrought in Vietnam had no rational relationship to a serious assessment of our national interest or to the demonstrated involvement of our national security.[10]

Values and Goals

Liberal values may be analyzed in two categories. First are the values that concern creation of the good life or the good man. Because liberalism views the economic world (and, within it, the free market) as primary, natural, and fulfilling, these values are much like the basic values of capitalism. Second are the values associated with the kind of political process that will succeed in defending both the economic and the political markets from such artificial forces as concentrations of power, particularly from concentration of power in government. These values closely resemble liberalism's images of the American political process. Descriptions merge with prescriptions, and the "is" (as perceived) sounds very much like the "ought"

---

[10] *Ibid.*, pp. 174–175.

that is desired. What starts as an objective description becomes a celebration of achievement; such is the power, and the occasional defensiveness, of a dominant ideology. Almost any high school civics text, and most college American government texts, readily illustrate this process.

(1) VALUES PRIMARILY ASSOCIATED WITH THE QUALITY OF PRIVATE LIFE

The central value of liberalism, as noted, is individualism. Individuals are entitled to serve their own interests in order that both they and the society might develop and progress. Their entitlement is absolute, part of their birthright; it belongs to them solely by virtue of their existence as persons and not through the benevolent grant of any outside source. Thus it is appropriate to speak of "rights" of the individual, such as the right to hold property, the right to take part in politics, or the right to personal liberty.

To assure freedom and the openness of the political processes, the individual must be protected against encroachments upon his rights from those sources of power in the society that might reduce the area of personal freedom surrounding him. Individual rights are secured against government by framing them into legal descriptions and expressing these as prohibitions in the basic contract by which government is created. The Bill of Rights of the Constitution is the leading example of the expression of individual rights by American liberalism.

The principal rights of the individual, however, represent independent values in themselves. In effect, liberalism sees a comprehensive package of rights surrounding the individual. But these rights are valued in order of priority—they are not all of equal significance to liberal ideology. Two rights or values that have long contended for top place in the liberal priority ranking are *property* and *equality*. Property is essential to permit men to retain the fruits of their labor and to enable them to be truly independent individuals. Equality usually has been defined as an equal right to take part in the contest for advantages that the market institutionalizes. It is also seen as necessary to enable citizens to take part as equivalent units in the political marketplace. But on occasion, the rights of some to retain the advantages gained through the free and competitive market may conflict with the rights of others to compete on an equal basis. Any effort to truly equalize the opportunity of some to compete may result in the reduction of the freedom and property rights of others. In actual practice, property rights usually have triumphed. Support of equality, which always has been strong, hardened during the last decade; nevertheless, it is probably accurate to say that progress has been more in the realm of rhetoric than of reality.

Liberalism has juggled these two potentially conflicting values, generally succeeding in harmonizing them. This is no easy task, for the two can be quite contradictory. In the 1960s, for example, the efforts of blacks to advance the value of equality by means of civil rights legislation such as open housing laws ran up against the claim of some whites for observance of the value of the property right of owners to sell houses to whomever they pleased. The clash occurs over and over again in this subject area: in public accommodations laws, in fair employment laws, and in claims for "compensation" or "reparations" for blacks. Property rights as a paramount value are manifested also in resistance to controls on pollution, to zoning regulations, to taxation, and to social legislation generally. Equality manifests itself in demands for "one man, one vote" election arrangements, for full citizenship for blacks, and for "participatory democracy" in neighborhood governments.

Equality has been expanding in meaning, particularly in the last two decades, and its challenge to property rights increasingly is forcing this potential conflict within liberal ideology out into the open. At first, equality was understood to mean only the formal or legal equality of opportunity to take part in political affairs such as the right to vote. Even then, its scope was limited to property-owning males. The right has been expanded to include all citizens, although it was extended to blacks only after the Civil War and to women as recently as 1919. But two types of further expansion in the concept of equality also have occurred, converting it into something perhaps better called "human rights." First, the concept has acquired more than a formal or legal dimension, reaching as well to the tangible reality of the existence or nonexistence of the right for people in the circumstances in which they live. Black citizens in the South, for example, had a formal right to vote long before they were allowed to participate in the real sense in elections. Second, the concept has been expanded from its original role of assuring participation in public affairs to include the social and economic conditions of people. For many liberals, equality now means the rights of people to have some minimum share in the economic prosperity of the American society. Government's obligation to assist individuals in regard to economic security *and* opportunity is very clear. With such developments in the understanding of human rights or equality, the tension arising from the conflict between property and equality rights is becoming increasingly evident.

(2) VALUES PRIMARILY ASSOCIATED WITH THE POLITICAL PROCESS THAT IS CAPABLE OF DEFENDING THE ECONOMIC AND POLITICAL MARKETS

To keep the political and economic markets open and competitive, concentrations of power, particularly in government, must be prevented. One way is to limit government through legal prohibitions; another is to foster a social process that will give meaning to such limitations. Thus, one major value is the principle of limited government. Government has been erected by many individuals to serve and protect their rights. Its powers stem from the voluntary grant of those individuals, and it has no other powers. It is thus a government of limited powers, capable only of doing what it has been set up to do. In short, it is a servant, subject to dismissal for failure to perform its task adequately or for taking on tasks not assigned. The question of whether it is empowered to do particular acts is one that may be resolved by reference to the basic creating instrument, in this case the Constitution. The virtue of this is that the acts of government may be challenged at any time by a single individual, and the process of public action must stop while the authority of government is determined in court.

Another major value of liberalism, also expressed as one of the natural rights of individuals, is the individual's right to be secure against arbitrary government interference with life, liberty, or property. This is the right to *due process*. It means that government power may not be applied to limit or take the individual's life, liberty, or property *except through due process*—that is, in accordance with the procedures established by law for such action. The distinction is between regular, accepted, authorized ways of operating and arbitrary, discretionary, or whimsical uses of power by government officials. Before a man may be jailed and deprived of his liberty, for example, there must have been a properly enacted law on the books prohibiting his act, and he must be shown to have committed that act so clearly that a jury of ordinary citizens finds after presentation of all the evidence in an open trial that he did so. In emphasizing due process, liberalism seeks to accomplish two things: first, it achieves another dimension of protection for the freedom of the individual; and second, it renders the actions of government more mechanical exercise and less a personal or discretionary vehicle for men to employ.

Underlying the values just discussed, and making possible their realization, is the strong liberal faith in *legalism*—the capacity to express rights and prohibitions in contractual terms and to enforce them through legal and judicial means. Elaborate legal mechanisms are seen as enabling the avoidance of society-splitting conflicts and securing individual rights even under circumstances where people care deeply about conflicting goals. "The law" takes on a special quality of its own in liberal ideology, becoming something more than the acts of men and, therefore, worthy of special respect and regard. Answers to deep value conflicts are said to lie within the reservoir of wisdom represented by the law. Its neutrality is asserted, and neither the circumstances of its enactment nor the disputes of learned lawyers and judges over its proper interpretation are permitted to legitimate others' denial of validity to particular laws that may appear to them unjust or selfish. Only where law receives such independent regard is it possible to realize the values of individualism, property, equality, due process, and limited government in the manner that liberalism endorses.

But the major value to be served through law, and through the interest group type of social process, is the creation and maintenance of *fair procedures* for decision-making. Every man's opinion and preference in politics is just as good as any other's, just as all wants are equal in the economic marketplace. There is no way to choose between possible alternative policies on moral or ethical grounds. Indeed, it would be dangerous to try to do so, for bitter disputes would arise. One man's version of morality may be utterly repugnant to another's. Far better to have an utterly impartial process of decision-making, similar to the economic market, where impersonal decisions (and not judgments on the *merits* of claims) determine results. Justice and fairness are thus defined in terms of consistency and neutrality of decisional standards, not by the advantages conferred or purposes served by the decision itself. In effect, liberalism places its confidence in the *method* by which decisions are made rather than in the people who make them or in the inherent quality of the decisions themselves. A complicated system of checks, balances, division and limitation of powers, resting ultimately on majority-rule elections but with multiple opportunities for individual impact, becomes in itself the solution to the problem of conflict. Deep value conflicts that are likely to excite and divide people and threaten stability, not all conflicts, are avoided in this way. At least some basic issues are muted, while others are held and resolved within the more "responsible" leadership echelons.

This brings us to liberalism's values regarding the social system that will support effective limits on power. The basic premise may be seen in the words of Robert A. Dahl, a leading political scientist:

> The fundamental axiom in the theory and practice of American pluralism is, I believe, this: Instead of a single center of power there must be multiple centers of power, none of which is or can be wholly sovereign.[11]

These multiple centers of power, in social terms, are to be found in the interest groups into which the society is divided and in the method by which such groups are consulted in decision-making. The good system, in which natural self-interest is harnessed (much as occurs in the case of individuals), produces the greatest good for the greatest number.

The pluralist process achieves this, according to liberalism. In effect, all groups share an investment in maintaining the fairness and openness of the process through which they seek to attain their ends. Each wants to be able to be heard when it is seeking something, and in order to assure such opportunity, it must help at all times to defend the rules of the game by which the polity is conducted. These rules involve fair hearings for all, tolerance for all views, and regular procedures for making decisions. Above all, every party to this process should be willing to try to see the other side's problems and

---

[11] Dahl, *Pluralist Democracy,* p. 24.

to compromise somewhere short of its own goals—and, also, short of absolute disaster for the other side. When each group knows in advance that its needs and interests will not be totally ignored or eradicated by the other if that side should win, the debate loses some of its bitterness.

The merits of this system are enormous. It channels goal-seeking, promotes compromise, and makes for flexibility and progress. Not only does it mute conflict and stabilize politics, but it leaves officeholders free to act wisely and in the "public interest." The "public interest" in this case is understood as being *whatever* policy emerges from open and fair procedures. The established legal procedures and the pluralist social process that supports and defends the rules of the game acquire the status of an independent political value. For liberalism, the rules become a kind of test of loyalty to the entire process: those who adhere may continue to play; those who do not are beyond redemption and properly may be punished. In the words of a former Supreme Court justice:

> Procedure is the bone structure of a democratic society. Our scheme of law affords great latitude for dissent and opposition. It compels wide tolerance not only for their expression but also for the organization of people and forces to bring about the acceptance of the dissenter's claim. Both our institutions and the characteristics of our national behavior make it possible for opposition to be translated into policy, for dissent to prevail. We have alternatives to violence.[12]

It is vital that the rules be enforced and that conflict be reduced or absorbed in this manner because agitated masses otherwise may threaten stability. The authors of a major voting study, applauding low levels of interest and knowledge among the electorate as functional for democratic politics, ask:

> How could a mass democracy work if all the people were deeply involved in politics? Lack of interest by some people is not without its benefits, too. True, the highly interested voters vote more, and know more about the cam-

---

[12] Abe Fortas, *Concerning Dissent and Civil Disobedience* (New York: New American Library, 1968), p. 60.

paign and read and listen more, and participate more; however, they are also less open to persuasion and less likely to change. Extreme interest goes with extreme partisanship and might culminate in rigid fanaticism that could destroy democratic processes if generalized throughout the community.[13]

They call for a balance of stabilizing groups and multiple attachments of other kinds so that most citizens are not led to excessive involvement in politics:

> For political democracy to survive, (certain) features are required: the intensity of conflict must be limited, the rate of change must be restrained, stability in the social and economic structure must be maintained, a pluralistic social organization must exist, and a basic consensus must bind together the contending parties.[14]

This concern is broadly shared, particularly among liberal social scientists. Many see the group structure as the principal bulwark against extremist actions by masses. Civil liberties are believed to depend on the more sophisticated support of elites, many of whom will have learned the rules of the game in their interest group activities. They also depend on competition between elements of elites. These principles are well summarized in the words of a leading sociologist:

> Civil liberty requires considerable social autonomy of *both* elites and non-elites. This means specifically that elites and non-elites must have the following characteristics:
> (a) There must be extensive self-government, private as well as public, and individuals must belong to several self-governing units.
> (b) There must be extensive opportunities for elites to formulate policies and take action without *ad hoc* interefence from the outside.
> . . . social pluralism is a social arrangement which performs this function. A plurality of independent and limited-func-

---

[13] Berelson et al., *op. cit.*, p. 314.
[14] *Ibid.*, p. 313.

tion groups supports liberal democracy by providing social bases of free and open competition for leadership, widespread participation in the selection of leaders, restraint in the application of pressures on leaders, and self-government in wide areas of social life.[15]

The other major return to be realized from a multiplicity of groups and strong support for the established procedures is the provision of some autonomy and discretion for governing elites. The advantages of decision-making by elites are that elites take into consideration policy continuity, that they are insulated from the influence of the potentially emotional, irrational masses, and that they generally possess at least a degree of expertise. Liberals assert that there are difficult decisions to be made and that only a few people are qualified to make them. Pluralist democracy is also seen as providing these opportunities through its many layers of authority and its development of a kind of "subculture" of elites. The latter is an essentially self-perpetuating group of specially adept persons who carry the principal responsibility for keeping the system on an even keel, making the crucial decisions, and setting the agenda for mass political actions. In the words of political scientist V. O. Key, Jr.:

> The longer one frets with the puzzle of how democratic regimes manage to function, the more plausible it appears that a substantial part of the explanation is to be found in the motives that actuate the leadership echelon, the values that it holds, in the rules of the political game to which it adheres, in the expectations which it entertains about its own status in the society, and perhaps in some of the objective circumstances, both material and institutional, in which it functions.[16]

(3) GOALS

The goals of liberalism may be succinctly stated. In general, they are that as many individuals as possible realize as many of their

---

[15] Kornhauser, *op. cit.*, pp. 230–231.
[16] V. O. Key, Jr., *Public Opinion and American Democracy* (New York: Knopf, 1961).

private preferences as possible. This means, first, that the American economy must generate material prosperity on an ever-increasing level and, second, that individual freedoms inherent in the rights of property, equality, and due process must be maintained. The American system is seen as being in constant and steady motion toward greater and greater realization of these goals of individual freedom and self-fulfillment. Material possessions and the less tangible rights to take part in the political affairs of the nation are expanding steadily and, soon, very few people will remain unintegrated into the mainstream of an increasingly affluent and harmonious society.

Some specific goals that liberal ideology holds out for the political system as such really are intended as means to private and individual ends. The chief goals of political activity are stability and the avoidance of disruptive conflict. In order to achieve stability, the basic framework of procedures must be defended and violations promptly punished. At the same time, however, the procedures must be sufficiently flexible to give promise of successful attainment to the individual goals of most people, and the policies formulated by government must move marginally in the directions preferred by unsatisfied groups of people possessing significant fragments of power. Stability is thus a product of insistence upon maintaining established rules while delivering at least some of the goals sought by individuals who might otherwise be tempted to break the rules. *Liberalism offers half a loaf to many and a whole loaf to very few; but it hopes that there are even fewer who receive nothing at all, and that everybody will find working within the system preferable to challenging it.*

Other goals are taken to flow more or less naturally from the unconfined efforts of many individuals toward their private ends. For example, progress is a desirable goal as well as one which may be anticipated from individual effort. The freedom from restraint that is achieved in the liberal system will permit a maximum of inventiveness and experimentation, not just in technological and economic affairs, but also in literary, social, artistic, and political matters. Attainment of levels of material comfort, aesthetic employment, and political civility unknown in other societies will be the result. And in this case, the people will share very widely in all of these attainments because part of the definition of progress is the broad and increasing distribution of all the desired products and achievements of the system. Continuing movement toward realization of these goals will foster increased recognition of the virtues of our system and promote harmony and national pride within the society.

Not least among goals of this kind is the final goal of overcoming communism in the battle for men's minds. The material achievements of our economy and the associated levels of individual freedom, social harmony, and national pride that they generate will, in time, demonstrate to the attentive world that our economic and political institutions are better—more worthy of emulation—than are those of the Soviet Union or China. Such a showing, coupled with the maturation of both Communist and Third World nations, will result in increasing acceptance of democratic methods and a lasting peace.

This is not to say that there will be an easy time for the United States in the continuing conflict with communism. Because the proper role of government is the protection of the market and of the growth of the economy abroad as well as at home, there are bound to be clashes. Anticommunism and the promotion of business interests are taken for granted, although liberalism sees itself as moderate in these respects. For example, a recent work by Arthur Schlesinger, Jr., states the proper balance of goals:

> I would regard anticommunism as a moral necessity for any believer in democracy. After the last thirty years of world history, one hardly need insist that liberalism and communism have very little in common, either as to the means or ends of government, either as to principle or practice. But it is essential to distinguish between *rational* and *obsessive* anticommunism: between anticommunism as an element in a larger position, . . . and anticommunism as a total position.[17]

Nevertheless, the liberal implementation of this principle retains a firm, if not hard, line with regard to serving the American national interest in international affairs. Schlesinger offered the following guidelines in 1969 for future American foreign policy:

---

[17] Schlesinger, *op. cit.,* p. 161.

We should undertake military intervention only (a) when the national security of the United States is directly and vitally involved, (b) when the people whom we think we are supporting display a capacity for resistance themselves, and (c) when, in addition, there are reasonable prospects for success.[18]

Social Change and Tactics

Liberalism's world view, values, and goals merge and find expression in its image of how change comes about. To begin with, it assumes that all legitimate interests are heard under conditions of fairness, mutual tolerance, and realistic assessment of others' needs and power. No group will win all it wants all of the time, but the assumption is that it will win something some of the time. In such a context, reasonable men can arrange a compromise that nearly all will consider acceptable. Then the problem of change reduces to one of implementation—of finding the rationally best means to generally shared ends. Thus, pragmatism and rationalism in both policy making and administration characterize liberalism's approach to change.

This emphasis on pragmatism and rationalism carries several implications. Liberalism regards all absolutes with profound skepticism, including both moral imperatives and final solutions produced through factual analyses. The criteria for a sound decision involve the manner in which it is reached more than the substance of what is done; the solution that is appropriate is one that is realistic in the sense of being responsive, *first,* to the established or evolving pattern of power and preference in the society and, *second,* to the merits of the problem involved. Insistence upon any particular solution is the mark of an ideologue, one who does not understand liberalism's method. In Schlesinger's words, "those who rush around ladling out moral judgments quickly arrogate to themselves an alarming and repellent sense of their own moral infallibility." [19] Further, liberalism's effort to avoid extremes causes it to see as best that decision

---

[18] *Ibid.,* p. 191.
[19] *Ibid.,* p. 89.

that strikes the middle path between polar positions. Because it acknowledges no particular solution to be intrinsically best or ethically superior, liberalism is uniquely able to shift its ground, balance demands and pressures, and emerge with a compromise that can be universally accepted. On occasion, action may be delayed until such polar positions are taken and the middle path is identifiable. Finally, decisions must be uniformly applied to all who are similarly situated or neutral. They must not be deliberately discriminatory, even with benevolent intent. This principle ("If we do it for one, we must do it for all") flows from the previously discussed emphasis on consistent, impartial standards of decision-making that do not take results into account.

These standards for decision-making emphasize not only mechanical characteristics of the process by which they are made, but also technical aspects of the decisions themselves. Because of the importance of such technical characteristics—the specific implementing means whereby the shared ends are to be achieved—liberalism sees a special role for intellectuals and their principal home, the universities. Social scientists, in particular, have rational and administrative skills that serve to effectuate and interpret liberalism's policies. The kind of change that is best from liberalism's perspective is one for which empirical data point the way and suggest improved techniques for attaining agreed goals.

In the years since World War II, the universities have come to serve more and more as bases for research in both the natural and social sciences. This is a natural outgrowth of liberalism's emphasis on maximum use of rational and technical skills. At the same time, the desire to be of service animates the universities. In his famous *The Uses of the University,* Clark Kerr (then head of the University of California) declares, "Knowledge is now central to society. It is wanted, even demanded, by more people and more institutions than ever before. The university as producer, wholesaler, and retailer of knowledge cannot escape service." [20] At the same time, of course, Kerr recognizes that the university's directions "have not been set as much by the university's visions of its destiny as by the external envi-

---

[20] Clark Kerr, *The Uses of the University* (New York: Harper & Row, 1966), p. 114.

ronment, including the federal government, the foundations, the surrounding and sometimes engulfing industry." [21]

Emphasizing the uses of pragmatic, rational, relativistic means of dealing with problems helps liberalism avoid confrontation with potentially insoluble conflicts. By stressing the established rules, seeking a middle path, avoiding absolutes, balancing contending forces, and relying on technical sophistication to produce solutions, the peaceful continuity of the society is advanced. Conflict must be avoided where possible—particularly class, religious, or racial conflict—because of the prospect that it cannot be managed, or its results foretold.

Perhaps ironically, liberalism's efforts to deflect and avoid the intrinsic merits of issues lead to a complementary emphasis on flexibility and change. To avoid confrontations, it is desirable to try to satisfy every group that is pressing a claim and has some political power to apply within the system. Once it has been established that the group is powerful and unsatisfied, reaching an accommodative solution is preferable to being forced to debate the merits of the issue. Today's public policy has no necessary ethical or moral standing; it is merely the product of yesterday's configuration of power, which is now out of date. The policy should therefore now be modified to register the new pattern of power. In the long run, assuming the political processes remain open, this means a steady process of incremental change. On occasion, it may be necessary to act to reopen temporarily closed units of the political process, but this can usually be accomplished without serious difficulty because of the widespread agreement on the propriety of the familiar rules of the game of politics.

One of the major accomplishments of such a continuing process of change in the character of government activity is that the primary initiative toward change continues to come from the private sphere. Government responds to thrusts generated by individuals and groups whose changing power and interests reflect shifting trends in technological, social, and economic affairs, rather than taking the initiative to shape the society in somebody's image of what it should be like. This, in general, should be the role of government. It is both

---

[21] *Ibid.*, p. 122.

more natural and more likely to encourage the individual diversity and achievement that, in the aggregate, spell progress for the society.

As we have noted, however, there are firm limits to what individuals may do when it comes to the rules of the game of politics or to the economic market that those rules are designed to protect. Violators of the rules of the game in domestic politics are legitimately subject to harassment and legal or physical coercion. The system is sufficiently important to justify violent tactics to defend it when necessary. The use of violence by change-seekers is untenable, for it not only seriously threatens the integrity of the system but creates the danger of provoking violent reactions from others, which could destroy the system. Nonofficial violence, in other words, is always wrong, regardless of context, provocation, or consequences; official violence, however, may be necessary to prevent or repel challenges to the system.

This attitude toward violence is even more visible in international affairs. The needs of the economy apparently include trade and investment in foreign countries. Communism, socialism, nationalism, and general social unrest threaten to interfere with such opportunities. Social change and unrest in foreign countries frequently involve violence. Because the American government's role is the protection of the market economy, such violence, or even peaceful change deemed inimical to American interests, may set the stage for use of military violence. Of course, other goals also are involved, such as defense of "the free world," self-determination of peoples, and preservation of democratic liberties, but these may be less central than the basic protective function of government. In any event, liberalism sees violence as a legitimate tactic in international affairs even more readily than in domestic matters. In an amoral world, the only lasting standard is one's own national interest, and under most circumstances, only military force ultimately can assure that it is served.

Liberalism and the Challenges of the 1970s

Advocates of dominant ideologies do not welcome challenge, particularly when the ideologies have been highly successful in their own terms. Capitalism encountered three serious but factually undeniable crises—the Great Depression, the rise of the integrated corporation-government economy, and "stagflation." In each case, a healthy liberalism helped it adapt to the new realities. Liberalism's crisis still is not acknowledged as such by many of its spokesmen. This is so partly because they do not see such tangible evidence of the irrelevance or contradictions of their beliefs amid developing circumstances. The crisis dates only from the mid-1960s, but already, it seems likely that it will be more severe than the crisis that capitalism experienced and, ultimately, will have a more drastic impact. For one thing, since the current challenge is directed at both capitalism *and* liberalism, neither can draw upon the other. Moreover, escalating social tensions may make it impossible to develop any practical adaptations within the liberal framework.

Essentially, liberalism is now charged with being not much more than a rationalization for unwillingness to solve pressing problems and/or a facade for maintaining an economic and social status quo that is unjust and destructive. Problems such as race relations, poverty, pollution, and war are laid at liberalism's door, and its utility as a basis for political practice is continually questioned, sometimes through violent means. The nature of these allegations and the alternatives offered will be explored in subsequent chapters. But liberalism is not defenseless against such challenges to the viability of its doctrines and the legitimacy of the political system that embodies them. It is an ideology in crisis, but it shows a vitality appropriate to its longevity as part of the American mainstream. This spirited defense serves to highlight some important aspects of liberalism and of the present conflict of ideas in the United States.

Liberalism's response to its challengers is an integrated defense of the established political system and practices, particularly of the values and purposes that they serve. It demands that its challengers recognize that most people do not agree with them and asserts that the great diversity of interests in the United States means that those who challenge liberalism are no more than a tiny minority. They should therefore realize that their chances of achieving their goals are dependent upon preservation of the established procedures.

The other side of liberalism's emphasis on following those procedures is the question of what happens if they are *not* followed. When they *are* followed, the result, by definition, is right, appropriate, or at least the best possible under all the relevant circumstances.

Bitter conflicts are channelled into arenas where they can be safely ventilated, compromised or absorbed; the mechanism remains flexible and responsive, and a large and heterogeneous society is enabled to go on living together. The resultant change may be neither swift nor fully satisfying to those who seek new and unfamiliar goals, but it *is* change, and it is accomplished peacefully and with the consent of all concerned. If the established procedures are *not* followed—if change is not carried out peacefully and with consent—fatally disruptive agitation and conflict may ensue. Finally, if force, rather than law and due process, becomes the final arbiter, the reactionary Right will wipe out the gains made through decades of patient effort on behalf of the underprivileged. Wide distribution of economic rewards, observance of civil rights, and meaningful political participation will be ended in the wave of reaction and repression that will follow a takeover by those who hold the major resources of power in the society.

Liberalism's adherents are not unaware of the costs of placing such paramount emphasis upon established methods and procedures. They acknowledge the three major points that often are made in criticism of its procedural fetish. First, the established procedures did not spring full-blown from either a divine or a neutral source: they were created by powerful men who were satisfied with their achievements (and probably concerned to defend them). Therefore, they permit only such behavior and types of change as those men were willing to allow and did not see as a threat to their positions and possessions. Second, the social and economic realities that lie behind the laws and procedures of any nation at any given time do not represent an ideal world, but rather a particular structure of advantages for some and hardships for others. Some people may justifiably consider this situation reprehensible and desperately in need of change. Following the established procedures, assuming they permit the desired change at all, will mean delay and incomplete attainment of goals. Finally, established laws and procedures must be enforced only through the acts of policemen, prosecutors, judges, and other public officials. Since public officials are charged with the duty of making judgments, their selfish interests and perspectives on ethics are likely to reflect the more advantaged segments of the population and, thus, favor the status quo. A decision of a court, then, may be tainted by the preferences of the person who made it—

neither a neutral product embodying justice nor a solution designed to be responsive to the problem.

Liberals are aware of all these facts. Nevertheless, they place their faith in the established methods and procedures, particularly in the machinery of the law. This is so not because the legal method is foolproof or really mechanical (indeed, official violation of procedures is recognized as perfectly possible), but *because there is no better way*. Any other method of resolving disputes raises the prospect of the assertion of one brand of morality upon other people, or the use of power on behalf of a cause or a goal essentially self-selected by those who happen to hold the power. Because there is no way to choose who is right or whose solution is best, the only way to solve the dilemma of action is to accept whatever emerges from a recognizable and agreed on set of procedures. The citizen may not like a law, but he ought to obey it until it is changed through the regular procedure. To ignore the established procedure is to raise the prospect that others will do the same—in which case the next prospect is the mutual use of force to achieve goals. Presumably, the side that first mobilized the overpowering force would be victorious. The fabric of civilized society is very fragile, and every effort must be made to keep conflicts within the framework where they can be dealt with without causing upheaval.

This condemnation of nonofficial violence is made with particular vigor in an unusually blunt little book by former Supreme Court Justice Abe Fortas.

> Violence is never defensible—and it has never succeeded in securing massive reform in an open society where there were alternative methods of winning the minds of others to one's cause and securing changes in the government or its policies. In the United States, these avenues are certainly available. Our history, and specifically the remarkable story of the present social revolution show that the alternatives of organization and protest . . . are open and effective. They may be long processes. They may be difficult. But they can produce lasting results.[22]

---

[22] Fortas, *op. cit.*, pp. 76–77.

Not only is violence undesirable from the point of view of the system and of the change-seekers themselves, but it also poses the threat of reaction:

> This sort of assault is ultimately counterproductive. It polarizes society, and in any polarization, the minority group, although it may achieve initial, limited success, is likely to meet bitter reprisal and rejection of its demands.[23]

Liberalism also sees the established procedures as already providing a potentially incendiary level of individual freedoms and opportunity to seek change in established policies. Exercises of free speech and dissent frequently create highly volatile situations, even riots. Defense of this set of opportunities provides liberalism with a further justification of requiring efforts toward change to conform to the prescribed limits. Freedom of speech, press, assembly, and the right to vote are regularly celebrated as providing ample opportunity for minorities to become majorities or to mobilize sufficient support to cause changes in public policies. Indeed, liberals expend much of their energies in defending these opportunities against those who would entirely prevent any efforts to change the status quo. Thus, liberalism sees itself as holding firm to a middle path that succeeds in maintaining an open political process against attacks from both left and right.

A second dimension of liberalism's response is an affirmative counterattack based on the inherent superiority of middle-line solutions. Neither left nor right extremes, but a popularly grounded, problem-sensitive middle course offers a realistic means of achieving the multiple goals of Americans. In one sense, extremists on both sides share the same oversimplified view of politics. Schlesinger says,

> the New Left and, less clearly, the New Right share a common view: that is, that the American democratic process is corrupt and phony, that it cannot identify or solve the urgent problems and that American society as at present organized is inherently incapable of providing justice. . . . the

---

[23] *Ibid.*, p. 62.

New Left and the New Right are agreed in their condemnation of the central institutions of American power, whether
real (the national government), semimythical (the Establishment) or mythical (the power elite). However much they
detest each other, the two extremisms have common methods and common targets. . . . For all their vast differences
in values and objectives they end as tacit partners in a common assault on civility and democracy.[24]

But liberalism (here, the "New Politics") understands the existing system and knows how to make it produce the greatest good
for the greatest number. Again, Schlesinger tells why the middle
path is superior:

The New Politics acknowledges the existence and urgency of the questions that fill the extremists with apoc-
alyptic despair. But it believes that these questions can be
met and resolved by democratic means. . . . No one should
ignore the fundamental difference between, on the one hand,
the determination to master and use the existing political
system and, on the other, the determination to reject and
overthrow that system. A test question would be whether the
Vietnam War is seen as the result of particular decisions
taken by particular men in a situation where other men
might have taken other decisions; or whether it is seen as
the predetermined expression of an evil system that would
have imposed an imperialistic policy on whatever body of
men sat in the councils of state.[25]

Thus, drawing on both dimensions of response, liberalism, in
essence, says that it has *not* merely elevated form over substance or
been more concerned with *how* things are done than about *what* is
done. Instead, it has found a way to tread the very delicate line between stability and change; it achieves all that can be done on behalf
of the deprived of the society while it retains the consent of a substantial majority and avoids serious, perhaps fatal, conflict. The
merits of the problem receive every possible consideration, and

---

[24] Schlesinger, *op. cit.*, pp. 250–251.
[25] *Ibid.*, pp. 251–252.

action taken to solve such problems is all that can be done in the context of the situation and given the real risks involved. To some, the costs of adhering to established procedures may be particularly salient and the costs of failing to do so less obvious. But failure to understand the crucial importance of recognized and neutral (liberal) standards raises the prospects of the most drastic costs possible to civilized society.

A primary source of support for liberalism's unwillingness to violate its own standards even in an intensely pressured situation comes from its image of the social and economic worlds as distinct from the political world. Only with the utmost caution should government seek to alter the structure or complexion of the social and economic worlds. Although conditions of life are not ideal or even tolerable for many people and a relative few hold most of the resources and benefits available, such conditions are the product of private activities over time. Imperfect as they are, they represent individual striving under conditions that are more free and less coercive than would be the case if government tried to specify exactly what the results of social and economic activity should be. Thus, liberalism takes existing social and economic patterns as established and hopes to make marginal improvements that will expand equality steadily in all its dimensions. The operative principle is to permit all to join and enjoy, rather than to seek to reconstruct, the basic economic and social order in the United States. Liberalism insists that this is more practical, humane, and just than any other approach to politics today.

Liberalism thus deemphasizes the role of politics as a means of redressing grievances and attaining ethically superior ends; it stresses instead the primacy of private economic life and individual striving. In so doing, it takes direct issue with the developing emphasis among its challengers upon community. As we shall see, all of liberalism's challengers adhere to some version of community, either in the sense of rejecting as outmoded the emphasis of capitalism-liberalism on individualism and self-interest or in affirming some form of cooperation, sharing, and mutual assistance among men. Self-interest and profit motivation and a system built to serve such ends do not command the loyalty of adherents of the challenging ideologies. Procedures, pragmatism, and realism are not important to them; they hold instead to more idealistic, humanistic, and fraternal visions of what life could be like. They see men not as atomized, self-seeking units, but as mutually supporting and fully participating members of a larger universe, capable of creative development in many dimensions other than material achievement. This contrast lies at the heart of the split between the mainstream ideologies and all the others. The latter display great diversity, of course, but they are united in their rejection of what they see as the incapacity of capitalism-liberalism to embody moral aspirations for an uplifting social life.

Annotated Bibliography

Bunzel, John. *Anti-Politics in America.* New York: Random House, 1967. A statement of the liberal conception of politics, its hostility to absolute principles, and its celebration of procedures. Directed against the new left protest activities of the 1960s.

Cawelti, John. *Apostles of the Self-Made Man.* Chicago: University of Chicago Press, 1965. An interesting survey of American letters from Franklin to Dewey focused on the American faith in individual self-improvement. Shows the extent to which the Horatio Alger myth (and its variations) have penetrated American thinking.

Chase, Harold, and Paul Dolan. *The Case for Democratic Capitalism.* New York: Crowell, 1964. A defense of liberal politics and capitalist economics.

Connolly, William, ed. *The Bias of Pluralism.* New York: Atherton Press, 1969. A collection of articles from conservative, reform liberal and new left points of view critical of liberal pluralism.

Dahl, Robert A. *Pluralist Democracy in the United States: Conflict and Consensus.* Chicago: Rand McNally, 1967. An extended essay developing and applying the pluralist image to American national politics.

Finer, Herman. *Road to Reaction.* Chicago: Quadrangle Books, 1963. A progressive liberal's reply to individualist-conservative Hayek (*The Road to Serfdom*). Argues the need for public welfare, progress, and national security programs to maintain a democratic nation.

Fortas, Abe. *Concerning Dissent and Civil Disobedience.* New York: New American Library, 1968. A brief and forceful defense of liberal procedures from a legal perspective.

Girvetz, Harry K. *The Evolution of Liberalism.* New York: Collier Books, 1963. An authoritative historical analysis, with suggestions for future liberal policies and practices.

Hook, Sidney. *Political Power and Personal Freedom*. London: Criterion Books, 1959. A standard liberal's appraisal of democracy, communism and civil rights.

Johnson, Lyndon Baines. *The Vantage Point*. New York: Holt, Rinehart and Winston, 1971. A liberal President's reflections on the problems, programs and events of his tenure in office.

Kennan, George F. *Realities of American Foreign Policy*. Princeton, N.J.: Princeton University Press, 1954. A good short statement of the role of national interest and realism in foreign policy.

Kennedy, John F. *The Strategy of Peace*. New York: Harper & Bros., 1960. The proper stance for liberalism in foreign policy.

Kerr, Clark. *The Uses of the University*. New York: Harper & Row, 1966. A good statement of the integration between the state and education that results in the liberal state.

Lerner, Max. *America as a Civilization*. New York: Simon and Schuster, 1957. A two-volume celebration of the achievements of liberalism.

McCarthy, Eugene J. *A Liberal Answer to the Conservative Challenge*. New York: MacFadden, 1964. A response to the individualist-conservatives, setting forth the merits of liberalism and progress.

Macpherson, C. B. *The Real World of Democracy*. London: Oxford University Press, 1966. A brief historical analysis of three very different ideologies, each of which legitimately refers to itself as a "democracy." Argues that the Western liberal variant is intimately and historically tied up with capitalism.

Moynihan, Daniel P. *Maximum Feasible Misunderstanding*. New York: Free Press, 1968. A liberal's critique of those who would create conflict by seeking to force change in established structures.

Roosevelt, James, ed. *The Liberal Papers*. Garden City, N.Y.: Doubleday Anchor Books, 1962. Standard collection.

Schlesinger, Arthur M. Jr. *The Crisis of Confidence: Ideas, Power and Violence in America*. Boston: Houghton Mifflin, 1969. Staunch defense of liberal principles against the challenges of the late 1960s and 1970s.

Smith, Duane, and William Gerberding, eds. *The Radical Left: The Abuse of Discontent*. Boston: Houghton Mifflin, 1970. Collection of articles criticizing the new left from the liberal point of view.

Spitz, David. *Patterns of Anti-Democratic Thought*. New York: Macmillan, 1949. A liberal analysis and criticism of conservatism and socialism as antidemocratic.

Waldman, Sidney. *Foundations of Political Action: An Exchange Theory of Politics*. Boston: Little, Brown, 1972. An example of a recently fashionable approach to politics which seeks to ground political analysis in the individualist rational-choice assumptions that originated in classical capitalist thought.

4

Reform Liberalism

Reform movements regularly have been generated by specific problems or needs felt by segments of the American population. In cases such as the granger, populist, progressive, labor, and civil rights movements, they have been partially successful in gaining their policy goals. To a lesser extent, they have affected the dominant ideologies as well. For the most part, however, such movements have been blunted by being thus partially incorporated (or "co-opted") by liberalism's flexible style. Nevertheless, beliefs in the need for reform within the general framework of established ideas and practices are an enduring strand of American ideology.

We use the category "reform liberalism" to encompass contemporary versions of reform ideology. Today's reformers are set apart from capitalist-liberals chiefly by matters of degree, but these differences are quite capable of generating tensions between them. Reform liberal beliefs are *liberal* at their base because they are rooted in individualism, civil liberties, faith in the reason and capacity of all men, perception of a pluralist political process in the United States, and acceptance of continuing unresolved tension between the values of equality and property. They are *reformist* in character because they seek the realization (or modest change) of long established values by means that accept the procedures and affirm the validity of the established political process. The distinctions from orthodox liberalism are visible in the reform liberal conviction that politics can be purposeful—it can be the means toward societal solution of shared problems and attainment of qualitatively different and more important ends than those sought by liberalism. Reform liberalism also is distinguished by the beginnings of shifts it urges in the priorities assigned to familiar liberal values and the beginning of an analysis that finds the causes of problems in the character of the political system itself.

Reform liberalism is perhaps best characterized by an acute concern for contemporary social problems—poverty, war, racism, deterioration of the physical and natural environment—coupled with the conviction that the established ideologies cannot or will not cope with them adequately. Reform liberalism also is impatient with what it sees as patchwork solutions tardily arrived at by current capitalist-liberal methods—"solutions" that succeed only in perpetuating those features of the status quo that helped create the problems in the first place. It holds that capitalism-liberalism is not really living up to the generally sound values which it espouses and that the selfishness or obtuseness of leaders has blocked the generally responsive and adequate political system from taking actions of the necessary kind. *Revitalization of the basic values* (with some changes in emphasis) and *reopening of the political processes* (with some modernizing improvements) are thus the keys to reform.

Reform liberalism is particularly critical of what it sees as capitalism's and liberalism's complacent, business-as-usual approach to problems. Over time, it has thus developed a continuing tension with these dominant ideologies: it complements them, as it strains to improve them. The resulting conflict-ridden but mutually sustaining relationship reveals much about the real priorities and limits of all three ideologies, and reform liberalism represents one of the major directions in which capitalism and liberalism may evolve. We shall examine the distinguishing features of reform liberalism in each of our three categories of analysis. Then we shall briefly explore the sometimes acute dilemma of ideologies that are critical of many of the consequences of capitalism and liberalism, but nevertheless act entirely within their framework and on the basis of the same values.

World View

(1) THE CONTEMPORARY ECONOMIC ORDER

Reform liberalism sees a highly technological economy of super-corporations, with government as a kind of junior partner assigned the task of stabilizing, promoting growth, and ameliorating the most severe hardships suffered by individuals. It accepts American capitalism, at least in this form, as basically desirable or permanent. But it is not content with what it sees as an excessive private capacity to maximize profits or otherwise employ corporate power at the cost of public needs and convenience. Nor is it acquiescent in the present balance of initiative in private hands, which it sees as producing chaotic consequences for economic growth, equitable distribution of income, and the quality of life in the nation.

Contemporary capitalism tends to celebrate the aspects of Keynesianism that concern welfare capitalism and management of the economy, but reform liberalism sees a misapplication of Keynesian principles which has the effect of serving the wrong values and/or creating danger of depression. In a highly complex technological society, industrial giants begin to shape the society to their needs. They require from government the absorption of risks, assurance of stability and predictability, promotion of growth, and maintenance of demand; these needs make it imperative for such industries to convert government into the agent of the productive enterprises and not of popular goals and needs. Two major consequences follow.

(a) Some see this corporate domination of government as bringing with it a *redistribution of power*. In *The New Industrial State,*[1] for example, Galbraith argues that power has really drifted into the hands of the experts within the industrial economy, the "technostructure." Neither stockholders, owners, nor top managers —and certainly not legislators—can exercise control over the technostructure. By virtue of their skills, they cannot be controlled externally; the motive forces for the economy and society thus stem from the values which they hold uppermost. Galbraith sees their basic goals as autonomy and assured earnings. To ensure attainment of these individual goals, the corporate economy must be successful. This, in turn, requires that societal goals be increased production, a higher standard of living, technological progress, and economic growth.

(b) Others see the abundant productivity of the new economy

---

[1] John Kenneth Galbraith, *The New Industrial State* (rev. ed.; Boston: Houghton Mifflin, 1972).

as creating *unprecedented new problems*. In spite of great abundance, there are fewer and fewer jobs, a shortage of demand, and unjust patterns of distribution. The abundance that could be shared widely is not really shared at all. To make matters worse, government's frantic effort to maintain full employment by promoting growth only postpones the day when Keynesians will finally face the fact of abundance. For example, Robert Theobald argues that Keynes himself saw that when the stage of abundance was reached, societies would have to change their values and adjust distribution to principles of equity and justice. He quotes and endorses Keynes as follows:

> When the accumulation of wealth is no longer of high social importance, there will be great changes in the code of morals. We shall be able to rid ourselves of many of the pseudo-moral principles which have hag-ridden us for two hundred years, by which we have exalted some of the most distasteful of human qualities into the position of the highest values. We shall be able to dare to assess the money-motive at its true value. . . . All kinds of social customs and economic practices affecting the distribution of wealth which we now maintain at all costs, however distasteful and unjust they may be in themselves . . . we shall then be free, at last, to discard.[2]

The dangers that Theobald foresees are (1) increased unemployment because of automation and cybernation and (2) government efforts to promote full employment that merely reemphasize private consumption, chain men to meaningless jobs, and ignore public needs. He summarizes his analysis in these words:

> We saw that although there were major unfulfilled public needs, these would not be met unless changes in the socio-economic system took place. In addition, we saw that continuation of the drive for the maximum rate of economic growth would be not only ineffective in meeting our goals but also increasingly destructive of Western values, for it

---

[2] Robert Theobald, "Policy Formation for New Goals," in Robert Theobald, ed., *Social Policies for America in the Seventies* (New York: Doubleday, 1968), p. 165. (Quoted from J. M. Keynes, *Essays on Persuasion* [New York: Harcourt, Brace, 1936], pp. 369–70.)

would not avoid a rising rate of unemployment, and would not even succeed in averting a worldwide slump.[3]

Reform liberalism thus sees and condemns an ongoing process of adapting men to the needs of the productive mechanism in the society rather than vice versa. Public needs are not being served, even though the economy could do so with ease if it were properly organized. Unnecessary unemployment and economic hardships are being experienced. The basic causes are unperceived changes in the character of the economy, outdated ideas about the proper relation of government to the economy, and faulty premises about how man's true needs can best be served.

(2) THE DOMESTIC POLITICAL PROCESS

Reform liberalism sees the American political process as essentially pluralist in character; that is, many groups exist and through aggressive and sophisticated efforts, all can make themselves heard under conditions of fairness. Elections offer further opportunities for participation and impact on the direction of government policies. But reform liberalism also sees an increasingly complex society developing bureaucracies, technical expertise, and other unresponsive accumulations of power that insulate official decision-making from popular preferences. Although most stop short of explicit class conflict analyses, reform liberals do see unequal distributions of political power and uncontrolled powerholders (chairmen of Congressional committees, old political party leaders) sitting astride the channels that are assumed to be the means of communicating popular wants to officeholders. If these obstacles were removed, however, the political system would be sufficiently responsive to achieve their goals. Failure of capitalist ideology to provide for socially responsible planning and goal-setting through government action and the blockages that exist in the liberal political system mean that the nation is incapable of coping either adequately or democratically with its problems. These problems are so severe that failure to take remedial action that will reach their causes (and not just their superficial symptoms,

---

[3] Robert Theobald, *Free Men and Free Markets* (New York: Doubleday, 1963), p. 111.

such as riots or poverty) may threaten the stability and even the continuity of the American polity. No current program is sufficiently drastic, innovative, or massive in scale to solve these problems. Today's policies are hopelessly trapped in the assumptions, precedents, and self-imposed limitations of the increasingly irrelevant past.

Reform liberalism sees liberalism as experiencing a hardening of the arteries as the result of excessive time in power. This is manifested in several ways. One is a kind of excessive realism in which the moral dimension is excised from politics and officials become capable of legitimating practically anything they desire in the name of efficiency or realism. Citizens are urged to be quiescent and to trust in the wisdom of the experts—in short, to see politics as the art of the possible, rather than as an arena of hope and aspiration. Reform liberalism challenges current images of democracy in particular, arguing that democracy has been redefined to fit the modest and unimpressive conception offered up by empirical investigations of democracy as it "actually" is in the "real world." Too little emphasis is placed on citizen participation, on what might be possible through enlightened leadership, and on the growth of individuals through sharing in power. Too little real concern is felt for the reality of the civil liberties that lie at the center of the democratic political process. And, most serious of all, too little attention is paid to citizens' demands for change; entrenched liberal elites delay, deflect, and ultimately deny opportunities for change in the status quo.

In many cases, reform liberalism joins battle with liberalism over specific policy questions. Often, the depth of analysis of causation employed and sometimes the timetable for solution are the issues that separate these two ideologies. Liberalism sees crucial conditions as requiring a cure. It attributes such problems, however, to the acts of public officials—to their poor judgment, to the problems that confront them, and to the other legitimate interests they must serve—and it says it will do the best it can as soon as practicable to solve the problem. Reform liberalism believes that to set aside or play down such crucial social problems is to give reason to doubt the sincerity of one's claim to believe in equality or other human values. Reform liberalism attributes such problems to *more systematic causes* such as regular patterns of recruitment of men into office, shared ideology among officeholders, or the economic interests of decision-makers. The solution of these problems is an immediate necessity, even if it means the loss of other desirable goals or the production of political tensions. Except under the most extreme conditions of official obstinacy or willful disregard for established procedures, however, reform liberalism does *not* endorse illegal actions. It believes in a full use of all the major civil liberties, broadly defined, but stops short of resort to other forms of pressure for action.

(3) THE INTERNATIONAL SCENE

Reform liberalism sees liberalism as obsessed with anticommunism and as hopelessly outdated in its perceptions of the nature and varieties of communism in the world. Because this is so, the United States is committed to a disastrous, counterrevolutionary posture in the world that constitutes a severe danger to world peace. Where liberalism sees unity in the Communist world, reform liberalism sees diversity; where liberalism suspects Communist instigation behind local insurgencies, reform liberalism sees nationalism rooted in social injustice; and where liberalism seeks to promote capitalism and stability, reform liberalism seeks economic viability and popular self-determination.

Again, reform liberalism's assignment of causes for American difficulties in international affairs is more systematic and somewhat deeper than liberalism's, but it does not reach to the level of basic values or economic imperatives. One major critique of American policy toward the Third World, for example, attributes U.S. policy to an ideology shared among "National Security Managers." [4] This ideology holds that the United States has a duty to suppress revolutions wherever they occur on behalf of peace and stability in the world; according to this analysis, "the prevailing official view is that there is no way for a great country to relate to a small one other than as manipulator or exploiter." [5] Thus, the United States pursues an undesirable policy because its policy-makers have faulty perceptions

---

[4] Richard J. Barnet, *Intervention and Revolution: America's Confrontation with Insurgent Movements Around the World* (New York: New American Library, 1968).

[5] *Ibid.*, p. 262.

of the world around them. By implication, replacement of such men would make for a clearer view and a more flexible policy.

A similar type of analysis distinguishes reform liberalism's attitude toward military expenditures in the United States. The armed forces and their allies in industry are seen as having usurped initiative and control from Congress and other popularly responsive institutions, in effect constituting a military-industrial complex in which the balance of initiative lies with the military. Their self-maintenance needs, together with the liberal emphases on anti-communism and patriotism, have caused them to exceed their proper bounds—aided of course by the eagerness of businessmen and Congressmen to secure the contracts to build their expensive weapons. But there is nothing fixed or inevitable about this predominance, and either Congress or the people are capable of recapturing control over the defense establishment at will.

Thus, the "super-realism" with which reform liberalism charges liberalism is evident in both domestic and international policies and practices. Operating exclusively in terms of national interest standards and obsessed with the need for security against real and imagined dangers, liberalism completely has abandoned the moral dimension in politics. Reform liberalism insists that politics cannot and should not be amoral, that there are bounds beyond which no government can go without vitiating its claim to integrity and democracy. Repeated incidents of espionage, duplicity, and subversive activity with regard to other nations serve to escalate the tensions between the reform liberal and the liberal position in international affairs. Reform liberalism is neither naive nor ignorant about communism; it simply sees both a greater necessity and a livelier prospect of being able to practice peaceful coexistence.

Values and Goals

VALUES

Reform liberalism essentially endorses the basic values of capitalism and liberalism, but it reserves the right to modernize them and perhaps to adjust the order of priority in which they are held. Impatience with patchwork solutions contributes to this questioning, both about the sincerity of capitalist-liberal commitments and about the order in which they should be ranked. First, reform liberalism questions the sincerity of the capitalist-liberal commitment to equality in the sense of both broad sharing of power and broad distribution of wealth. It asks whether liberalism means what it says about political equality when the "one-man–one-vote" principle encounters so much delay, political parties are run from the top down, the Congress is controlled by committee chairmen and the seniority system, and effective citizen participation is short-circuited. It asks whether capitalism is honest in its stated goal of widespread distribution when wealth remains tightly concentrated among the top one or two percent of the population and millions live in poverty. For most reform liberals, it would be enough if capitalism and liberalism were to live up to their oft-stated values and if the system could be made to work for all.

Second, however, reform liberalism tends to put forward an alternative priority ranking among the basic capitalist-liberal values. Equality is raised to share the top position with property rights, or even to have primacy over property rights. In the "human rights" sense, equality is defined in terms of the actual social and economic circumstances of people's lives, not just in terms of the right to take part in public affairs or the opportunity to compete in the economy. Two other differences in value· rankings or definition are closely associated with this development. First, reform liberalism is no less individually oriented than is capitalism-liberalism, but it emphasizes the moral, humanistic, and qualitative dimensions of individual achievements and circumstances rather than the more strictly material side. Concern for the ecology, aesthetic amenities, and public facilities that make individuals' lives enjoyable wins out over concern for the individual's possession of tangible goods in excess of those that are necessary for satisfaction of his needs. Second, reform liberalism is committed to the established rules and legal procedures of politics, particularly to democratic civil liberties, but it does not overlook the importance of the substance of what is done through these processes. Indeed, just because reform liberalism looks so carefully at the contents of the policies produced and compares them with the depth and urgency it sees in the problems that exist, it has become impatient with the current value priorities and the slow and uncertain style of capitalism-liberalism.

The net result of these changes in the priority ranking and/or definition of well-established liberal values is to reduce the harshness of the capitalist-liberal emphasis on competition, effort, and privately generated solutions to problems of societal use of resources. In its place, a stronger emphasis on communitarian action to solve shared problems emerges, particularly, a more legitimate role for government as the conscious agent of popular will. For the first time, two other values begin to compete for high position in this context. One is the social side of the value of freedom: in the past, it was assumed that freedom meant the opportunity to gain individual goals, particularly the possession of property that would permit one to be independent, and thus was linked closely to capitalism. Reform liberalism speculates that a more qualitative understanding of freedom would hold that it is not complete unless a multitude of aesthetic and humanistic opportunities actually are available and that they can be made available only through a conscious social use of government to provide them. The other is an increasingly internationalist view of the problems and obligations of the American economy. Capitalism and liberalism assume the nation as the unit, with the external world important chiefly for purposes of resources and trade; they also place a high value on nationalism, patriotism, and integration into a single national community. Reform liberalism, on the other hand, tends to see the American economy as interdependent with that of the rest of the world, to take on a larger share of moral responsibility for other nations' economic circumstances, and to give a lower priority to protecting American security through military power, militant anticommunism, and intervention.

GOALS

The goals of reform liberalism move beyond liberalism's hopes for steady extension of existing benefits to wider and wider populations. Where an ideology develops a world view that stresses the social problems of the present, it is likely to speculate also on innovative ways of solving them. Reform liberalism is committed to significant enlargement of the public sector (schools, housing, recreation facilities, transportation, and the like) as well as to gaining control over the military-industrial complex and restructuring foreign policy. Recently, reform liberalism has begun to address itself to the problem of democratizing large corporations and forcing on them policies more oriented toward the public interest. In addition to embracing the cause of "consumerism" and endorsing the watchdog activities of public interest groups, reform liberalism also has attempted to speak out forcefully in support of various minority groups and thus to draw these groups into its struggle for orderly but visible social change. Reform liberalism assures these groups that it has their struggle at heart, but encourages them to accept the strategies, hopes, and values of reform liberalism. It also emphasizes the need for tax reform that would close loopholes that benefit the rich, raise corporation taxes, and favor progressive taxation over regressive taxation. But its goals extend farther, to a qualitatively different set of aspirations. In Galbraith's words, the proper goals are "those that serve not the production of goods but the intellectual and artistic development of man." [6] A meaningful leisure and a socially determined rate and process of development are other reform liberal goals; they should replace the work ethic and the chaotic and essentially regressive manner in which the economy now evolves.

For a time, a constitutional guarantee of the individual right to an income sufficient to provide an acceptable standard of living was a major goal of reform liberalism. This proposal was geared not to replacement of the welfare system, but to the need to replace the work ethic, distribute surplus, and enable new and more humanistic activities to develop. This position was forcefully advocated in a series of books by Robert Theobald, who saw it as a remedy for the job loss caused by cybernation and as a means of setting new values in the society and releasing man from economic bondage. Individuals would be more free and, because purchasing power would be more widely distributed among the population, the economic market would also work better. In Theobald's words:

> The only way of preserving both free men and free markets is to recognize that the economic system needs to divorce the productive function from the distributive function and therefore allow each to work in a way which will be of maximum benefit to society. . . . Once the obligation to provide market-supported jobs for all was lifted, the frantic search for

---

[6] Galbraith, *op. cit.*, p. 378.

ways to stimulate sales and thus employ surplus productive
capacity would no longer be necessary. The level of production could then be determined by desired levels of consumption, rather than consumption being forced by the
existence of unused productive capacity. We would, therefore, have the power to determine economic policy on the
basis of our social goals rather than continuing to be forced
into social actions because of what are, at present, economic
necessities.[7]

What is distinctive here is the desire to reshape values through policies that qualitatively differ from those that now exist. The ultimate
goal is not incompatible with liberalism; indeed, the kind of life
envisioned by reform liberals might very well be endorsed by liberals.
But the interim goals and the innovations in policy that are characteristic of reform liberalism indicate a bolder, more imaginative,
less constrained approach to reaching the good life.

Another characteristic goal of reform liberals that illustrates
the qualitative difference from liberalism is the firm insistence upon
reviving the moral and uplifting dimensions of politics. Officials
and citizens alike should realize that politics cannot be amoral, for
one's morals inevitably enter his perceptions and judgments in many
ways; they shape what he sees, his self-interests, his commitments,
and his ideology. Nor *should* politics be amoral: political actions
are never neutral, and criteria of citizen judgment should include
explicit examination of the moral quality of government action. Not
to do so results in such morally vicious pursuits as the Vietnam war.
But the realization that politics is a real route toward noble ends
will be simultaneous with the reintroduction of morality. Through
understanding and extension of the traditional civil liberties, substantial accomplishments on behalf of the underprivileged are possible; many vital gains have been recorded in the United States
through effective struggle in the past. Arnold Kaufman's *The Radical
Liberal* shows the mixture of realism and hope that characterizes
reform liberalism in addressing this very point:

What has been won is due to the genius with which America's
powerful and privileged elites have, since the Civil War,

---

[7] Theobald, *Free Men,* p. 132.

been able to buy off discontent through peripheral remedy of grievances. Yet enough peripheral movement equals substantial social change.[8]

What is required, according to Kaufman, is recognition of the importance of the goals available through existing political processes and recognition that many "half-loaves" add up to more than a whole loaf. With the return of morality and idealism, the rejuvenation of the political system may be possible in short order.

Social Change and Tactics

The impatience that reform liberalism feels for the capitalist-liberal capacity to deal with today's acute problems does *not* carry it outside the established rules and procedures. Essentially, the reform liberal position is that the political system would be capable of solving all existing problems if selfish and/or obstinate individuals located in key positions of power could be replaced by better men *and* if people could be alerted to the dangers that face them, either directly or through the astute actions of the "new" leaders. Reform liberals envision a more substantial role for government in the immediate future: they see it as setting new and better goals, as involving greater economic planning, as rationalizing popular wants with productive capacity, and as drastically redirecting resources toward problems of race, poverty, the cities, etc. But they see such changes coming about through the existing political mechanisms, principally by means of rational education and persuasion of the general public to install and support new leaders through the elective process.

Reform liberalism is aware that the sweeping nature and drastic scope of the changes called for make attainment a difficult goal. It recognizes that established powerholders are not likely to be enthusiastic about such changes, especially when restructuring will mean a deprivation of existing privileges and a new role for government in the society. Furthermore, the task of first persuading and

---

[8] Arnold Kaufman, *The Radical Liberal* (New York: Atherton Press, 1968), p. 53.

then enabling the public to find and elect the right kind of leaders is not expected to be an easy one. But in spite of the prospect of long delays, reform liberals cling tenaciously to such methods, partly because they see no better route. Under some circumstances, violence does speed up the process of change, but it also involves grave risks of counterviolence and chaos. Most important, reform liberals place democratic civil liberties on a pedestal so high that no other path seems valid.

Reform liberals might emphasize the need for grassroots or "open" politics and criticize what they call the "old" politics to a greater degree than do their liberal brothers. Nevertheless, when it comes to the process of change, reform liberals are very much like liberals: they endorse the established procedures because they fear the alternative. Their method is to convert leaders who are amenable to the views of reform liberalism by persuasion. They call for greater popular participation, such as in new political parties and interest groups, as one means of reducing the influence of present obstinate leaders. They stoutly defend the liberties of free speech, press, and assembly that contribute to making change possible. And they fear that prescriptions for change that involve non-liberal tactics or go outside the established procedures may lead to conditions worse than those that exist; consequently they operate sincerely and consistently within the rules and practices of liberalism.

To some extent, the process of change envisioned by reform liberals may be a product of their conviction that mass-based change movements either are unlikely to develop or are undesirable. Perhaps reform liberalism merely exaggerates liberalism's faith in rationality and persuasion. But it is clear that reform liberalism places its confidence in a process of change that is rooted in education and the universities and is essentially centered around elites. In some cases, this reliance is explicit. In others, there is a kind of "necessity will provide" emphasis which seems to lead in the same direction.

The process of change envisioned by Galbraith, for example, is entirely dependent on the intervention of a new set of values through the vehicle of the technostructure and "the educational and scientific estate." The latter, as the supplier of the productive agent for the economy, is a vital source of power and potentially the key to the society's future values and purposes. It is the new agent of change:

For this emancipation, education—higher education in particular—obviously is strategic. Among other things, it is an apparatus for affecting belief and, hopefully, inducing more critical belief. By making trained and educated manpower the decisive factor of production, the industrial system requires a highly developed educational system. If the educational system serves generally the beliefs of the industrial system, the influence and monolithic character of the latter will be enhanced. By the same token, should it be superior to and independent of the industrial system, it can be the necessary force for skepticism, emancipation and pluralism.[9]

The industrial system exerts a strong influence on colleges and universities to celebrate the system and serve its needs ("One is led to inquire whether education remains education when it is chained too tightly to the wheel of the industrial system"[10]). Nonetheless, these institutions can teach potential leaders new values and goals, especially if they succeed in gaining control of their own budgets and insist on maintaining their independence. Individuals must simply "opt out" of existing values and frames of reference. The new values can then be communicated by way of the mass media and through the political activity of the new educational and scientific elite. Once the determination exists, the channels may be found or made and the political system redirected and revived to serve the new goals.

Other specifications about change sound more mass-based and democratic, at least initially. Some call for a combination of particular interest groups, a coalition built around specific goals and operated under specified principles. This is essentially an effort to use the pluralist framework and extract maximum rewards from that effort, apparently on the ground that no other tactics are really effective. In *The Radical Liberal,* for example, Kaufman calls for

a new politics of radical pressure that synthesizes in mutually reinforcing ways welfare politics, coalition politics, and

---

[9] Galbraith, *op. cit.,* p. 372.
[10] *Ibid.,* p. 324.

participatory democracy—a politics of radical pressure which operates on the principle that when one of these three vital constituents of a total liberal strategy is formally absent or defective, everything, short of rebellion, required to provide informal substitutes for them ought to be done—but done *effectively*. . . . Morally and politically, the development of a more deliberative process of coalition politics, the growth of participatory institutions, and the completion of the welfare state are concomitant enterprises—none more important from a theoretical point of view than any of the others, all three absolutely indispensable conditions of a good American society.[11]

The coalition would be held together by policy commitments such as compensation for blacks, support for the black power movement, higher education for all in universities converted into bastions of social criticism, and morality in foreign policy.

Less specific but similar images of the process of change are those that assume that public belief systems can be changed through rational persuasion by the more alert and educated individuals. Somewhere, somehow, some individuals must first free themselves from existing values and attitudes and then do the same for others. But political movements drawn from masses are not the vehicle preferred by reform liberals. Robert Theobald manifested this conflict: first, he emphasized that "the critical problem of our time is that of powerlessness [on the part of] the poor, the aged, students, the Negro, those in poor countries";[12] he then went on to disclaim intent to transfer power to such people, arguing instead that power should be eliminated and replaced by the willing and unanimous consent of the people. It may be that, pragmatically, he was looking for time in which to reshape values through particular policies (such as his guaranteed annual wage) that may be justified on other grounds:

Proposals that fail to appear conservative of existing values have no opportunity of success, and proposals that will not

---

[11] Kaufman, *op. cit.*, pp. 72–73.
[12] Theobald, "Policy Formation," p. 163.

be trail-blazing have no relevance. The task is to discover those measures that appear conservative and will be trail-blazing.[13]

What seems to be emerging here is not so much political inexperience as an affirmative judgment that the best route to desired ends is through converting policy-makers and other powerholders to the new values and priorities. Whether that "best" is attributable to the practical difficulty of mobilizing masses promptly or to a feeling that this would be dangerous or undesirable on other grounds is not clear. Perhaps it is a natural outgrowth of the fact that the principles of reform liberalism are espoused chiefly by middle-class intellectuals. But it calls into question reform liberalism's expressed concern for greater participation, raises the question of whom the more open political processes are intended to serve, and reinforces the impression of reform liberalism as a "within the system" ideology.

The Dilemma of Reform Liberalism

In many ways, reform liberalism severly criticizes capitalism and liberalism. In the face of serious, society-splitting social problems, it charges, these ideologies make complacent assumptions about the benignity and efficiency of the American economy, the responsiveness of the political system to demands for change, and the sufficiency of current values and priorities. Reform liberalism sees instead a faltering economy, a stagnant political system with faulty policies, and outdated and excessively materialistic values dominating action. Without some sweeping changes, reform liberalism foresees drastic, perhaps ruinous, consequences for the United States. Because the industrial system now dominates the government and is forcing people to shape themselves into the kinds of beings needed for the benefit and perpetuation of that system, the only real prospect is a constantly accelerating worsening of the situation.

The kinds of goals contemplated are also substantial, even though they are presented in terms of a return to, or true realization

[13] *Ibid.*, p. 158.

of, the familiar values of liberalism. A different priority among those values is contemplated, with equality rising to unprecedented levels and other humanistic values receiving attention along with the more established material standards. Morality, idealism, and participation are to be revived. And many policies—most of which have been in effect for a sufficient number of years to have developed supportive constituencies from among those who benefit economically or otherwise from their provisions—are to be drastically reshaped.

The nature of the critique of capitalism and liberalism that reform liberalism makes and the kinds of goals it advocates suggest that in contrast with those ideologies, change will be dramatic— and difficult. But the *means of change* that reform liberalism sees as adequate to its needs are exclusively those of the established political system—the same procedures that have given rise to the intolerable situation that reform liberalism now seeks to alter. This is the central dilemma of reform liberalism. Because it accepts so many of the premises and values of capitalism and liberalism, it is forced to endorse only limited means of achieving relatively marginal goals. Two examples may suggest dimensions of this dilemma. (1) Reform liberalism complains about the patchwork solutions of liberalism, alleging that the marginal changes possible within the capitalist-liberal framework succeed in treating some symptoms but perpetuate the real causes of problems. But all it really asks for are *many* such changes, on a wider front and on a more continuing basis, apparently in the belief that enough instances of such changes over a sufficiently sustained period of time will bring about the qualitative transformation that is sought. (2) Reform liberalism's conviction that the existing structure of civil liberties is complete, operative, democratic, and fully protective of the rights of all to bring about desired change holds it to only limited (and perhaps containable) types of efforts toward its goals. It cannot justify going outside the established procedures, both for reasons of principle and because it sees such acts as self-defeating.

These self-imposed limits in the scope of change sought and the means by which it is sought stand in rather sharp contrast to reform liberalism's view of current American problems and the critique of capitalism-liberalism it reflects. One example of such contrast may be seen in John Kenneth Galbraith's prescriptions for

achieving control of the military-industrial complex. After detailing
the scope of military dominance over the economy, specifically over
Congress, and the dangers associated with such conditions, Galbraith
offers suggestions:

> My instinct is for action within the political framework. This
> is not a formula for busy ineffectuality. . . . if sharply fo-
> cused knowledge can be brought to bear on both weapons
> procurement and negotiations; if citizen attitudes can be
> kept politically effective by the conviction that this is the
> political issue of our times; if there is effective organization;
> if in consequence a couple hundred or even a hundred mem-
> bers of Congress can be kept in a vigilant, critical, and
> aroused mood . . . and if for the President this becomes
> visibly the difference between success and failure, survival
> and eventual defeat, then the military-industrial complex
> will be under control. It can be made to happen.[14]

Reform liberalism's self-imposed constraints appear to flow
from three sources: acquiescence in liberalism's principles; assumptions about the efficacy of existing procedures; and a judgment that
any other route would be self-defeating. Like liberalism, reform
liberalism defines the real danger to progress as coming from the
potential reaction of the right, if it is aroused and if the veneer of
civility provided by the democratic procedures is once removed.
The unhappy result is a posture that continues to condemn liberalism
for failing to achieve reform but, in many respects, shares the commitments that prevent liberalism from doing more. In one sense,
the dilemma is that of democracy itself: where a political system is
responsive to the wishes of the people, reformers who are also democrats must await broad popular conviction that reform is needed
before it can be instituted—even if they believe sincerely that such
reform is long overdue. But the key to this dilemma is the premise
on which it rests. If the political system as presently constituted is
not responsive to the wishes of the people, or if they have been in
some way prevented from understanding their true interests, must
even the truest democrat be bound to follow the procedures of that

---

[14] John Kenneth Galbraith, *How to Control the Military* (New York:
Signet Books, 1969), p. 84.

system? May he not be free to base his tactics on the principle of what works best to gain the democratic ends he seeks? The issue of the nature of the current political process thus becomes a crucial element in an ideology's system of thought, as we shall see in the ensuing chapters.

Annotated Bibliography

Alinsky, Saul D. *Reveille for Radicals.* Chicago: University of Chicago Press, 1946. A major work showing how to use the system to produce results amounting to significant redistribution; a model of reform tactics at work.

Bachrach, Peter. *The Theory of Democratic Elitism.* Boston: Little, Brown, 1966. An incisive summary of the way in which empirical researchers have consciously or unconsciously employed pluralist ideology to redefine democracy into what they found to exist.

Barnet, Richard J. *The Economy of Death.* New York: Atheneum, 1969. A strong criticism of the military-industrial complex and its effect on policy and budgetary decisions. Argues that Americans must become well-informed on the activities of the groups involved if disaster is to be prevented.

———. *The Roots of War.* New York: Atheneum, 1972. Roots of war are the national security bureaucracy, the owners and managers of big business, and the manipulation of public opinion. Optimism prevails, however. The bureaucracy can be pared down, budgetary priorities redirected and the people informed.

Beam, George. *Usual Politics.* New York: Holt, Rinehart and Winston, 1970. A criticism of liberal pluralist and procedural democracy and an argument in favor of a substantive conception of democracy based on the good life for all. Believes demonstrations, legislation, and electoral process are ineffective as means and defends instead an infiltration of those groups and organizations—government and non-government—that actually carry out undesirable policies.

Chamberlain, John. *Farewell to Reform.* New York: Liveright, 1932. A useful summary of the experience of a major reform movement.

Dahl, Robert A. *After the Revolution.* New Haven, Conn.: Yale University Press, 1970. A discussion of participation and authority with a view towards a realistic and optimal extension of participation in various areas of life, for example, the workplace.

Douglas, William O. *Points of Rebellion.* New York: Random House, 1969. Endorses protest against injustice, repression, inequality, pollution, and the like and argues that unless fundamental and wide-ranging reform is undertaken, rebellion is likely.

Galbraith, John Kenneth. *The New Industrial State,* rev. ed.; Boston: Houghton Mifflin, 1972. An important analysis of the shifting character of the economy and the shifts of power and purpose that follow.

Gardner, John. *Excellence.* New York: Harper & Row, 1961. Gardner is now head of Common Cause, a "public-interest lobby." In this book he expresses concern for the achievement of equality, but not in such a way that excellence—the result of individual striving informed with moral purpose—is compromised. Criticizes the loss of purpose, meaning and commitment in American society and ascendancy of mediocrity, conformism, apathy and cynicism.

Greenfield, Jeff, and Jack Newfield. *A Populist Manifesto.* New York: Praeger, 1972. A survey of the ills, inequalities and injustices of contemporary American life and a program of reform based on "opening up the political process."

Hicks, John D. *The American Nation.* Boston: Houghton Mifflin, 1941. Sets background of American history from 1865 to 1940 with attention to the role of reform movements.

Kaufman, Arnold. *The Radical Liberal.* New York: Atherton Press, 1968. Good sketch of how the reform liberal distinguishes himself from orthodox liberals, written by a philosopher-activist of the "New Politics."

Ridgeway, James. *The Closed Corporation: American Universities in Crisis.* New York: Random House, 1968. A series of allegations about the perversion of universities by the operations of the liberal state.

Weinstein, James. *The Corporate Ideal in the Liberal State.* Boston: Beacon Press, 1968. A valuable study of the penetration of the state by business under the guise of reform.

Wolff, Robert Paul. *The Poverty of Liberalism.* Boston: Beacon Press, 1968. A powerful analysis of the philosophical weaknesses of liberalism.

5

Conservatism

In taking up conservatism at this point, we may appear to be following a change-seeking ideology with one that is change-resistant. In practical effect, conservatism in the United States must be so characterized. But in terms of its own beliefs and principles and in the contemporary American context, conservatism is as change-oriented—though in a contrary direction—as is reform liberalism, and it shares many of its perspectives on the present. It, too, sees American political thought and practice dominated by capitalism and liberalism as they have evolved. It too interprets current problems as the product of failures in the values of these ideologies and calls for their replacement by a new set of governing principles. In short, if properly understood, conservatism is far more than a convenient rationalization for inertia or mere resistance to change. It is, quite simply, a change-seeking ideology with a contrasting set of goals from those most often voiced in the American context.

Conservatism has many problems in the United States, not least of which is that of gaining a fair hearing. On many occasions, its principles are seized upon by reactionaries or by others who seek merely to defend a particular status quo that happens to serve them well at the moment. Without adopting its values or goals, and certainly without following its consistent principles or even appreciating its real qualities, those who so use conservatism as a rallying point do it a major disservice. But its principles themselves do lend themselves to this use and contribute to this effect because they run contrary to the mainstream of American egalitarianism, majoritarianism, and idealism.

In analyzing American conservatism, we are really dealing with two very distinct ideologies. They are alike in their apparent change-resisting effects and in the manner in which they are misunderstood —as we have just described. They also share a similar problem: they are consistent and firm in their opposition to "social engineering" and "the welfare state" and, thus, effectively cut themselves off from most potential business *and* popular support. They enjoy much less past or potential impact in American politics (in terms of achieving the goals they seek) than the space allocated to them in this book would suggest. But analysis of these two very different forms of conservatism will help to explain why capitalism and liberalism, and the ideologies that would *accept* and *extend* their principles more widely, have been so dominant in the United States.

One form that conservatism takes may be called *individualist-conservatism*. It is an ideology closely approximating early liberalism and classical economics in its emphasis upon individual self-fulfillment in material terms and pure laissez-faire limitations on government. It is frequently used in the most platitudinous defenses of features of contemporary capitalism or liberalism. If there were no more substance to the ideology than suggested by such usage, we would dismiss it from consideration. Or we would note in passing that, though much honored in rhetoric, it was abandoned in practice by governments throughout the United States. But deeper analysis shows that most rhetorical usage is without understanding of the humane concern for individual freedom that animates consistent efforts to create a setting in which men can indeed be free of restraints, from whatever source. It is on individualist-conservatism at this latter level that we shall focus in this chapter.

The other form of conservatism may be called *organic conservatism* in order to stress its sharply contrasting emphasis on the organic unity of the society and its roots in the eighteenth century conservatism. This ideology rejects individualism entirely as a basis for political thinking. Instead, it sets up the society as an ongoing independent entity with a life and needs of its own, needs that should be served by those who happen to inhabit it at any given moment. Essentially irrational and emotional individuals must be provided order and guidance through the wise actions of talented men in government. The progress of the society depends on making the correct decisions (often involving physical hardship) for its defense or improvement, and not on individual material satisfactions or ultimately self-destructive egalitarianism or majoritarianism. In most cases, the correct decisions are those that draw upon the traditions and experience of the society and apply those principles to its future needs.

Although the premises and goals of these two categories of thought are very different, the confusion that leads to labeling both "conservative" is understandable. Both take the same stands on some continuing issues of American politics. They insist upon a hard line against Communist expansion, tending to view communism as an integrated and very dangerous threat that can only be checked through decisive force. They share a special concern for the protection of private property and commensurate resistance to social welfare legislation, and they oppose any widening of popular control over or involvement in the process of government. In addition, the two lines of thought have very similar problems. As we shall see, they have real difficulty in formulating attractive, affirmative programs, either for acquiring power or for building popular support. There is relatively little in the American past that fulfills their standards, so a backward-looking approach to gaining guidance for present action is often unsuccessful. On the rare occasions when their adherents are in positions of power in government, they frequently find that the complex of forces and existing momentum to which government is subject prevents them from carrying out their principles. But in spite of these shared issue positions and problems, the two ideologies' basic premises, values, and goals are widely separated—even diametrically opposed to each other. We shall consider the underlying principles of each in turn, and the differences will be readily evident.

Individualist-Conservatism

Our analysis of the individualist-conservative ideology can be brief, for it is essentially the same as that described as bedrock capitalism (pp. 27–32, above) together with the basic framework of liberalism, with a deeper sense of purpose. It is sometimes known as Manchester Liberalism, after the writings of a group of classical capitalist-liberal thinkers of Manchester, England in the nineteenth century. Perhaps the leading exponent in the United States was William Graham Sumner, who joined laissez-faire capitalism, individualism, and Darwin's theory of evolution into the doctrine known as

Social Darwinism. In its contemporary form, individualist-conservatism still draws heavily from the basic tenets of nineteenth century capitalism. It remains firmly committed to individual striving for self-satisfaction (conceived in chiefly material dimensions) as the principal dynamic of the society, and all other priorities and principles flow from that.

Individualist-conservatism does not represent simply a case of arrested development in which some people have managed to resist awareness of contemporary conditions or of the evolution of liberalism to more social uses of government. Instead, it reflects the considered judgment that the early principles of capitalism are still valid for the United States, if only they would be properly and consistently applied. Further, they would create a better world than now exists under today's "pragmatic" or "problem-solving" approach to politics and economics. Three related premises and values support and give impetus to this conviction.

(1) The market is a sufficient regulator and distributor when it is left truly free to do its work. Indeed, the market is both the *source* of *economic* freedom and a kind of *precondition* of *political* freedom. Milton Friedman, a professional economist and perhaps the leading modern exponent of laissez-faire capitalism, states this principle emphatically in his major work, *Capitalism and Freedom*:

> On the one hand, freedom in economic arrangements is itself a component of freedom broadly understood, so economic freedom is an end in itself. In the second place, economic freedom is also an indispensable means toward the achievement of political freedom. . . . I know of no example in time or place of a society that has been marked by a large measure of political freedom, that has not also used something comparable to a free market to organize the bulk of economic activity.[1]

For individualist-conservatives, the principal problem of social life is coordinating the economic activities of a large number of people while at the same time maintaining freedom of choice and action

---

[1] Milton Friedman, *Capitalism and Freedom* (Chicago: University of Chicago Press, 1962), pp. 8–9.

for all individuals. The free market—voluntary exchanges among mutually benefiting individuals—is the only instrument that can assure simultaneous achievement of both goals. Notice that the notion of a "free market" is meant to preclude not only government interference, but also monopoly power.

(2) Coercion of every kind is to be avoided, and the principal source of coercion is government action. Freedom consists of the absence of coercion upon the individual. It can be assured only by avoiding or controlling the use of political power as much as possible. In particular, this means reducing the economic role of the government to that of enforcing contracts, maintaining law and order, and umpiring the rules of the game (which includes breaking up monopolies). An operating free market renders government organization or management of the economy unnecessary and thus reduces the prospect of coercion on individuals. Further, free market capitalism assures wide distribution of economic power and helps to prevent centralization of either economic or political power— thereby promoting political freedom. It also provides protection against economic sanctions for political activities. Friedman makes this point through extended examples and concludes:

> No one who buys bread knows whether the wheat from which it was made was grown by a Communist or a Republican, by a constitutionalist or a Fascist, or, for that matter, by a Negro or a white. This illustrates how an impersonal market separates economic activities from political views and protects men from being discriminated against in their economic activities for reasons that are irrelevant to their productivity—whether these reasons are associated with their views or their color. . . . The groups in our society that have the most at stake in the preservation and strengthening of competitive capitalism are those minority groups which can most easily become the object of the distrust and enmity of the majority—the Negroes, the Jews, the foreign-born, to mention only the most obvious.[2]

(3) There exists among individuals an ultimate harmony of interests, which will lead to satisfaction and fulfillment of all men if

---

[2] *Ibid.*, p. 21.

the conditions of freedom from coercion are realized. This ultimate harmony does not flow from a recognition of shared needs and community actions to serve them, but from the articulation of the infinitely different but interdependent needs and desires of millions of satisfaction-seeking individuals. Their varied interests, when permitted to mesh through independent pursuit of their personal goals, will form a harmonious social system. Individualist-conservatives visualize men as naturally competitive and self-seeking and see progress as dependent upon their freedom to follow such inclinations. Equality of opportunity, therefore, is to be sharply distinguished from equality of condition: the latter is a brake on progress and a block to freedom. Again, Friedman illustrates this point very nicely:

> The heart of the liberal philosophy is a belief in the dignity of the individual, in his freedom to make the most of his capacities and opportunities according to his own lights. . . . This implies a belief in the equality of men in one sense; in their inequality in another. Each man has an equal right to freedom. This is an important and fundamental right precisely because men are different, because one man will want to do different things with his freedom than another, and in the process can contribute more than another to the general culture of the society in which many men live.
>
> The liberal will therefore distinguish sharply between equality of rights and equality of opportunity, on the one hand, and material equality or equality of outcome on the other. . . . But [the egalitarian] will defend taking from some to give to others, not as a more effective means whereby the "some" can achieve an objective they want to achieve, but on grounds of "justice." At this point, equality comes sharply into conflict with freedom; one must choose. One cannot be both an egalitarian, in this sense, and a liberal.[3]

Thus, individualist-conservatism is far from a crass rationalization for the existing pattern of distribution of wealth and power, although some may seek to use it as such. It rests on a principled

[3] *Ibid.*, p. 195.

foundation of commitment to a particular definition of freedom and how it may best be achieved. Its renascence in the post-World War II United States flowed in part from a conviction that European efforts at managing economies and societies through the use of government inevitably led to some form of totalitarian coercion and consequent elimination of freedom. The crucial definitional question to be asked is: does freedom consist of the absence of coercion exercised by other men through the instrument of government (but with the possibility of economic hardship or market-applied pressures), or does it consist of the absence or reduction of economic hardships (but with the possibility of political restraints)? The question is not factual, of course; it is a complex value problem that may depend on whether an observer identifies with the *haves* or the *have-nots*. The individualist-conservatives opt firmly for the first definition of freedom. Contemporary capitalist-liberals reach uncertainly toward the latter and end up vacillating between the two.

Individualist-conservatives see an inevitable intrusion upon individual freedom every time men undertake to act on behalf of others through the vehicle of the United States government. With the most benevolent of intentions and the most democratic of impulses, leaders can only institute one set of priorities or policies. Efforts to institute society-wide planning or to provide security against various economic and social hazards inevitably lead to coercion, diminution of freedom, and tyranny by those that dominate the party. The most sincere and public-spirited advocates of government help for the weak may be innocent totalitarians, but however humanitarian their motives, eventually, they impose their standards and preferences upon the lives of others. In one of the major works of individualist-conservatism, appropriately titled *The Road to Serfdom,* Friedrich Hayek argues for abandoning attempts at social engineering through government and making a new start at achieving the old goals of freedom:

> It is more important to clear away the obstacles with which human folly has encumbered our path and to release the creative energy of individuals than to devise further machinery for "guiding" and "directing" them—to create conditions favorable to progress rather than to "plan progress." . . . Though we can neither wish nor possess the power to go back to the reality of the nineteenth century, we have the

opportunity to realize its ideals—and they were not mean.
. . . If in the first attempt to create a world of free men we
have failed, we must try again. The guiding principle that a
policy of freedom for the individual is the only truly progressive policy remains as true today as it was in the nineteenth century.[4]

As articulated by Friedman, Hayek, and others, individualist-
conservatism is a consistent ideology resting upon concern for individual freedom (absence of external restraint) and a concern for
economic freedom (free-market capitalism) as the indispensable
source of political freedom. This consistency means, for example,
that government is not to be used for the private advantage of *any*
sector of the economy and that trade should move freely across
national boundaries. Subsidies, trade barriers, monopolies, collusion
between management and labor, government regulation of rates or
quality equally impair operation of the American free market and
should be eliminated. Clearly, some who seek to ally themselves
with the individualist-conservative position are not so consistent
and seek the alliance in an effort to rationalize the status quo, oppose government assistance to others, and preserve their advantages.
Others adopt some portion of the individualist-conservative posture
and avoid the reciprocal obligations or implications for their own
behavior. Because of such propensities, confusion and uncertainty
about the nature of this variant of conservatism is probably inevitable.

There are also variants of individualist-conservatism that contribute to the blurring of the ideology. U.S. Senator Barry Goldwater, for example, in a much-read book entitled *The Conscience
of a Conservative,*[5] argues that continued freedom requires vigorous
efforts in defense of freedom—that is, a powerful stance against the
spread of communism. The potential conflict with the consistent
laissez-faire-limited government principles of individualist-conservatism should be clear. Preservation of military strength requires that

---

[4] Friedrich Hayek, *The Road to Serfdom* (Chicago: University of Chicago Press, 1944).

[5] Barry Goldwater, *The Conscience of a Conservative* (Shepherdsville,
Ky.: Victor, 1960).

a large sector of the economy be dependent upon the government and independent of all market forces. A society mobilized around nationalism and anticommunism is unlikely to eliminate trade barriers or grant internal individual freedoms. In other respects, Goldwater is much the consistent individualist-conservative. Even at the cost of appearing unsympathetic to racial discrimination, he insisted that government legislation to force people not to discriminate was an undesirable infringement upon individual freedom.

Perhaps the best-known variant of individualist-conservatism is that of Ayn Rand, whose many writings revolve around the principle of the individual's absolute entitlement to gain and hold all that he can in the way of material goods. Rand maintains that capitalism is "an unknown ideal" which if actually instituted would fulfill all of the highest needs and goals of individuals, properly conceived. Titling one of her books "The Virtue of Selfishness," [6] she argues for frank avowal of the efficacy and propriety of self-seeking. She maintains that the individual has the right to compete and to retain all the fruits of that competition and that enforcement and preservation of those rights are the government's function. Evil in the United States and the world, she believes, stems largely from the exercise of government power—particularly from the acts (however well intentioned) of those who hold such power. Only a rigidly enforced emphasis on individual self-service and the utter absence of government interference with the free market can eliminate the prospect of war, coercion, and limits on self-fulfillment.

But these variants merely serve to demonstrate the scope and appeal of the basic ideology of individualist-conservatism. It is deeply sunk into the capitalist-liberal origins of American thinking. In its pure and consistent form, as we have described it here, it touches strongly held values of freedom and individual independence. Whether it is truly *conservative* in the sense of preserving and extending values or traditions of the past is less clear, and perhaps not important. Individualist-conservatism is a distinct ideology, and in its general resistance to most contemporary changes in the status quo, its effects are conservative.

---

[6] Ayn Rand, *The Virtue of Selfishness* (New York: New American Library, 1966).

Organic Conservatism

Organic conservatism is what we historically understand as classical or Burkean conservatism; it lays claim to being "true" conservatism. This brand of conservatism explicitly lays claim to being "conservative" in the sense of deliberately seeking to conform contemporary change to perceived fundamental traditions and principles of the society. It is also totally different from all other American ideologies in that it conceives of the society as an entity *distinct from* and *superior in importance to* the individuals who happen to make it up at any given moment. Organic conservatism, as the name suggests, views the society as an intangible unit or organ, proceeding semimystically through time and having needs and goals independent of the ever-transitory group of people who temporarily live in it. Understanding the premises and approaches of this form of conservatism requires a substantial wrench out of the standard forms of thinking that characterize other American ideologies. Let us revert to our three-stage analytical framework.

WORLD VIEW

Organic conservatism begins with the society, not with the individual. The society, having evolved out of the dim past, contains within its traditions and practices the accumulated culture and wisdom of generations that guide an individual's life, give it meaning, and make civilized existence possible. Organic conservatism is both pessimistic and fatalistic about man, collectively and individually. Men are born with talents, interests, and propensities that are inherently unequal. They are irrational, self-serving, and fated to struggle with each other unproductively. In effect, they are touched with original sin. Only the firm guidance of well-considered principles can create the order and conditions of civilization within which men can realize some happiness and fulfillment. "Freedom" implies the presence of such order, within which at least some of the more talented men can develop and not only carry forward the culture and other qualities of the society, but also, by contributing to its betterment, add to their own contentment.

The principles that can bring order and civility amidst these propensities for evil are those that the society has generated over the centuries of its existence. As the society moves through time, a kind of partnership develops between those members now dead, the present incumbents, and generations as yet unborn. The duty of the living is to devote their talents to discerning and applying (with modifications if necessary) the principles from the past that are appropriate to the conditions of the present. Change is inevitable, and those who insist on preservation of any particular status quo do not understand the nature of the world. But precipitate change, change for which the society is unready or which is inconsistent with that long line of practice extending from the past through the present and into the future, must be avoided.

Where are the necessary guiding principles to be found in actual practice? Organic conservatism finds them in history, in natural law, in religion, or in other standards that are external to any particular situation. In other words, organic conservatism denies that rational analysis can generate plans capable of achieving important long-term goals because such plans require assumptions about cause and effect relationships and the predictability of human behavior that are at odds with all experience and the elements of chance and fate that shape events. Instead, guidance must be found in the principles of the American past that have been proved successful.

One prominent organic conservative, the author-columnist Walter Lippmann, terms his source of guidance (and his major book) *The Public Philosophy*.[7] He argues that there was once a distinct public philosophy, a set of moral standards for political action that man could deduce through logical process and to which all adhered. According to Lippmann, these principles have been forgotten and ignored in the United States with the effect that the prevailing view is that all positions on questions of purpose and moral standards in politics are equally valid. He insists that the public philosophy must be revived to guide man in determining what is right and proper and in the general interest. He describes the principles of this "public philosophy" in this way:

---

[7] Walter Lippmann, *The Public Philosophy* (Boston: Little, Brown, 1955).

They are the laws of a rational order of human society —in the sense that all men, when they are sincerely and lucidly rational, will regard them as self-evident.

When we speak of these principles as natural laws, we must be careful. They are not scientific "laws" like the laws of the motions of the heavenly bodies. They do not describe human behavior as it is. They prescribe what it should be. They do not enable us to predict what men will actually do. They are the principles of right behavior in the good society, governed by the Western traditions of civility.[8]

In the next section, we shall explore the specific content of these natural laws or public philosophy. The point to be noted here is that organic conservatism firmly subscribes to the belief that *somewhere* there is a fixed set of principles by which man should be guided. Measured by these principles, the United States is a patchwork melange of ad hoc solutions and superficial rationalizations.

The existence of such a fixed and eternal guiding standard is both confirmed and made necessary by the imperfect nature of man and the uncertain conditions of his stay on earth. No principles of action devised on the spot by such men could lay claim to moral validity, so there must be firm and transcendental standards somewhere that can point the way toward civility. Lippmann reaches this conclusion by positing a "confusion of two realms"—two conceptions of the human condition. One is the state that is attainable on earth, the other is the condition that is theoretically possible and for which men yearn. The predicament of modern man, Lippmann says, is that "the harder they try to make earth into heaven, the more they make it into a hell." [9] The way out is to recognize the difference between the "two realms" and reduce worldly aspirations accordingly:

The radical error of the modern democratic gospel is that it promises, not the good life of this world, but the perfect life of heaven. The root of the error is the confusion of the two realms—that of this world where the human condition is to

---

[8] *Ibid.*, pp. 95–96.
[9] *Ibid.*, p. 109.

be born, to live, to work, to struggle, to die, and that of the
transcendent world in which men's souls can be regenerated
and at peace. The confusion of these two realms is an ultimate disorder. It inhibits the good life in this world. It falsi-
fies the life of the spirit.[10]

This excerpt is characteristic of organic conservatism not only
in its pessimistic view of man and his terrestrial prospects, but in its
explicit contrast of the spiritual and material worlds. Organic conservatism's modest expectations concerning individual capacity lead
to reliance on religion as a means of obtaining guidance and developing faith that can light man's ways in the darkness of the
world. There must be some way of divining the truth, and some justification for finding it in a particular way; the necessarily mystical
dimensions of this act naturally converge for some organic conservatives with religious faiths. The act of governing thus acquires
some of the moral glow associated with religion and requires very
special talents. Clearly, the necessary skills and wisdom are not the
same as those that lead to success in other fields of endeavor.

The distinctiveness of the moral insight and culturally generated sense of public needs that are requisite to governing mean
that only a few persons within the society are likely to be candidates
fit for administering the public responsibility. Neither election, self-
selection, nor appointment has proved satisfactory, and the few
true conservatives who have acquired power in the United States
have done so almost by accident. In particular, businessmen—with
their exclusively materialistic and profit-seeking orientation—are
ill-suited for governmental responsibility. Though many serve in
American government, particularly in the executive and legislative
branches, they are short-sighted, likely to avoid hard decisions that
might cost immediate profit or support, and unwilling to sacrifice
profit and material gain to protect and improve the society. Peter
Viereck, one of the most prolific of modern conservatives, dismisses
the business community in this fashion:

Our distinction between rooted conservatives and root-
less, counter-revolutionary doctrinaires is the measure of

---

[10] *Ibid.,* p. 110.

the difference between two different groups in contemporary America: the humanistic value-conservers and the materialistic old-guard Republicans. The latter are what a wrong and temporary journalistic usage often calls "conservative." It is more accurate to call them nineteenth-century Manchester liberals with roots no deeper than the relatively recent post-Civil War "gilded age." [11]

Organic conservatism, tracing its origins to the founders of the Republic and back through them to earlier English, Roman and Greek principles, has little patience for short-sighted or self-serving behavior. Only those whose sense of the society's needs is finely developed and whose vision is informed by understanding of its future needs are capable of charting its course. That this is a relatively small number of persons with unique characteristics seems clear; identifying them within a society at any given time is not so easy, however.

VALUES AND GOALS

Organic conservatism's highest values are freedom and authority. From the proper definition and arrangement of freedom and authority flow such goals as societal order, individual achievement, and the kind of progress that succeeds in improving the culture. Property plays a vital role in sustaining freedom and permitting societal improvement and is, in effect, a subsidiary value.

Freedom is a general condition in which men are guided and encouraged to do that which they ought to do. It is nearly the opposite of the individual's exercise of free choice, which constitutes the essence of the liberal definition. It is what results from willing acceptance of authority, and the two must be understood together. The essence of organic conservatism's definition of freedom is captured by a single paragraph from Viereck:

> Liberties versus "liberty." Concrete liberties, preserved by the chains of ethics, versus abstract liberty-in-quotes, be-

---

[11] Peter Viereck, "The Philosophical 'New Conservatism,'" in Daniel Bell, ed., *The Radical Right* (Garden City, N.Y.: Doubleday Anchor, 1964).

trayed by messianic sloganizing, betrayed into the far grim-
mer chains of totalitarianism. "Man was born free" (said
Rousseau, with his faith in the natural goodness of man)
"but is everywhere in chains." "In chains, so he ought to be,"
replies the thoughtful conservative, defending the good and
wise and necessary chains of rooted tradition and historical
continuity, upon which depend the civil liberties, the shared
civil liberties of modern liberals and conservatives, and
parliamentary monarchists, and democratic socialists. Without the chaos-chaining, the id-chaining heritage of rooted
values, what is to keep man from becoming Eichmann or
Nechayev—what is to save freedom from "freedom?" [12]

By thus embracing Rousseau's famous image of man in chains,
Viereck points to the central theme of organic conservatism's view
of freedom: structure, order, and guidance. The appetites of man
must be controlled somehow, and until they are, he is not free.

Thus, freedom involves not the *absence,* but the *presence,* of
restraint. Such restraints, however, must be consistent (not arbitrary), purposeful (not whimsical), and in the public interest (appropriate to the *society's* needs, that is). Restraints of this kind, it
is argued, are not really restraints at all, for they merely prevent
man from giving in to his baser instincts and release his creative
capacities to proceed in productive directions. In this sense, they
are *freeing* chains. They do not just permit, but affirmatively lead
men toward, the kinds of activities that are most likely to produce
societal advancement. And they create the conditions that make
individual existence reasonably tolerable. As Lippmann says, "We
are free if we have the faculty of knowing what we *ought* to do and
the will to do it." [13]

Authority is essential to social existence; without it, there can
be no organized continuing relationships among men, no order, and
hence no freedom. Organic conservatism charges liberalism with undermining respect for authority by misusing it, turning it into the
mere instrument of temporarily dominant groups of men—and thus
robbing it of its majesty. The nature of man is to rebel against the

---

[12] *Ibid.*
[13] Lippmann, *op. cit.,* p. 111.

people and institutions to which he owes most, and to cast off authority wherever possible. When liberalism encourages self-serving behavior on the part of individuals and asserts that majorities can by rational determinations employ government to serve their mutual needs, it creates the prospect of whimsical or aggrandizing action by men holding political power and lends support to the belief that all are equally capable of deciding what should be done—or equally *incapable* of doing so. If a man sees no greater claim to determine government policies in others than he does in himself, he is not likely to obey except through the application of force. In this way, the authority of the government becomes eroded, a condition that organic conservatives allege now exists in the United States.

Where is authority to be found, once it has been lost, as in the United States? Russell Kirk, a major conservative thinker, declares that the sources are prescription and tradition. Prescription means "those ways and institutions and rights prescribed by long—sometimes immemorial—usage." Tradition means "received opinions, convictions religious and moral and political and aesthetic passed down from generation to generation, so that they are accepted by most men as a matter of course." These twin sources are apparently to be applied through firm use of government, and in this way restored to the level of habitual acceptance. Kirk concludes:

> It is through respect for tradition and prescription, and recourse to those sources of knowledge, that the great mass of men acquire a tolerable understanding of norms and conventions, of the rules by which private and social existence is made tolerable.[14]

Once authority has been established, order and freedom again become possible.

The concept of order held by organic conservatism involves not just obedience to established legal requirements, but an order of things among people. Those who are more talented should be able to acquire and hold material possessions and other perquisites

---

[14] Russell Kirk, "Prescription, Authority, and Ordered Freedom," in Frank S. Meyer, ed., *What Is Conservatism?* (New York: Holt, Rinehart and Winston, 1958).

according to their success in amassing them. Whatever inequalities among men are natural should be permitted to run their course. If the more energetic are *not* allowed to develop and apply their skills to the fullest, some form of tyranny over them is threatened; in effect, it is to enforce mediocrity, which is what organic conservatives see occurring in the United States. When this natural order of relationships among people has been institutionalized, firm enforcement of necessary and just laws regulating individual behavior completes the imperative of order.

Contributing to several aspects of the freedom-authority-order pattern is the role of private property. Property has a moral validity all its own because it provides the base that assures independence and frees some individuals to devote their time and energy to developing understanding of the needs of the society. It fulfills natural human aspirations and marks the differences in capabilities among men. Its unequal distribution is thus part of the natural order of things, and its protection, therefore, a part of government's function. Property promotes freedom, helps to project the wisdom of the past into the present, and conforms to the needs and wants of men—and is therefore a building block of a well-ordered society.

The goals of organic conservatism center on the creation of a society in which these major values can be served, but they go beyond that. One continuing goal is the development of a process of change that respects the past and succeeds in fitting new policies and programs into forms that are consistent with it. Organic conservatism recognizes change as inevitable and frequently desirable, given the propensity of environmental conditions to change in sometimes drastic ways. Too much of value has been learned in the past (or should have been), however, to permit idle or hasty—and particularly abrupt—change which departs sharply from earlier ways. At the same time, not to change when there is need to do so is also dangerous. Kirk declares, "We possess tested political institutions; but for those institutions to endure, now and then reform is essential, lest the institutions atrophy." [15] This is why, for example, organic conservatives often part company with individualist-conservatives on specific issues, such as the reform of rules in the Congress.

Once the conditions of freedom, authority, and order have

---

[15] *Ibid.*

been established, individuals will be able to pursue their personal goals freely and fulfill their potentialities consistent with their capabilities. By doing so, they may be expected to contribute to the moral, intellectual, and material progress of the society. This is perhaps the highest mission to which any generation can aspire; to each is given the opportunity to add an increment of wisdom or of culture to the ongoing heritage, but not all make good on that chance.

The goals of organic conservatism must of necessity appear attractive to only a relative few. Nor will the route to achieving these goals be at all an easy one. This realism is a part of the understanding that organic conservatism has of the self-limiting nature of its leading principles. Lippmann sums up this realization aptly:

> The public philosophy is addressed to the government of our appetites and passions by the reason of a second, civilized, and, therefore, acquired nature. Therefore, the public philosophy cannot be popular. For it aims to resist and to regulate those very desires and opinions which are most popular. The warrant of the public philosophy is that while the regime it imposes is hard, the results of rational and disciplined government will be good. And so, while the right but hard decisions are not likely to be popular when they are taken, the wrong and soft decisions will, if they are frequent and big enough, bring on a disorder in which freedom and democracy are destroyed.[16]

The Logical and Tactical Dilemmas of the Two Conservatisms

Analysis of images of change and tactics on the part of organic conservatism alone would leave us with only a partial understanding of the nature of conservative ideology. Instead, we shall start from a broader focus and examine the self-limiting consequences of conservative principles as they affect tactics. Because individualist conservatism faces many of the same problems, we shall include that version in the analysis also. Although the premises and values of

---

[16] Lippmann, *op. cit.,* p. 124.

the two conservatisms are very different, they end up approaching the question of accomplishing their goals in much the same manner.

The two conservatisms face a dual problem. First, there is the task of developing an affirmative program of social and political action. But the values and goals of the two ideologies call either for *inaction,* in favor of letting individual striving run its course, or for particular types of guidance that amount to *unattractive restraints* on many individuals. In both cases, an affirmative program would call for the repeal or drastic revision of much of the social and economic legislation of the last forty years. Further, the two ideologies agree that there is now too much popular control over the power of government and that this power is being used unwisely—sometimes for the aggrandizement and special advantage of particular businesses and sometimes for social purposes that are destructive of the talent and will of capable individuals. Thus, the two conservatisms have inherent limitations, based on principle, on what they can stand *for,* and similar imperatives concerning what they must be *against.* It is very difficult to fashion an affirmative program of government action out of such principles and highly unlikely that it would be a very attractive one in the eyes of either business, entrenched politicians, or the people generally—the groups that are viewed as dominant in government. Although they might somehow be converted to new principles that run sharply contrary to their immediate economic interests, the more they learn about the practical implications of such conservative principles, the more they are likely to see their interests threatened.

Second, there is the task of acquiring power. The conservative perspective (i.e., that government is now dominated by private aggrandizers, whether they be particular corporations or the masses and their perhaps innocently totalitarian leaders) simply does not harmonize with the basic tactical implications of conservative principles. Both versions of conservatism are essentially prescriptions for "inside" or already-established elites to follow in governing. They tell how a government should be conducted, and why, but do not envision being out of power and having to acquire power in some way before the principles can be put into operation. Nor can conservatives consistently turn to a popular appeal as a means of acquiring power. Not only would their program be unattractive, as we have seen above, but, by definition, the people are likely to err and to follow their short-range interests to the exclusion of the less attractive long-range needs of the society. Only a talented few are capable of governing, and majoritarian control is wrong; but the talented few are not holding power in government now, and only something like a majority can put them there. Conservatism, an elite-centered, tradition-oriented ideology, thus finds it both inherently and practically difficult to appeal for majority support for imposing new restraints and disciplines upon the society.

The dilemmas are troubling, but not disabling. Both versions of conservatism insist upon maintenance and promotion of the established social, economic, and political structures, and their principles are generally acceptable to many men who hold power in government or elsewhere. Neither ideology is mass-based. As a consequence of these factors, the two conservatisms—even though rarely represented by officeholders—enjoy access to men of power. They provide useful rationales for *not* taking contemplated or proposed government actions, and public notice of both forms of conservatism usually is achieved in this negative sense. Their real problem is thus one of bringing men of power to acceptance of consistent, principled applications of their power in conformity with one of the two ideologies, instead of merely using the ideologies as rationalizations for opposition to particular changes in the status quo.

The tactic of rational argument in opposition to contemplated or proposed change is thus the most characteristic tactic of both forms of conservatism. This opposition provides the best chance of acquiring converts among men of power, and realistically the most that conservatism can hope for in the present world is to prevent the worsening of conditions as much as possible. For these reasons, both forms of conservatism oppose extension of government regulation, broadening of popular impact on policy, and centralization of power. At the same time, they both call for increased emphasis on maintaining order and enforcing rules of conduct, and for a firm military posture against communism. They both view government policies at present as insufficiently concerned with the protection of property rights and too ready to attempt to serve social ends. The increasing coercion visited upon the more talented individuals in this way, and the sapping of the will of the masses to improve themselves, diverts progress from its normal course and substitutes a kind of popular mania for unattainable earthly rewards that can only end in totalitarianism or societal fragmentation. Failure to make sufficiently determined efforts to preserve domestic peace and enforce obedience to necessary standards of behavior will continue the process of undermining the authority and capability of the government, to the point where (again) fragmentation will ensure. Survival requires constant military preparedness to counter Communist expansionism.

Thus, both by action and inaction, contemporary government policies endanger the future of the society. To correct such errors, however, rational appeals must be directed, first, at men of power and, second, at potential supporters among the general public. But under all circumstances, the laws and practices of the established systems must be followed; anti-traditional actions are not employed, and violence or disruption is not even considered within the framework of these ideologies.

Annotated Bibliography

Barzun, Jacques. *The American University: How It Runs, Where It Is Going.* New York: Harper & Row, 1968. The problems of the university, from the conservative perspective of the need to train only an elite.

Buckley, William F. *Up from Liberalism.* New York: Honor Books, 1959. A stinging critique of liberalism by one of the most incisive of contemporary commentators.

deGrazia, Sebastian. *The Political Community: A Study of Anomie.* Chicago: University of Chicago Press, 1948. An organic conservative criticism of liberal societies as competitive, anomic and ultimately destructive of human happiness and mental health.

Friedman, Milton. *Capitalism and Freedom.* Chicago: University of Chicago Press, 1962. A short but important explanation of the relationship between capitalism and individualist-conservative style freedom.

Goldwater, Barry. *The Conscience of a Conservative.* Shepherdsville, Ky.: Victor, 1960. Brief but much-read tract by the 1964 Presidential candidate.

Hacker, Andrew. *The End of the American Era*. New York: Atheneum, 1971. A conservative assault on the loss of a sense of common purpose; the impersonality, extravagance and power of the large corporations; the egotism that results from a pronounced emphasis upon equality and "individuality;" and the hypocrisy of sentimental liberal altruism.

Hayek, Friedrich. *The Road to Serfdom*. Chicago: University of Chicago Press, 1944. An individualist-conservative attack on collectivism and planning, liberal and socialist. A classic.

Kendall, Wilmoore. *Contra Mundum*. New Rochelle, N.Y.: Arlington House, 1971. Collection of writings of the late well-known conservative on a wide range of subjects.

Kirk, Russell. *A Program for Conservatives*. Chicago: Regnery, 1954. A good statement of the classic position.

Kristol, Irving. *On the Democratic Idea in America*. New York: Harper & Row, 1972. A defense of the status quo and a strident criticism of progressives, the counterculture, and the left in general.

Lippmann, Walter. *The Public Philosophy*. Boston: Little, Brown, 1955. One of the most important writings by organic conservative thinkers.

Lowi, Theodore. *The End of Liberalism*. Chicago: Norton, 1969. A perceptive modern conservative critique of liberalism, urging a return to "juridical democracy" as an alternative.

Rand, Ayn. *Capitalism: The Unknown Ideal*. New York: Signet Books, 1966. Marks the extreme individualist position.

Rossiter, Clinton. *Conservatism in America*. New York: Knopf, 1965. Perhaps the best single source tracing conservatism from its early manifestations to the present; reflects discouragement, but not unsympathetically.

Tucille, Jerome. *Radical Libertarianism*. Indianapolis: Bobbs-Merrill, 1970. A radical individualist manifesto arguing that the split between the individualist and traditional conservatives no longer can be reconciled and that the radical right has more in common with some forms of the radical left than with traditional conservatism.

Viereck, Peter. *Conservatism Revisited and the New Conservatives: What Went Wrong*. New York: Free Press, 1965. Critique of traditional or classic conservatism from a "modern" perspective.

PART II

Challenges of the 1960s and 1970s: Reform or Reconstruction?

6

Minority Liberation:
Blacks, Chicanos, and Indians

In the last decade or so, Americans have been forced to face up to the fact that various minorities systematically have been discriminated against and/or exploited throughout our history. Benevolent and self-congratulatory images of the "melting pot" and justice for all have been jolted by the realities of the current status of minorities. This awareness has been developed through efforts of these minorities themselves, not through some new insight generated within the dominant society. Blacks were the first to develop a significant movement and coherent liberation ideologies, but Chicanos and American Indians soon followed with public positions that are detailed but quite different, and Puerto Ricans and Asians also demanded status for their claims.

Each minority is truly distinct in the manner in which it became subjugated by the American orthodoxies, in the nature of its claims against the United States, and in the basic aspects of its culture and belief systems. In every case, the dominant ideologies have pressed on minority groups in the same insistent manner as they have on others in the society, and the effect has been to draw many minority members into one or another of those orthodox systems. But, also in every case, a distinctive indigenous liberation ideology has begun to develop out of the special characteristics of that culture and its experiences with the dominant society. These indigenous ideologies confront the American society and its orthodoxies today with nationalist and/or revolutionary demands. Nor have significant steps yet been taken to remedy either past injustices or present inequalities—primarily because the dominant society and its ideologies have had great difficulty in accommodating minorities on any but dominant society terms. This is the crux of the issue: minority liberation ideologies insist that they will not be incorporated into the dominant belief system on its terms; to do so would be to sacrifice the unique and distinguishing features of their cultures. But the dominant orthodoxies cannot adapt to anything else, so tension is inevitable.

In this chapter, we shall focus principally on the evolving black liberation ideology. We do so because blacks constitute the largest American minority and because the written record of the development of these views is more comprehensive than other minority records are. Nevertheless, the distinctive aspects of the liberation ideologies of both Chicanos and American Indians will be discussed in separate sections toward the end of the chapter, and the ideologies of all minorities will be conceptualized in terms of the problems they share in accomplishing their goals against a background of pressures exerted by the dominant American ideologies. In this manner, we hope to emphasize that blacks are not the only American minority with a coherent ideology and a distinctive culture. The manner in which this *variety* of different ideological and cultural claims is understood and perhaps accommodated in some fashion by the dominant society will determine much of the American future.

Black Liberation

The status of black people in the United States was one of the most critical areas of conflict in the 1960s and continues unabated during the 1970s. But the evolving political and economic ideology of black liberation often is neglected behind news coverage of sit-ins and riots. In the course of their struggle for freedom and equality, some black thinkers have presented an alternative view of the good society in the course of articulating profound criticisms of the American system. In this section, under the rubric of black liberation, we will describe the challenge to traditional American ideologies developed by contemporary black thinkers.

For a number of reasons, this is an extremely difficult task. First, there are intrinsic difficulties for the white person in attempting to analyze black thought. In *Soul on Ice,* Eldridge Cleaver eloquently describes the intense demythologizing experience he believes whites must undergo if they are to understand and accept what he calls "the black world's vision" of the United States.[1]

The second difficulty arises from the fact that the black critique is constantly evolving. *The Autobiography of Malcolm X,*[2] which traces the activist stages and intellectual development of one of the most dynamic black leaders, is striking testimony to the capability of black thought to push beyond old formulations. Because the black thinker is often an activist as well as an ideologist, his work often reflects the changing lessons of his immediate field experience.

A further difficulty arises from the fact that there are significant differences and disagreements within the black movement. These differences are most apparent on the level of tactics. Disagreements over tactical matters devolve ultimately from variations in the fundamental view of the American system and the related question of the proper goals of the black movement. Thus, in this section, we must try to present both what is general and what is diverse in black thought. To accomplish this, we will first describe black liberation ideology in a general manner, emphasizing themes that appear in some form in the work of all the prominent black leaders. Here, the emphasis is on what unites black thinkers and differentiates them from liberal and other mainstream ideologists. Second, we shall focus on the major areas of disagreement among black thinkers; the emphasis there will be upon the complexity and diversity of black thought.

World View

Black thinkers begin from a posture toward the American system that basically is critical rather than approving. The depth and

---

[1] Eldridge Cleaver, *Soul on Ice* (New York: Dell, 1968), pp. 77–79.

[2] Malcolm X with Alex Haley, *The Autobiography of Malcolm X* (New York: Grove, 1965).

tone of black disapproval that permeate the works of every black leader will serve as an appropriate frame for our analysis. Martin Luther King often is thought of as a moderate. He walked softly:

> When you have seen vicious mobs lynch your mothers and fathers at will and drown your sisters and brothers at whim; when you have seen hate-filled policemen curse, kick and even kill your black brothers and sisters; when you see the vast majority of your twenty million Negro brothers smothering in an airtight cage of poverty in the midst of an affluent society . . . when you are harried by day and haunted by night by the fact that you are a Negro, living constantly at tiptoe stance, never quite knowing what to expect next, and are plagued with inner fears and outer resentments; when you are forever fighting a degenerating sense of "nobodiness"—then you will understand why we find it difficult to wait.[3]

Malcolm X was not so tactful:

> Our people in this particular society live in a police state, a black man in America lives in a police state. He doesn't live in any democracy, he lives in a police state. That's what it is, that's what Harlem is. . . . Any occupied territory is a police state; and this is what Harlem is. Harlem is a police state; the police in Harlem, their presence is like occupation forces, like an occupying army.[4]

And Eldridge Cleaver expanded on both:

> The boxing ring is the ultimate focus of masculinity in America, the two-fisted testing ground of manhood, and the heavyweight champion, as a symbol, is the real Mr. America. In a culture that secretly subscribes to the piratical ethic of "every man for himself"—the social Darwinism of "survival of the fittest" being far from dead, manifesting itself

---

[3] Martin Luther King, *Why We Can't Wait* (New York: New American Library, 1964), pp. 81–82.
[4] Malcolm X, quoted in George Breitman, ed., *Malcolm X Speaks* (New York: Grove Press, 1966), p. 66.

in our rat race political system of competing parties, in our
dog-eat-dog economic system of profit and loss, and in our
adversary system of justice wherein truth is secondary to the
skill and connections of the advocate. The logical culmina-
tion of this ethic, on a person to person level, is that the
weak are seen as the natural and just prey of the strong.[5]

As these examples suggest, the images of freedom, order, justice, and plenty that comprise conventional descriptions of American society are not to be found in black thought. Instead, the vision
is one of prisons, suffering, brutality, starvation, and decay. A unifying theme runs throughout black ideology: the United States presents a social environment that is fundamentally dehumanizing for
black people. From the outset, the traditional ideological image of
the United States as the land that provides a maximum opportunity
for the fulfillment of human potential has been reversed. With this
general image in mind, let us turn to a consideration of three specific concepts used by black thinkers to describe and analyze this
society: racism, exploitation, and white political dominance.

(1) RACISM

The most basic characteristic of society from the perspective
of the black thinkers is that it is racist: it systematically assigns one
ethnic group an inferior position in the social structure. Most traditional ideologies would also recognize racism, particularly in the
past, as a regrettable flaw in the system but view it as a peripheral
characteristic of the system that is well on the way toward being
eliminated. Black thinkers do not share this view. For them, racism
is a basic characteristic of American life, woven deep into both its
past and its present. It is the fundamental concept they employ for
the description and analysis of the American social structure.

The major uses and meanings of the term racism as used by
black thinkers have been well summarized by Stokely Carmichael
and Charles Hamilton in their book *Black Power*.[6] They begin with
a basic definition of racism as "the predication of decisions and

---

[5] Eldridge Cleaver, *op. cit.*, p. 84.

[6] Stokely Carmichael and Charles V. Hamilton, *Black Power: The Politics of Liberation in America* (New York: Vintage Books, 1967).

policies on consideration of race for the purpose of *subordinating* a racial group and maintaining control over that group." [7] They then distinguish two forms of racism. The first is individual and overt. It consists of violent destructive acts by individuals against individuals, such as the bombing of a black church and killing of black children. It is easily identified and often condemned. It is this aspect of racism to which whites are most sensitive, and the fact that such acts of individual racism are relatively rare allows whites to assert that racism is declining.

The second form of racism is termed "institutional." It is found in the "operation of established and respected forces in the society." [8] This racism takes the form of support for societal procedures that keep black people underemployed and confined to ghettos, procedures that are not overtly racist but have racist effects. Carmichael and Hamilton point out that respectable individuals can consider themselves blameless because they are not sensitive to racism of this type. "*They* would never plant a bomb in a church; *they* would never stone a black family. But they continue to support political officials and institutions that would and do perpetuate institutionally racist policies." [9] Because institutional racism is structural rather than individual, its consequences can be both more devastating and more difficult to combat than are the consequences of individual racism. Carmichael and Hamilton consider death caused by failure to provide blacks with proper food, shelter, and medical facilities a consequence of institutional racism.

Underlying and supporting individual and institutional racist acts are the racist attitudes that permeate the society. Carmichael and Hamilton describe the basic feeling among whites that they are better than blacks. This racist attitude has its root in the history of the slave economy, when the very humanity of slaves was questioned, and continues into the present in the form of the conviction of white group superiority.

Black thinkers are concerned with the numerous destructive consequences of individual and institutional racism upon blacks. The first, and most obvious, is the material deprivation that blacks suffer

---

[7] *Ibid.*, p. 3.
[8] *Ibid.*, p. 4.
[9] *Ibid.*, p. 5.

as a result of racism. Black leaders emphasize the fact that by any indicator of economic well being—employment, wages, housing, education, and mortality—blacks as a group are deprived relative to white Americans. This deprivation is the result not of the unwillingness of black people to work or lack of ability, but of the systematic economic discrimination to which they are subjected.

But black thinkers also emphasize the social and psychological as well as the material consequences of racism. Denied all status and respect in the society, the black man questions his worth as a human being. Accepting the white-imposed negative vision of himself, he begins to despise, devalue, and even hate himself. This process psychologically damages the individual black person and reinforces the negative attitude of the dominant white group.

(2) EXPLOITATION

Closely linked to this view of the American social system as racist is the image of it as exploitative. In applying the concept of exploitation to the United States, black thinkers have departed significantly from the traditional principles and assumptions of American capitalist ideology. For example, where mainstream thinkers extol the unparalleled wealth and power that the economic system created, black thinkers focus on the material deprivation it bred. Beginning with different images of the consequences of the capitalist economy, they stress the poverty, hunger, and misery that are often obscured by images of "the affluent society."

Mainstream thinkers describe a society in which free individuals compete and are rewarded on the basis of labor and merit. For the individual, upward mobility is theoretically unlimited. Black thinkers start with the fact of a slave economy in which human beings were treated as property and denied the fruits of their labor. They assert that the use and exploitation of this slave labor enabled the United States to lay the foundations of today's powerful economy. Malcolm X, speaking to a black audience, described the origins of American economic strength in this fashion:

> Our mothers and fathers invested sweat and blood. Three
> hundred and ten years we worked in this country without a
> dime in return—I mean without a dime in return. You let

the white man walk around here talking about how rich this
country is, but you never stop to think how it got rich so
quick. It got rich because you made it rich.[10]

Even in the more moderate Martin Luther King we read that "few
people consider the fact that in addition to being enslaved for two
centuries, the Negro was during all those years robbed of the wages
of his toil." [11]

With this perspective on the historic development and contemporary workings of the economy as their basis, black thinkers
challenge the justice of the present distribution of economic rewards
in the society. From this challenge, at least in part, flow demands as
diverse as the $10,000,000,000, "Freedom Budget" proposed by
A. Philip Randolph and the Urban League and the Nation of Islam's
demand for exclusive possession of six or seven southern states.
From it, in addition, comes a demand for economic equality in fact
rather than mere equality of opportunity, and the related demand for
preferential treatment for blacks. Preferential or compensatory treatment of blacks is a demand endorsed by Martin Luther King and
many other black thinkers.

The black thinkers' demurrer from the basic assumption concerning the workings of the economic system and their assertion that
its processes are exploitative threaten to open a Pandora's box that
usually is not opened in mainstream ideologies' discussion of the
economy: the issue of alternative forms of economic organization.
Many, perhaps most, black thinkers continue to see the capitalist
economy as viable in theory although in need of modification. Their
position is much like that of reform liberals who assert that modification and reforms are necessary to eliminate the injustices sometimes wrought by the operation of the market but do not propose
an elimination of the market itself. However, a minority of black
thinkers has carried the black critique of the economy farther. Asserting that capitalism is intrinsically exploitative, they are search-
ing for alternative modes of economic organization, both for the
black community and for the United States as a whole. At this point,

---

[10] Malcolm X, *Malcolm X Speaks*, p. 32.
[11] Martin Luther King, *op. cit.*, p. 137.

the consensus in the black economic critique dissolves. These difficulties will be considered later.

(3) WHITE POLITICAL DOMINANCE

Black thinkers also view the political system differently than do mainstream thinkers. As we have seen, liberalism conceives of the political system as a pluralist democracy. All individuals are thought to have access to the basic democratic institutions such as political parties and the electoral process. Even more important, all major groups are represented in the bargaining and negotiation processes and therefore their interests are represented in government policy decisions. Power is viewed as diffused throughout the system rather than concentrated in a few individuals or a particular social class.

For black thinkers, the United States is an incomplete democracy at best. They view it as a system that systematically has excluded a major group from participation in its political processes. Black ideologists argue that, historically, black people in the South were legally excluded by law from democratic participipation in activities as basic as voting. When such laws were declared unconstitutional, informal norms sanctioned by economic power and terrorism were used. They point to the fact that as late as 1968, attempts by blacks to register to vote resulted in the murder of voter registration workers in southern communities. In the North, more subtle measures such as gerrymandering were and are used to achieve similar results. The consequence is that blacks continue to be excluded from the decision-making process on both local and national levels. The open processes of the pluralist society have remained closed to them. Carmichael and Hamilton coined the phrase "monolithic pluralism" [12] to describe a system in which power, while diffused, is denied to one group, in this case a racial minority.

A minority of black thinkers have gone farther in their critique of the American political processes and questioned the validity of the pluralist model in its entirety. In its stead, they propose a ruling class model in which power is concentrated in a small group that makes decisions primarily in its own interests. The United States

---

[12] Carmichael and Hamilton, *op. cit.*, p. 7.

thus operates as a democracy neither for blacks nor for the majority of whites. This viewpoint, while probably not widely shared within the black liberation movement, has important theoretical implications that will be explored later.

Some black thinkers have begun to apply the concepts of racism, exploitation, and white political domination not only to the domestic processes of the United States, but also to its relationships with other countries, particularly those of the Third World. Rather than viewing international relations in terms of a conflict between the free world led by the United States and the encroaching Communist powers, they see it primarily as a struggle between white and colored peoples. The Western white nations led by the United States are seen as the exploiters and colonizers of black, brown, and red peoples on a worldwide scale. For a century, this exploitation has been a fundamental aspect of U.S. foreign policy. During the 1950s and 1960s, Third World peoples were struggling, often successfully, to regain their political and economic freedom. Black thinkers who subscribe to this international perspective make a connection between the struggle of blacks in the United States and the struggling Third World peoples. They consider the Third World, particularly the African nations, as actual or potential allies. The implication of this international perspective also will be considered later.

Values and Goals

In spite of the apparent similarity between mainstream values and those of black thinkers, the latter typically see the traditional values and goals as different from or even an obstacle to their own. The mildest critique of prevalent U.S. values and goals offered by black ideology is one that questions the extent to which the articulated values and goals are implemented in the present social order. Mainstream thinkers see the society as actually operating on the broad principles of freedom, justice, and equality. Black thinkers see instead a society that hides oppression in this rhetoric. How, they ask, can a social system claim to promote equality when it denies equal access to job opportunities? How can it speak of a commitment to justice when black citizens seeking to exercise their right to vote are brutalized? The American social system fails to live up to its own most frequently articulated standards. Thus, for some black thinkers, a major goal of the black liberation movement is to move the American social system toward an implementation of those values and goals upon which it is supposedly founded.

A second common critique of traditional values and goals is one that questions priorities among the values found in capitalism-liberalism. Black thinkers see a society that emphasizes property rights to the extent that the American system does as particularly likely to sacrifice human values. American society is seen as improperly stressing materialistic values and goals and placing humanistic values second in order of priority. Black thinkers emphasize the conflict already noted above between the right to acquire property and the right to equality and liberty embedded in the U.S. Constitution. They see an unacknowledged conflict between the two values which, in practice, is resolved in favor of property rights. Therefore, a major goal of the black liberation movement is the reorientation of the American system to an emphasis on the equality strand of the value system.

However, some black thinkers deny that such a reorientation is possible because they hold to the belief that there really is such a value conflict in American society. These thinkers assert that American society is almost exclusively motivated and defined by property values. To speak of a conflict between the two values vastly overemphasizes the extent to which a humanistic dimension is present at all in the American value system. Carmichael and Hamilton have written that as a whole, middle-class America is "without a viable conscience as regards humanity. The values of the middle class permit the perpetuation of the ravages of the black community. The values of that class are based upon material aggrandizement, not the expansion of humanity." [13]

For black thinkers of Carmichael's and Hamilton's persuasion, the values and goals of liberalism and capitalism are intrinsically flawed rather than merely inadequately implemented or improperly emphasized. The stress these values place upon individualism, competitiveness and conflict is seen as flowing from a view of man that is fundamentally incorrect. This incorrect vision is the basis for a

---

[13] Carmichael and Hamilton, *op. cit.*, p. 40.

social system that in its emphasis upon material accumulation prevents men, both black and white, from developing as full human beings. As these black thinkers analyze American society, the race problem in the United States does not result from a failure to implement American values but is a logical and predictable extension of those values.

It follows from this analysis that a fundamental task of the black liberation movement is articulation of an alternative set of values and goals that can serve as the basis for a society that is truly humanist in its orientation. James Baldwin expressed the feelings of many black thinkers: "White people cannot, in the generality, be taken as models of how to live. Rather the white man is himself in sore need of new standards, which will release him from his confusion and place him once again in fruitful communion with the depths of his own being." [14]

These alternative standards have been attributed to several sources. The young organizers of SNCC saw the poor black people of the South as possessing a beautiful and morally superior life style. Others have pointed to the distinctive culture of the northern black ghetto. Finally, there are those, like Carmichael, who see the Third World, and especially Africa, as the source of the appropriate new model. Common themes are found in these partial formulations of alternative values. There is a universal rejection of the cult of individualism and the cult of materialism which are considered basic tenets of American and white western value systems. It is asserted that wherever black culture is found, it is based upon the cooperative, rather than the competitive, aspects of human nature. The group is characteristically seen as having value—value that complements, but does not deny, the development and freedom of the individual. The communal and egalitarian organization of the African tribe is often cited as an example of a social structure based upon a superior conception of human nature.

Black thinkers argue that the right to reject the dominant values, goals and norms of white society and to create new ones that will accord with the cultural and historical experience of black people is the most important right that can be established by the

---

[14] James Baldwin, *The Fire Next Time* (New York: Dial Press, 1963), pp. 110–111.

black liberation movement. Black thinkers who subscribe to this view are separated by a considerable distance from those who see the implementation of traditional American values as the critical task of the movement. This brings us to consideration of one of the most important issues dividing black leaders, the issue of integration versus some form of nationalism.

Substantial agreement among black thinkers as to the goals of the liberation movement on a general level begins to cease when more proximate goals are considered. The most dramatic and important point of departure is the debate between integrationists and nationalists. We shall explore it shortly, but its history also is important.

This debate is not a new development. It is a theme that weaves throughout the works of black thinkers from the time of the Civil War. During the 1950s and early 1960s, integration was the universal goal. The NAACP and other black organizations dedicated to integration were given wide coverage by the press. Then the media discovered the Nation of Islam, which preached a separatist ideology, and SNCC and CORE, advocates of "black power," and the situation was transformed suddenly and radically. The "black power" issue in particular touched off bitter debate among black liberation leaders concerning the proper goals of the liberation movement. This debate is rooted in the differences in world view and understanding of values which, as we have just seen, permeate the black movement.

Social Change and Tactics

The ideology of black liberation obviously is concerned with extensive change in the American social system. For even the most moderate black movements, the disparity between the reality of life for blacks and the values and goals to which blacks aspire is very great. The elimination of racism and the various forms of economic and social discrimination woven into American society is seen as a task that requires intense commitment and the mobilization of societal resources on an unprecedented scale.

Black thinkers often describe the scope and pace of the social change that they demand as revolutionary. Leaders as diverse as Malcolm X and Martin Luther King referred to the black movement as revolutionary. As we have seen, black thinkers do articulate sweeping criticisms of the present social system. It remains to be seen, however, which of them if any really fit our definition of revolutionary ideology. We will consider this question further when we deal with variations in black thinking. Here, we need only note that there is a consensus among black leaders that, in some sense, revolutionary change is a necessity in the United States.

Like the area of goals, the area of social change and tactics is one in which the differences among black thinkers are dramatic. Disagreement among black leaders over the question of violent as opposed to nonviolent tactics and the proper relationship of whites in the black movement has received a great deal of public attention. However, when black thinkers' general approach to social change is contrasted with traditional ideologists' views on methods of social change, it is clear that there are unifying themes in black ideology.

In general, black thinkers are far less convinced of the efficacy of following established procedures than traditional American thinkers are. They begin from the position that the traditional methods of social change through the electoral process or legal channels have broken down in relation to blacks. They see few indications that American society is equipped to handle a problem of social change of the magnitude of racism in the peaceful and semi-mechanical manner pictured by mainstream ideologies. From their perspective, the genius of American politics has not been its ability to change when necessary, but its ability to preserve the status quo and, at the same time, present the illusion of change.

While there are major black spokesmen who still view the traditional procedures, particularly the courts, as major instruments of social change, the focus of emphasis appears to have shifted decisively to collective methods. Bayard Rustin has suggested that Martin Luther King's Birmingham campaign represented the victory of the concept of collective struggle over individual mobility as the road to black freedom.[15] While the emphasis had been on breaking down legal barriers and winning such individual token victories as the admission of one black student to a southern university, the em-

---

[15] Bayard Rustin, "From Protest to Politics: The Future of the Civil Rights Movement," *Commentary*, Feb. 1965, p. 25.

phasis has changed to the mobilization of *group* economic, political, and at times physical power.

The black liberation image of change differs also in that a majority of its adherents take it as established that under certain conditions, extralegal methods will be used. In 1966, when Martin Luther King suggested that civil law is at times superseded by a higher moral law and led his followers on illegal marches and sit-ins, he was considered an extremist. The direct action approach is now a common tactic that is considered controversial only when accompanied by deliberate acts of violence or property destruction. This position is clearly in stark contrast to the liberal emphasis on following established procedures and preserving the sanctity of the law.

Variations in Black Ideology

The following sections elaborate differences among black thinkers: their varying attitudes toward capitalism, the relationship of their struggle to Third World liberation movements, the integration-nationalism argument, and their claims to types and processes of change that may be properly understood as revolutionary. Our discussion will be organized around the disagreements over goals and tactics, which we have already noted, because these differences reflect most faithfully the way in which black thinkers themselves experience them. In the section on goals, four different types will be examined. In regard to tactics, we shall concentrate on the issues of coalition versus independent black organization and violent versus nonviolent methods.

Contending Goals: Four Formulations

INTEGRATION

Proponents of integration, the most familiar of black goals, hold that black freedom and equality can be achieved only by full admission of the Negro into the mainstream of American life. Forced segregation of blacks into separate institutions is viewed as the major obstacle to progress, and the goal of integrationists is the destruction of each and every barrier that separates whites and blacks.

At various times, different institutions have been the focus of attack. All integrationists point to the 1954 Supreme Court decision in *Brown v. Board of Education*[16] ordering integration of schools as a major landmark in the black liberation movement. The dramatic sit-in movements in the early 1960s had as their object the integration of dime store lunch counters. But realization that economic handicaps prevented full enjoyment of the new legal rights soon followed. Many blacks could not afford to eat in integrated restaurants and use other public accommodations integrated by the Civil Rights Act of 1964, for example. Nor were they able to compete fairly for jobs without adequate training. Integrationist leaders have therefore come to focus increasingly on the problem of jobs, education, and housing, seeking to open up unions, universities, and white-collar opportunities. Bayard Rustin has suggested that the focus has shifted from relatively peripheral institutions to those that are basic to the social and economic order.[17] In spite of the shift in the types of institution that are the specific targets, the integrationist goal remains the same: black progress through the opening of white institutions to blacks.

The integrationist perspective emphasizes the essentially *American* character of the struggle for black liberation. Martin Luther King wrote, "Abused and scorned though we may be, our destiny is tied up with America's destiny." [18] Integrationists take the Declaration of Independence as their model and see the black movement as forcing the United States toward the realization of the values and goals stated in that document. The Third World and Africa enter into integrationist thinking only very peripherally. The development of free African nations is seen as an inspiration for blacks in the United States, but concrete connections between the black struggle in the United States and the Third World are not made.

While integrationist thinkers share the goal of creating black pride and dignity, they do not relate these qualities to the distinctiveness of Afro-American culture as other black thinkers do. Martin Luther King saw blacks as exercising their right to self-definition

---

[16] 347 U.S. 483 (1954).
[17] Rustin, *op. cit.*, p. 25.
[18] Martin Luther King, *op. cit.*, p. 93.

through participation in nonviolent direct action. Through such participation, the black man rejects the American eye-for-an-eye ethos, and by creating his own means of changing society, generates self-respect and wins the respect of others. It is through the fulfillment of traditional Christian values that the black man frees himself. In a direct attack on the nationalist tendency to advocate pride through black distinctiveness, Bayard Rustin wrote that "pride, confidence, and new identity cannot be won by glorifying blackness or attacking whites; they can only come from meaningful action, . . . from good jobs, and from real victories." [19]

Integrationist leaders see the American system as at least moderately responsive to black demands for change. Martin Luther King considered the Birmingham mass action a success, pointing to the token integration of formerly segregated facilities and the promises of the white business sector to begin to open jobs to blacks. Passage of the Civil Rights Act of 1964 and the Voting Rights Act of 1965 often is cited as proof of the ability of black pressure to elicit change. Although integrationist leaders are dissatisfied with the *rate* of change, they do argue that there is movement in the desired direction.

This is not to say that the integrationist leaders are uncritical of the present social structure of the United States. Leaders such as Whitney Young and Bayard Rustin share the view of American society as racist and exploitative and therefore in need of basic change. Martin Luther King represented the civil rights movement as potentially accomplishing the moral rejuvenation of the United States. He wrote that

> the civil rights movement will have contributed infinitely more to the nation than the eradication of racial injustice. It will have enlarged the concept of brotherhood to a vision of total interrelatedness. [20]

King was concerned with change on a cultural and moral level. He contended that in rejecting segregation and accepting and promoting integration, American society is correcting the perversion of its

---

[19] Bayard Rustin, " 'Black Power' and Coalition Politics," *Commentary,* Sept. 1966, p. 39.
[20] Martin Luther King, *op. cit.,* p. 152.

values and turning toward the positive American values. His formulation is a good example of a black leader who views American values as essentially sound but in need of implementation and reemphasis.

Bayard Rustin, taking a more pragmatic approach to the question of societal reorientation, has suggested that black demands cannot be objectively satisfied within the framework of existing political and economic relations and that the black liberation movement ultimately will lead to a "refashioning of the political economy." [21] Rustin argues that the insistence of the black movement that emphasis be placed on equality of condition rather than equality of opportunity will accelerate the existing tendency toward the expansion of the public sector and result in substantial social change. In spite of these arguments, the complaint of Harold Cruse that "Negro leadership is not really fighting *against* the system, but against *being left out of* it" [22] is more applicable to the integrationist perspective than is any other subideology within the black liberation movement. The final vision of Rustin and many other integrationists appears to be the creation of an inclusive welfare state within the capitalist framework. Theirs is a vision of change similar to that of the reform liberal, rather than the kind of call for the total reordering of the system that distinguishes revolutionary goals.

SEPARATISM

The ideology of Elijah Muhammad's Nation of Islam (Black Muslims) presents a dramatic contrast to the integrationist perspective.[23] This ideology completely rejects any solution for the black man within the context of the American social system. Muhammad's doctrine advocates complete withdrawal of the black man from the governmental and territorial jurisdiction of the United States. It de-

---

[21] Rustin, "From Protest to Politics," p. 25.

[22] Harold Cruse, *The Crisis of the Negro Intellectual* (New York: Morrow, 1967), p. 371.

[23] The description of the ideology of the Nation of Islam that follows is drawn from Malcolm X, *The Autobiography of Malcolm X*; Louis Lomax, *When the Word Is Given* (New York: Signet, 1964), especially pp. 169–180; E. Essien Udon, *Black Nationalism: A Search for Identity in America* (Chicago: University of Chicago Press, 1967).

mands that the United States relinquish several southern states, out of which an independent and separate black state is to be established. The ultimate goal of its adherents, then, is separatism in its purest (geographical) form.

As a more proximate goal, voluntary separation of blacks into the black ghetto or community is advocated. There, through a program of self-help, the black man will prepare himself spiritually and economically for the coming complete separation from white society. Unlike the integrationist perspective, which directs its energies to the opening of the institutions of white society, the Nation of Islam focuses upon developing and strengthening the existing black community.

An involved and sweeping religious creed is the underlying rationale for both the ultimate and proximate goal. Elijah Muhammad preaches that humanity is divided on a worldwide basis into the Black Nation and the white race. Conflict between the two is continuous. The original man created by Allah or God was black and the white race was grafted from the black. The inferior and evil white race fought the black race and eventually enslaved it. Recent history has witnessed the struggle of the Black Nation to free itself from white enslavement. American Negroes, collectively constituting the Nation of Islam, occupy a special position in that they have been chosen by Allah to redeem the whole black nation from evil before the coming apocalypse in which the white race and a portion of the black nation will be destroyed by the wrath of Allah. Specifically, they must lead the American Negro to the realization that his true spiritual and temporal home lies with Islam and with its center in the Arab world and Mecca.

Although much of the ideology of the Nation of Islam is framed in religious mystical language, many of the themes that run throughout more secular black thinking are clearly present. The speeches of Elijah Muhammad and, even more, those of Malcolm X (during his Muslim period) contain the most sweeping condemnation of the United States to be found in black writing. The white man's treatment of the black man, historically and in the present, is offered as proof that the white race is evil, cannot be redeemed, and has earned the wrath of Allah. Although they themselves are vehemently opposed to integration, Black Muslims point to the white man's continual refusal to allow it as proof of his evil nature. Again and again, the moral degeneracy of the white man is emphasized and America is termed the modern Babylon. Their rejection of integration is seen as a refusal to integrate with evil.

The second theme, often stated by Malcom X, is less overtly religious and mystical. Malcolm emphasized the cultural identity of American blacks with Arabian and African cultures. Malcolm told his audiences that they descended from civilizations that were rich and flourishing when the white Europeans still inhabited caves. Blacks were stolen from their "culture of silks and satins" and enslaved in the United States. The Nation of Islam invites black people to renounce their slave names, their Christianity, and their American identity, and to regain their true identity in Islam.

The Nation of Islam asserts that blacks must identify with Arabian civilization. Both Elijah Muhammad and Malcolm X traveled to Mecca. These trips emphasized the cultural roots of blacks in Muslim lands. In Black Muslim schools, black children are taught to speak Arabic and Muslim religious rituals are performed in Black Muslim homes. The demand for southern states is seen as an expedient, albeit one completely justified by white exploitation of blacks, rather than as an acknowledgment of black identification with the United States.

It is difficult to classify the Nation of Islam as a revolutionary ideology in spite of its sweeping condemnation and the character of its demands. The eschatology certainly envisions drastic change— in fact, the destruction of the white world. But Elijah Muhammad appears to have no specific program for either forcing separation or destroying white civilization. The Black Muslims are withdrawn from politics at any pragmatic or practical level. The apocalypse is awaited fatalistically. Apparently, this passivity was at least partially responsible for the split between Elijah Muhammad and Malcolm X. We will consider Malcolm's more secular goal formulations for the black liberation movement shortly.

BLACK POWER

The "black power" slogan often is equated with a shift in the black liberation movement from nonviolence to violence. This is a very superficial characterization, and in any event, the real significance of this development may lie in its reflection of the attempt to formulate new goals within the framework of nationalism. The ideology of black power embraces many of the themes of the Nation of Islam, but expresses them in a secular and political, rather than religious, manner. In addition, black power advocates draw the thinking of Third World revolutionary writers such as Franz Fanon into the black liberation movement, applying their concepts to the relations of blacks and whites in the United States. In describing black power thinking, we shall rely principally on two sources: the speeches of Malcolm X after his break with the Nation of Islam and the more extended statement of Stokely Carmichael and Charles Hamilton in *Black Power*.

Like the Nation of Islam, black power thinkers emphasize the cultural distinctiveness and need for independence of black people and reject integration as a degrading solution. Nevertheless, they recommend development of an independent black community within its present boundaries rather than complete territorial independence from the United States. They call for blacks to take control of the political, economic, and social institutions of their communities. As Carmichael and Hamilton put it, "the goal of black self-determination and black self-identity—black power—is full participation in the decision-making processes affecting the lives of black people." [24]

This goal, a kind of modified separatism, is based upon an analogy to the colonial situation of other nonwhite peoples of the world. Blacks in the United States are seen as the colonial subjects of the white rulers; they are not an integral part of the United States, but constitute a separate nation within a nation. Like other oppressed peoples, they must throw off the oppressor, reject their colonial status, and assert their identity as a nation of free and independent people. Integration is not a possible solution, for it would destroy, rather than recreate, the black nation.

Carmichael and Hamilton detail three characteristics of the black-white relationship in the United States. In combination, these characteristics define the colonial situation. First is the political powerlessness of American blacks. They assert that whites always have made the black man's political decisions. Through the manipulation of political boundaries, indirect rule, and terrorism, he has been denied political power systematically. Despite the fact that in

---

[24] Carmichael and Hamilton, *op. cit.*, p. 47.

many geographic areas blacks constitute a majority of the population, they possess almost no political power. Second, like a colonial subject, the black man has been economically exploited. As a laborer, he is assigned to the menial jobs and compensated at a minimal level. The meager housing and business resources of the ghetto community are owned by whites and operated for profit. Like all colonies, the black ghetto exists for the sole purpose of enriching the colonizer.

Finally, the black man in America resembles the oppressed colonial because he is assigned a socially inferior status. The colonial social structure acts to convince the native colonial of his inferiority. Values and traditions are derided and basic social structures such as the family or tribe are destroyed. Because black people have been denied respect since they were brought to the United States as slaves, they doubt their worth as human beings. The mark of a colonial subject is that he has succumbed to myths of his own inferiority and been led by its acceptance to self-hatred.

Closely related to the black power analysis of the race problem in colonial terms is the tendency to place the problem in an international context. The struggle of blacks in the United States is equated with Third World (particularly African) struggles to free themselves from white oppression by the West. Malcolm X expressed this connection to a black audience as follows:

> You can't understand what is going on in Mississippi if you don't understand what is going on in the Congo and you can't really be interested in what is going on in Mississippi if you don't understand what is going on in the Congo. They're both the same.[25]

This strong internationalist perspective of the black power ideology has a number of significant implications. First, it leads black thinkers to a particularly bitter condemnation of the United States. This country is seen not only as the oppressor of American blacks, but as the exploiter of the colored peoples of the world. At the same time, it offers black thinkers a vision of their people not as a hopelessly outnumbered minority, but as at least potential members

---

[25] Malcolm X, *Malcolm X Speaks,* p. 125.

of a worldwide majority, a majority which every day grows more restless. Finally, it provides American blacks with concrete models of other economic, political and cultural forms.

The colonial analogy made by the black power thinkers serves to integrate many of the general views of other black leaders. White racism, exploitation, and failures of democracy may be seen as related phenomena, adding up to a relationship between blacks and whites that can be described comprehensively only as colonial. As in the Third World countries, the existence of a colonial situation in the United States is seen as implying and justifying a revolutionary situation. Black power ideology asserts that like other colonized subjects, the black man in the United States can alter his status only if he self-consciously asserts his own value and frees himself through the creation of group political and economic power. It is realistic for blacks to unite and take control of local structures such as city councils, schools, and economic institutions. They can create enclaves within the United States in which they will be free to define themselves culturally and create political, social, and economic institutions of their own design. Thus, their goal is not, like integrationists', to eliminate the ghetto, but to transform it into an independent community that will operate under a set of values formulated to fill the needs of the black community and necessarily different from those of the majority white society.

Black power ideology places particular stress upon the cultural and social dimensions of oppression. Carmichael and Hamilton assert that it is essential for blacks to reclaim their history and identity. The struggle in America is conceived less in material terms than in terms of the struggle for the right of self-definition, a struggle "to create our own terms through which to define ourselves and our relationship to the society, and to have these terms recognized." [26] Throughout the works of Carmichael and Hamilton and of other black power advocates are scattered references to the different forms that the black community will take. As we have seen, on a very general level, it is usually presented as a community that will be organized around a true concept of humanity and brotherhood rather than around a competitive struggle for material goods. "Reorientation," Carmichael and Hamilton write, "means an em-

---

[26] Carmichael and Hamilton, *op. cit.*, p. 35.

phasis on the dignity of man, not on the sanctity of property." [27] More specifically, they call for collective economic institutions and a return to communal rather than private forms of property relationships. Late in his career, Malcolm X specifically suggested that some form of socialism was the proper goal of the black liberation movement.

The black power movement is clearly an example of the tendency in black liberation thinking to reject the legitimacy of American values. It does not, however, provide a full articulation and description of alternate values and institutions. For this reason (and a number of others) we can only tentatively classify black power as seeking a degree of change properly understood as revolutionary. In spite of black power's vehement denunciations of the United States in both domestic and foreign policy terms, the ultimate goals of black power ideology are ambiguous and/or contradictory. Carmichael and Hamilton, for example, make statements concerning the basic reorientation of the American system that encourage their classification as revolutionaries. But, in concrete terms, their goal appears to be transformation of the ghetto rather than of society as a whole. They speak of blacks receiving a proportionate share of societal power but not of a total change in power distribution. Finally, their failure to specify the values and goals clearly in terms of which the ghetto is to be transformed has allowed a number of alternate definitions of "black power" to develop. Among them is the very *non*-revolutionary concept of black capitalism or the creation of a parallel capitalism in the ghetto. The limited nature of these prescriptions for changes appears to be based upon more than a pragmatic calculation of what is possible. It seems to grow also out of the character of black power's analysis of the American system—a view that sees the system as brutal and dehumanizing in relation to blacks but is unconcerned with its effect on whites. Whites, with the possible exception of poor whites, are assumed by Carmichael and Hamilton to have power and to escape exploitation. It therefore becomes difficult to assert a need for revolution on a nationwide basis in a country where a majority of the population is admittedly not oppressed. These assumptions appear to exist side by side with a tendency to denounce both capitalism and pluralism

---

[27] *Ibid.*, p. 41.

in more general terms. But it is the former, more limited, conception on which concrete goal prescriptions seem to be based.

It is perhaps the ambiguity of the black power position combined with what many black thinkers perceive to be growing intransigence and racism among whites that has led one of black power's major spokesmen, Stokely Carmichael, to endorse a new position, revolutionary Pan-Africanism. The essence of this position is the establishment of a land base in Africa to which American blacks can return and join African and other Third World countries in their struggle against U.S. imperialism and capitalism. This perspective ultimately involves revolution on a world scale, with the United States as the principal target. But the timetable is a long one. Carmichael sees this as a natural development of black power and the black struggle generally.

> I think that, in terms of reality and history and my own ideology, all of the movement that we have been building up in terms of black nationalism, from the sit-ins to "black power" runs straight to Pan-Africanism. . . . We need a land base. . . . In the final analysis, all revolutions are based on land.[28]

REVOLUTIONARY NATIONALISM

The Black Panther Party led by Huey P. Newton and Bobby Seale represents a distinctive subideology of the black liberation movement that terms itself revolutionary nationalism. The ideology of this group, formed in Oakland, California in 1966, has carried the internationalist perspective and colonial analogy of black thinking to an unambiguously revolutionary conclusion. Like the black power advocates, the Black Panthers specify the goal of self-determination for the black community but place it within the context of a nationwide socialist revolution that will totally transform the economic and political systems. They argue that freedom, justice and self-determination for blacks are possible only if the capitalist system is replaced by a socialist one. Panther ideology reaches this

---

[28] Stokely Carmichael, "Pan-Africanism—Land and Power," *The Black Scholar,* November 1969, p. 39.

conclusion from an analysis of the U.S. system that employs both the class terminology of Marxism and the colonial terminology of black liberation. As in the black power analysis, racism, exploitation, and powerlessness are seen as intimately linked, but in Panther ideology, capitalism is explicitly identified as the cause of the other ills.

Black Panther spokesmen argue that racism and capitalism were linked in the past as they are in the present. The capitalist system created racism and maintains it so that it can continue to rationalize economic exploitation. One Panther spokesman expresses it thus:

> We understand we have two evils to fight—capitalism and racism. We rightly view one as "cause" (capitalism) and the other as "effect" (racism). The Black Panther Party knows that racism has always existed in lower forms, but that capitalism has institutionalized, commercialized, and mass-produced racism to such a high degree that it is sometimes thought of as a separate entity.[29]

While not denying the reality of racism as a psychological and structural characteristic of the American system, Panther ideology asserts that it can be eliminated only if capitalism is eliminated.

In addition to these links between capitalism and racism, the Panthers see the capitalist system as intrinsically exploitative and oppressive because it is motivated by a production for profit rather than production for human use. In such a system, the masses of people become tools. Denied the opportunity to participate in decisions concerning production, they are, in fact, slaves.

This analysis of capitalism as intrinsically oppressive leads the Black Panthers to break, on one level at least, with the black liberation vision of black people as uniquely oppressed. "We realize," Huey Newton writes, "that not only are blacks kept in a slave condition, all persons in this country are essentially in that condition. In order for us to become free, all citizens will have to be free." [30]

---

[29] Sylvester Bell, "Who's on the People's Side," *The Black Panther*, August 30, 1969, p. 9.

[30] Huey P. Newton, in *The Black Panther*, August 23, 1969.

Therefore, freedom of the majority of members of the society, both black and white, becomes the goal of black liberation. To express this, the Black Panther Party has replaced the slogan "Black Power" with the expression "All Power to the People," indicating that a total redistribution of power is necessary. The image of a white, open democratic society from which blacks are excluded, which runs throughout much of black thinking, is decisively abandoned by the Panthers in favor of a ruling class image. The capitalist business-men, the owners of the means of production, are seen as politically dominating blacks and whites alike. The majority of blacks and whites are equally excluded from real power, although they may differ in the degree of material deprivation and overt oppression to which they are subject. Eldridge Cleaver writes that "the black and white communities are controlled by the same ruling class. Towards black people, this ruling class uses racism as a tool of oppression, turning this oppression into a National Question. In the white com-munity oppression is a Class Question, provoking the response of Class Struggle." [31]

Although the Black Panthers insist on the importance of de-fining the goals of the black liberation movement in national revo-lutionary terms, they continue to emphasize the view of the black community as a colony. It is in the black community that capitalist oppression is seen as most overt and, as the quotation above from Eldridge Cleaver indicates, the processes of oppression are distinc-tive in that they are based on racism. The Panthers see the black community as a nation within a nation, and they express the colonial analogy in one of its most militant forms. Like Malcolm X, they re-gard the police as an occupying army operating to ensure the qui-escence and subservience of the colonized people through brutality and terror. The early activities of the Black Panther Party included the formation of armed black patrols to protect ghetto residents from police harassment. Although this practice has been discon-tinued, the prevention of police brutality remains a focus of Party activity.

Black Panther spokesmen have added to the demands of many black leaders for control of community institutions the demand that

---

[31] Eldridge Cleaver, "On Meeting the Needs of the People," *The Black Panther,* Aug. 16, 1969, p. 4.

police departments be subject to the control of the community. They also have challenged the working of the entire legal system, suggesting that it operates as an oppressive mechanism in the interests of the ruling class and that many black leaders accused of "crimes" are in reality political prisoners. In effect, while stating the long-range goal of total revolution, they specify decentralization and community control as more proximate goals in terms similar to those of the black power advocate. But they are precise and explicit about the form such community control should take, and they work in concrete ways to create what they consider revolutionary social structures in the ghetto communities they seek to serve.

In the early 1970s, perhaps as a result of the decimation of the party through police raids and court convictions, the Panthers turned to a longer range, less militant practice involving running for electoral office, registering black voters, and building black economic power in the ghettoes.

Tactical Differences

Our discussion of the variations in goal formulations of black thinkers establishes the context within which tactical differences should be understood. Both major tactical disagreements, the argument concerning the proper relationship of whites to the black movement, and the question of violence versus nonviolence generally follow the integrationist-nationalist split. For integrationist thinkers, with their lesser concern with the need for independent cultural definition and their less extreme view of necessary social change, viable coalitions between blacks and moderate whites, and nonviolent tactics, seem both necessary and fruitful. For the nationalists, with their emphasis on cultural differences and belief in the need for more fundamental social change, coalitions are suspect and violent methods are justified and necessary. We shall consider each of the disputed areas in turn.

RELATIONSHIP WITH WHITES

A number of black organizations always has refused membership to white individuals and declined to cooperate with white groups. The Black Muslims are an obvious example, and the rationale for this policy requires little elaboration if we recall the role accorded whites in their general world view. Until recently, however, the common form of organization for the best known black liberation groups has been interracial, and they have pursued a deliberate policy of coalition with liberal and left liberal groups such as labor unions and, in general, worked within the structure of the Democratic Party. However, in 1966, SNCC adopted the black power position, expelled its white members, and turned toward the organization of independent black political groups. In 1964, Malcolm X had announced his break with the Nation of Islam and formed the all black Organization of Afro-American Unity. The NAACP and other integrationist groups continued to maintain white membership and to pursue the traditional coalition policies. And the debate over the propriety and efficacy of different organizational forms was on.

In *Black Power,* Carmichael and Hamilton summarized most of the major arguments for rejection of the traditional coalition policy. Their major contention is that there is a lack of identity of interests between the goals of blacks and those of most whites. They argue that traditional coalitions were based on the assumption that what is good for white America automatically is good for black people. But this is an erroneous assumption because whites in general are opposed to the fundamental reorganization of the society that is the goal of the black liberation movement. Because it is in their interest, consciously or unconsciously, whites are dedicated to the preservation of the prevailing norms and institutions: it is difficult for whites to conceive of a society in which white Anglo-Saxon norms do not prevail.

Carmichael and Hamilton argue that, judged even by their own standards, supporters of the traditional coalition policy should admit their lack of achievement. They can point only to tokens as the accomplishment of the policy they have pursued. The material conditions of the black masses have remained unchanged or actually declined in recent years. In addition, the coalition policy has been positively destructive to black pride and dignity because it reinforces the prevailing image of black inability to progress without white leadership.

Black thinkers with an integrationist perspective have responded to this analysis with a number of charges and queries of their own. They reject the contention that past coalition policies have had little effect and suggest that the stronger, more militant coalitions of the present can be even more successful if the black liberation movement unites around them. They suggest that there is, in fact, an identity of interest between blacks and whites. They emphasize that material deprivation is shared by whites, who are thereby led to support considerable change in the society. Most emphasized, however, is their view that there is no realistic alternative to coalition politics. Black power advocates and other nationalists see the concentration of blacks in southern counties and northern cities as an untapped source of strength. Supporters of coalition politics see this strength as more illusory than real. They point out that on a national basis, blacks constitute a small minority of the population and need allies to move the federal government because critical decisions are made on the national level, not on the local level. They contend that alliances with Third World countries are unacceptable to the masses of blacks and impractical in any case. Third World countries are struggling for their own survival and are in no position to aid the American black liberation movement. Thus, proponents of the contending views reach an impasse over questions of both fact and ideology.

Often overlooked in the debate is the fact that Carmichael and Hamilton and other nationalist leaders have not rejected coalition politics per se, but have merely rejected the form that coalition politics has traditionally taken. In *Black Power,* the authors analyzed the reasons for failure of the traditional coalition politics and specified the criteria for viable coalitions. A minimum condition was that coalitions would be possible only with white groups committed to the total restructuring of the society. In fact, some of the more militant black liberation groups have made alliances with white radical groups. For instance, in 1968 the Black Panther Party formed a coalition with the predominantly white Peace and Freedom Party to run candidates in the 1968 presidential elections.

VIOLENCE VERSUS NONVIOLENCE

Like the dispute over coalition politics, the debate over violent versus nonviolent tactics generally has followed the split between integrationist and nationalist perspectives. Martin Luther King was the major spokesman for the nonviolent position. He tried to apply Ghandian principles of passive resistance to the black liberation struggle in the United States. Opposing him are leaders such as the late Malcolm X, Stokely Carmichael, and the Black Panther Party who insist that violence under some circumstances, particularly those of self defense, is necessary and justified.

At the core of the case for nonviolence is a moral and ethical argument. Martin Luther King expressed a moral standard in the following words: "Over the past few years I have consistently preached that nonviolence demands that we must be as pure as the ends we seek. I have tried to make it clear that it is wrong to use immoral means to attain moral ends." [32] Violent tactics, King argued, defeat the purposes of the black movement by reducing the freedom fighter to the level of the oppressor. By resorting to violence the black man might gain a few concessions, but he will not attain the pride and dignity that he can attain by passive resistance.

Describing the Birmingham marches, King wrote: "The brutality with which officials could have quelled the black individual became impotent when it could not be pursued by stealth and remain unobserved." [33]

King also used more pragmatic arguments to argue the case for nonviolent direct action methods. He pointed out that when combined with economic boycotts as they were in Birmingham, such tactics add economic power to the moral challenges raised by the other methods. Finally, and most pragmatic, he argued that violent attempts to produce social change are doomed to failure. The fate of the American Indian indicates the probable outcome of militant attempts to force social change. In any violent confrontation between blacks and whites, blacks, vastly outnumbered and possessing few technological resources, surely would be defeated.

More militant black leaders take exception to every point in the argument for passive resistance and nonviolent direct action. First, they reject the premise that self-defense is morally impermissible. They argue that man has the moral right and obligation to defend himself against attack. This is particularly true, they argue,

---

[32] Martin Luther King, *op. cit.,* pp. 93–94.
[33] *Ibid.,* p. 37.

in a society such as that of the United States where the brutalization of black people is commonplace and even the federal government has proven incapable or unwilling to protect them. Black dignity and pride are created not by turning the other cheek, but by commanding respect through strength. Malcolm X suggested that nonviolence is only justified where the oppressor himself is nonviolent. In his words, "you should never be nonviolent unless you run into some nonviolence. I'm nonviolent with those who are nonviolent with me." [34] In addition, many black leaders argue that it is inconceivable that white America, which itself has perpetrated so much violence and brutality on black people both in America and in the Third World, would be at all capable of feeling guilt for its acts. Leaders of white America are seen as hypocritical in their insistence that blacks limit themselves to nonviolent means of winning freedom while they waged violent war in Vietnam and justified it in terms of the necessity of defending freedom.

Many black thinkers contend that white America rejects violence only when blacks begin to organize themselves for self-defense. Any act by blacks to defend themselves is perceived by whites as a positive act of violence. At the same time, white America will not condemn itself for its treatment of American Indians, which stopped little short of genocide, or of American blacks and Third World peoples, which tends in that direction.

Finally, to the pragmatic argument that defeat is inevitable, they respond that there is little for blacks to lose in any case. The present situation of blacks is so intolerable that an honorable death in battle is preferable. Beyond this, they argue, violent means will not necessarily be defeated in spite of the obvious military advantages of white society. Black thinkers with an international perspective once again point to the Third World nonwhite majorities as a potential source of aid. More concretely, they suggest that the techniques of guerrilla warfare used in Cuba and in Vietnam have permitted revolutionary groups to defeat numerically greater and technologically more sophisticated enemies. The principles of guerilla warfare could be applied to the black liberation struggle in America with similar results.

In spite of the militant tone of some of these arguments, many

---

[34] Malcolm X, *Malcolm X Speaks,* p. 34.

black spokesmen who often are thought of as proponents of violence have done no more than advocate organized self-defense. That is, they have defended the right of American blacks to prepare to defend themselves when attacked. Their arguments often appear extreme because the groups that they are prepared to defend themselves against are often those to which the white society accords legitimacy, such as the police. As we have seen, many black leaders view the police as instruments of brutality and oppression in the ghetto, and they therefore advocate that the people organize in order to protect themselves against the police.

At some point, the argument for organized self-defense does shade over into a justification of positive acts of violence. Malcolm X, in one of his more militant statements, coined the phrase "freedom by whatever means necessary," a slogan which has been adopted by a number of black liberation groups. Leaders of this persuasion often have argued that freedom is a goal for which men traditionally have killed and been killed, that revolutionary violence is sanctioned even by the American Declaration of Independence, and that there is no reason to hold black men to any other standard. They are convinced that the condition of blacks in the United States is one that justifies revolutionary violence.

In spite of this assertion of the justification for positive violence, there still is a tendency for even the most militant black leaders to view violence as a last resort. They argue that the final choice of the means of social change remains with white society. If basic changes could be accomplished through peaceful means, violence would not be necessary. But black militants argue that white America has continually proved itself incapable of peaceful change. The inevitable result therefore will be violent revolutionary change.

Chicano Liberation

Integration of American blacks into the American culture has been so thorough that the most serious attempt to foster a black ethnic identity has taken the form of a rediscovery of the African or Islamic heritage. In contrast, retention of the Indian reservation has made the preservation of an indigenous Indian culture possible. Chicanos have not become "anglicized" to the degree that black people have, but they do not have the reservation Indians have. The primary goal of Chicano liberation is to maintain a cultural identity and, at the same time, to participate fully in American political, social, and economic life.

The distinction between assimilation and "Chicanismo" is relevant here. The assimilationist point of view holds that "altogether the Chicano movement is only another ethnic movement, at its bitterest a threat not to integrate which cannot stop the integration but which can wrest some reparations for the loss of old certainties." [35] This point of view regards Mexican Americans as on a par with other ethnic minorities such as the Polish, the Irish, and the Jews. It points to the gradual assimilation of Mexican Americans into American life. The success of such an assimilation is obscured somewhat by the ongoing arrival of new immigrants, but nonetheless, it is inevitable:

> But the trends now seem clear—that this "ethnic minority" is dissolving like the others into an "ethnic category," which within another generation will no more than statistically and nostalgically bring together people living in different classes.[36]

The outlook of Chicano liberation is somewhat different. In the introduction to *Aztlan,* Luis Valdez argues that the assimilationist point of view amounts to the imposition of "an immigrant complex" on Chicanos; it is just another form of American racism.[37] Assimilationism is a process in which "immigrants," people of other cultures or races, who come to the United States, take on the superior attitudes and values of the dominant Anglo culture; naturally, immigrants want to be Americanized, the faster the better. Chicano liberation insists that the Chicanos are not simply immigrants eager to be anglicized and integrated. Speaking for his people Armando Rendon argues that

---

[35] John Womack, Jr., "Who Are the Chicanos?" *New York Review of Books*, XIX, 3, p. 15.

[36] *Ibid.,* p. 14.

[37] Luis Valdez and Stan Steiner, eds., *Aztlan* (New York: Vintage Books, 1972), p. xxxii.

our ideals, our way of looking at life, our traditions, our sense of brotherhood and human dignity, and the deep love and trust among our own are truths and principles which have prevailed in spite of the gringo, who would rather have us remade in his image and likeness: materialistic, culture-less, colorless, monolingual, and racist. Some Mexican-Americans have sold out and become agringados, . . . like the Anglo in almost every respect. Perhaps that has been their way of survival, but it has been at the expense of their self-respect and of their people's dignity.[38]

In this view, the "melting pot concept is a sham," "the North American culture is not worth copying," and Chicanos must rally around "the unifying force of [their] nonmaterial heritage" and the "soul-giving myth of La Raza." Chicano liberation delights in pointing out that it is the Anglo-Americans who are the *true* "immigrants:"

Imagine, finally, white men marching into the light and darkness of a very old world and calling it new.

This was not a new world at all. It was an ancient world civilization based on a distinct concept of the universe.[39]

Chicano liberation goes far beyond the documentation of discrimination against and mistreatment of Chicanos. It asserts the integrity and validity of a world view of its own. Valdez says that "the Chicano can no longer totally accept as reality the white, western European concept of the universe. . . . Reason and logic are not enough to explain the modern world; why should it suffice to explain the ancient world of our ancestors?" [40]

Chicano liberation says that basically, Chicanos cannot be construed simply as another immigrant group pressing for assimilation because Chicanos do not accept the fundamental values or world view of Anglo culture. In fact, they are stridently critical of the Anglo culture, as this passage from Rendon indicates:

---

[38] Armando Rendon, *Chicano Manifesto* (New York: Macmillan, 1971), p. 46.
[39] Valdez and Steiner, *op. cit.*, p. xvii.
[40] *Ibid.*, p. xxxi.

The North American culture is not worth copying: it is destructive of personal dignity; it is callous, vindictive, arrogant, militaristic, self-deceiving, and greedy; it is a gold-plated ball-point pen; it is James Eastland and Richard Nixon; it is Strom Thurmond and Lyndon Johnson; it is a Mustang and old-folks' homes; it is Medicare and OEO; it is an $80 billion defense budget and $75 a month welfare; it is a cultural cesspool and a social and spiritual vacuum for the Chicano. The victims of this culture are not merely the minority peoples but the dominant Anglo group as well; everything that passes for culture in the United States is symptomatic of a people so swept up in the profit motive and staying ahead of the Joneses that true natural and humanistic values may be destroyed without their knowing it. Nationalistically, Anglo-America has come to believe that it is the supercountry, that it can do no wrong, that its might does make right. The United States suffers from a lack of perspective, a lack of humility; it is spoiled and immature without showing any signs that it is growing out of that stage.[41]

Luis F. Hernández, a professor of education at San Fernando Valley State College, described Mexican American values as being directed towards "tradition, fatalism, resignation, strong family ties, a high regard for authority, paternalism, personal relations, reluctance to change, a greater orientation to the present than to the future and a greater concern for being than doing." [42] Rendon refers to a rich and diverse folklore, and Valdez talks of "merging the very ancient with the very new to create new forms." All Chicano writers express the conviction that an ancient cultural tradition is a deeply rooted and inherent part of all Chicanos. They insist that it cannot and should not be snuffed out by Anglo culture. Most Chicano writers go farther and argue that the Chicano culture has much to teach the Anglo culture, that Anglo culture is corrupt and in the process of decay. Rendon expresses this viewpoint:

---

[41] Rendon, *op. cit.,* p. 178.
[42] Quoted in Ruben Salazar, from "A Stranger in One's Land," in Edward Simmen, ed., *Pain and Promise: The Chicano Today* (New York: New American Library, 1972), p. 165.

Americans now have more money and more leisure
than ever before in their history, but at the same time greater
tensions, less sensitivity toward a positive use of their money
and leisure, greater civil conflicts than ever, and social disintegration not only between minority and majority groups
but within the majority group itself. . . .

The Mexican-American . . . because he is what he is,
can also embody and bring together the white and the black
and the red for their mutual benefit and that of the whole
nation.[43]

Rendon acknowledges that some of the traditional Chicano
values are outmoded or incompatible with the current struggle for
justice. In particular, the emphasis on paternalism and obedience
to authority is an awkward value for a social group that emphasizes
equality and is challenging authority. He also acknowledges that
Chicano women have played a vital role in advancing the struggle,
and their role as the passive, submissive female no longer is appropriate. Yet values in all cultures become outmoded and undergo
change without calling into question the culture as a whole. The Chicano culture need concede nothing to the Anglo culture on this
account.

One basic question remains to be answered: to what extent can
a cultural group take part in the political, social, and economic life
of the Anglo culture without suffering annihilation of its own culture? Clearly, Chicanos can retain their ethnic identity easily when
their population is concentrated; they can do this even more easily
by using this concentration to achieve political control over their
lives, as La Raza Unida has done in many counties in Texas. But
many Chicano writers believe that Anglo culture has a "genocidal
tendency" that refuses to tolerate the existence of any culture other
than the Anglo one. Furthermore, the thousands of Chicanos who
do not live in areas of concentrated Chicano population are especially vulnerable to anglicization. The terms under which Chicanos
will eke out their existence in the United States are not yet clear,
but the fact that the Chicano movement embraces its own unique
culture and seeks openly to challenge Anglo culture is evidence that

---

[43] Rendon, *op. cit.,* p. 61.

it does not intend to accept the terms agreed to by (or forced on) Irish, Poles, and the other immigrant groups.

Chicano liberation is an attempt to formulate and assert a cultural world view that is fundamentally opposed to the dominant Anglo culture. It is an attempt to attract and unify Chicanos; to resist Anglicization; and to criticize and change Anglo culture. Whether the Chicanos will eventually follow, whether they will influence, or whether they will eventually lead Anglo culture is the essential question for Chicano liberation.

Chicano liberation has thus far been concerned mainly with unifying its ranks and expressing its cultural heritage as a fundamental criticism of Anglo culture. Now it must begin to formulate the precise conditions under which it can resist Anglo hegemony in positive rather than purely negative ways. That is, as long as it remains simply a refusal and a criticism, it risks a continuation of its present status as an excluded, powerless group. Its next step must be the formulation of an understanding that will provide it with *analytical* capacity—an ideology or an analytical framework that will give it insight into the nature of the society against which it struggles, suggest strategies for change, and create a vision of a society in which it can participate fully on terms it can accept.

The American Indian

Indians' beliefs have very little in common with those of blacks. Their culture has survived in somewhat fuller form, and it was distinctive to begin with. Their experience at the hands of the dominant society offers only some parallels. And the nature of their current claims is quite different. But because Indian beliefs and claims add such a distinctive dimension to the variety of minority demands on the dominant American ideologies, a brief consideration is well justified.

As the original inhabitants of the American continent, Indians view the developments of the last few centuries from a certain long-range perspective. The Indian watched the white man come to his country; he waited while the white man rationalized the destruction of a continent and perhaps the world in the name of "progress"; and then he saw the white man face a desperate racial, economic, and ecological crisis. A touch of "I told you so" animates the comments of Indians about the white man's culture and values, and a deep-seated cynicism of the white man's treaties and other legal apparatus shows through. Over the years, this cynicism has been turned primarily to the task of denying or circumventing the many commitments made to Indians over the years.

The most notable and central fact about Indian culture and beliefs is that they are profoundly different from orthodox American values and beliefs. Because the difference is so great, it exists at such a basic level, and it is so unrelated to specific strategies for "liberation," we do not use the concept of ideology with reference to Indians. The conceptual foundations of Indian thought—their habits, styles, or ways of thinking—are so distinctive that we can only present them in their own terms. For this purpose, we shall use as illustration a major work by perhaps the leading Indian spokesman, Vine Deloria, Jr., to illustrate the Indian culture. His work, *We Talk, You Listen,*[44] is much more than a statement of Indian beliefs and perspectives: it is an argument about the dominant society on behalf of *all* minorities and a call for specific change in dominant ideologies toward new forms based on contributions of minorities. But it also provides an invaluable window into the totally different world of the American Indian.

Deloria makes it clear that Indians do not share the empirical, logical rationality that is a part of capitalism-liberalism. Because they do not employ the same tools or units of thought, these differences start with the very definitions of words. For example, individualism to the Indian means the development and fulfillment of the self through and entirely within relationships to others in the community. Deloria sets forth the difference in this fashion:

> The vital difference between Indians in their individualism and the traditional individualism of Anglo-Saxon America is that the two understandings of man are built on entirely different premises. White America speaks of individualism on an economic basis. Indians speak of individualism on a social basis. While the rest of America is devoted

⁴⁴ Vine Deloria, Jr., *We Talk, You Listen: New Tribes, New Turf* (New York: Macmillan, 1970).

to private property, Indians prefer to hold their lands in tribal estate, sharing the resources in common with each other. Where Americans conform to social norms of behavior and set up strata for social recognition, Indians have a free-flowing concept of social prestige that acts as a leveling device against the building of social pyramids.

Thus the two kinds of individualism are diametrically opposed to each other, and it would appear impossible to reconcile one with the other. Where the rich are admired in white society, they are not particularly welcome in Indian society. The success in economic wars is not nearly as important for Indians as it is for whites, since the sociability of individuals with each other acts as a binding tie in Indian society.[45]

Deloria emphasizes that Indian society's concept of community completely changes the relationship of individuals to the society. Economic competition is eliminated, and "status depends upon the manner in which a person contributes to his community. . . . It becomes much more important that a person be wise and enter into the decisions of the group than that he know a great number of facts." [46] There is also a greater emphasis on spiritual, traditional, and long-range factors—and not much on the tangible, material, short-range matters that occupy capitalist-liberal society.

The Indians' attitude toward land clearly illustrates the difference between the cultures. Indians acknowledge no private property rights in land because it is one of the resources that sustain the lives of all. Because this is so, the land should be preserved and continually restored for the long-term benefit of all. Indians resisted the white man's persistent efforts to close off land and treat it as a commodity to be sold or "developed" for personal profit for centuries. But in the end, they were forced by the U.S. government to parcel off their own reservations into lots and homesteads so that they would have the means to learn to become capitalist individuals. Deloria draws a sharp and poignant contrast between the Indian view of land and natural resources and the results accomplished by the white man's developmental mania. He sees the latter

---

[45] *Ibid.*, p. 170.
[46] *Ibid.*, p. 172.

building an artificial universe totally at odds with the natural character and purposes of the environment:

> The Indian lived with his land. He feared to destroy it by changing its natural shape because he realized that it was more than a useful tool for exploitation. . . . All of this understanding was ruthlessly wiped out to make room for the white man so that civilization could progress according to God's divine plan.
>
> In recent years we have come to understand what progress is. It is the total replacement of nature by an artificial technology. Progress is the absolute destruction of the real world in favor of a technology that creates a comfortable way of life for a few fortunately situated people. Within our lifetime the difference between the Indian use of land and the white use of land will become crystal clear. The Indian lived with his land. *The white destroyed his land. He destroyed the planet earth.* (Italics in original.)[47]

The white man's "progress" has brought the United States and the world to the point of fundamental crisis. The use of land is at the center of this crisis, and the only solution is to reverse completely the way in which the land is used. This is not the only dimension to the crisis, to the solution, but the ecological crisis is fundamental to Deloria's analysis. The only way out, he insists, is to return to the Indian usage of land and restore the wildernesses. He is adept at irony:

> Every time we have objected to the use of land as a commodity, we have been told that progress is necessary to the American way of life.
>
> Now the laugh is ours. After four centuries of gleeful rape, the white man stands a mere generation away from extinguishing life on this planet.[48]

He sees no alternative but to restore the wildernesses and encourage "a great number of people [to] return to the life of the hunter,

---

[47] *Ibid.*, p. 186.
[48] *Ibid.*, p. 195.

living in the forests and hunting animals for food." [49] Consistent
with this viewpoint, he endorses the hippie communal lifestyle and
calls for a widening of the Woodstock spirit among youth generally.

But Deloria's analysis of the nature of the American crisis is
of a broader range. He also sees a major change in values, a change
in thinking of such proportions that ultimately, man will be viewed
in the Indian manner: as a member of a group. By multiplying culturally distinctive groups (tribalism), each free to think and act in
its own terms, both minorities and the society itself will be saved.
In his words,

> American society is undergoing a total replacement of its
> philosophical concepts. Words are being emptied of old
> meanings and new values are coming in to fill the vacuum.
> Racial antagonisms, inflation, ecological destruction, and
> power groups are all symptoms of the emergence of a new
> world view of man and his society. Today thought patterns
> are shifting from the traditional emphasis on the solitary in-
> dividual to as yet unrelated definitions of man as a member
> of a specific group. [50]

It should be obvious that much of what Deloria sees and welcomes
is happening in the countercultural movement among young people.

But Deloria is one of the few to carry the call for a multi-
cultural society to the point of actual description. He is not talking
about some version of the present society with the existing ideologies
in their dominant roles. The transformation he sees is a reconstruction of that society and elimination or drastic modification of its
ideologies to form a nation of tribes in which cultural minorities can
take their places as equals and within which the ecological problem
can be solved. The two principles are mutually complementary and
equally necessary. The land must be returned to wilderness, with
many people living simply off it. Simultaneously, values and living
styles must be reorganized into the tribal form. He sees today's increasing emphasis on the legal rights of distinct groups as a sign that
this tribal form might be achieved:

---

[49] *Ibid.,* p. 194.
[50] *Ibid.,* p. 16.

In view of the impending disaster in ecology, this development of group rights may prove to be the salvation of the survivors of modern technological society. If hostile elements are faced by a group, then integrity, customs, and semisovereignty can be built into smaller groups of people so that upon the final irrational dissolution of American society these people will survive. Whether the economic distribution system will be so thoroughly destroyed as to reduce modern society to absolute tribalism, or whether a fragment of that system will exist leaving us with a modified feudalism, is the question that we now face.[51]

At no point does Deloria suggest ways in which this reconstructed society might be achieved. Indians probably would answer any questions about the proper means of social action with the request that they simply be left alone. But Deloria appears to be prescribing for an entire society, and the only route toward change implied is that of the countercultural assumptions—inevitable, unplanned, yet widespread and effective fundamental value change.

Some Shared Aspects of Minority Liberation

Each of the minority groups that we have discussed in this chapter considers its particular history, problems, priorities, world view, strategies and the like to be unique. Nevertheless, some aspects of their struggles are common to all minorities. In our discussion of black liberation we tried to illustrate the full range of possible responses to the plight of black people—responses that ranged from the simple plea to be included in American political, social, and economic life as it is to the revolutionary nationalism of the Black Panthers.

Rejection of American society as it is today is precisely the factor that constitutes the "liberation" element of each of these minority groups. Minority liberation represents a profound criticism of what it perceives to be the materialistic, racist, and inhumane character of American society. Naturally, it is a criticism of inequal-

---

[51] *Ibid.,* p. 212.

ity, discrimination, and repression. But beyond that, it is a total rejection of the capitalist-liberal vision, a refusal of the terms on which American society offers "integration" to minority groups.

Annotated Bibliography

Acosta, Adalberto Joel. *Chicanos Can Make It*. New York: Vantage, 1971. A successful businessman believes that the Horatio Alger myth is applicable to Chicanos: individual striving will bring material and social success.

Allen, Robert L. *Black Awakening in Capitalist America*. Garden City, N.Y.: Doubleday, 1969. Author argues that the problem for blacks is capitalism and that a revolution to overthrow capitalism is the only remedy. But because such a revolution is not imminent, a transitional—not reform—program is called for.

Carmichael, Stokely, and Charles V. Hamilton. *Black Power: The Politics of Liberation in America*. New York: Vintage Books, 1967. The most detailed exposition of the black power position.

Cleaver, Eldridge. *Soul On Ice*. New York: Dell Publishing Co., 1968. A major cultural critique of the United States, from the perspective of prison and emerging political activism.

Cruse, Harold. *The Crisis of the Negro Intellectual*. New York: William Morrow, 1967. A somewhat difficult but rewarding work tracing the historical development of various strands of black ideology.
———. *Rebellion or Revolution*. New York: Morrow, 1968. A collection of several essays analyzing black culture and politics.

Davis, Angela Y., et al. *If They Come in the Morning*. New York: New American Library, 1971. A collection of articles by and about "political prisoners."

Deloria, Vine, Jr. *We Talk, you Listen: New Tribes, New Turf*. New York: Macmillan, 1970. Perhaps the most comprehensive articulation of the Indian position, written with wit and directed at whites.

DuBois, W. E. B. *The Souls of Black Folks*. New York: Dodd, 1970. A basic statement of the black world view by one of its earliest and most important spokesman.

Jackson, George, *Blood in My Eye*. New York: Random House, 1972. A revolutionary statement by a man whose prison experience transformed him from an ordinary street criminal into a compassionate and dedicated revolutionary. Written just before he was shot in an alleged prison escape attempt.

King, Martin Luther. *Why We Can't Wait*. New York: New American

Library, 1964. Perhaps the best of the many works by the leading exponent of integration and nonviolence.

Meier, Matt, and Feliciano Rivera. *A History of Mexican-Americans.* Emphasis on the Southwest during the last two centuries. Good background for understanding the current movement.

Neihardt, John G., ed. *Black Elk Speaks: The Life Story of an Ogallala Sioux.* Lincoln, Neb.: University of Nebraska Press, 1962. A subtle product of continued interviewing, this book presents the autobiography of an Indian chief in a manner that conveys the flavor of Indian thought and feeling very effectively.

Newton, Huey P. *The Genius of Huey P. Newton.* Berkeley, Cal.: Black Panther Party, 1970. A collection of the major statements of Black Panther ideology by the Party's Minister of Defense.

————. *To Die for the People.* New York: Random House, 1972. Selections from Newton's writings and speeches reflecting the development of his thought and that of the Black Panther Party.

Rendon, Armando. *Chicano Manifesto.* New York: Macmillan, 1971. A searing criticism of Anglo culture and a passionate defense of "Chicanoism." Covers many aspects of the Chicano history, culture, and struggle.

Rustin, Bayard. "From Protest to Politics: The Future of the Civil Rights Movement," *Commentary,* Feb. 1965. A brief but classic statement of the integrationist, coalition-seeking, traditional politics approach to black liberation.

Seale, Bobby G. *Seize the Time.* New York: Random House, 1970. A description of Black Panther Party history and ideology by the Party's Chairman.

Simmen, Edward, ed. *Pain and Promise: The Chicano Today.* New York: New American Library, 1972. An extremely wide and diverse collection of speeches and articles on the Chicano movement and Chicano life.

Steiner, Stan. *The New Indians.* New York: Dell, 1968. Perhaps the best historical and analytical description currently available. Contains a useful bibliography as well.

Valdez, Luis, and Stan Steiner, eds. *Aztlan.* New York: Vintage Books, 1972. Selections from Chicano literature with a perceptive introduction by Valdez.

Womack, John, Jr. "Who Are the Chicanos?" in *New York Review of Books,* 19, no. 3. A review of a number of current books on Chicanos and a discussion of the Chicano movement. Expresses the assimilationist point of view.

X, Malcolm. *Malcolm X Speaks,* George Breitman, ed. New York: Grove Press, 1966. The collected speeches convey the tone and substance of Malcolm's attempt to reformulate black ideology after his break with the Nation of Islam; a precursor of both black power and revolutionary nationalism.

X, Malcolm with Alex Haley. *The Autobiography of Malcolm X*. New York: Grove Press, 1965. A major critique of American society from the perspective of prison, and the Nation of Islam; traces Malcolm's own development as he moved to a more political and revolutionary stance.

Zinn, Howard, *SNCC: The New Abolitionists*. Boston: Beacon Press, 1964. A description of the activities of the Student Nonviolent Coordinating Committee and the early Southern phase of the civil rights movement.

7

Women's Liberation

The women's liberation movement as it exists today is of comparatively recent origin. The Woman's Rights Movement of an earlier time has much in common with the current movement, but the women's movement underwent an eclipse in American life sufficiently complete for us to treat the women's liberation movement of today as a *new* movement. The irritations of this movement's early followers, the condescending and mocking reception given them by the media and the general public, and the absence of program have given way to the organization of a movement that is striking out for various kinds of power for various reasons.

Almost none of the groups within the women's liberation movement finds it difficult to agree on the manifestations of the repression of women. Criticism was first directed at what Betty Friedan, one of the earliest spokesmen for the movement, called "the problem that has no name": the sense of desperation and profound frustration experienced by many middle-class women (especially those who are educated). They had no vocation other than that of housewife, a role they found dreary and unfulfilling, in spite of the fact that they were qualified to fulfill far more demanding jobs and lead interesting lives. From that point, it was only a short step to the realization that even when women did hold jobs, they worked under a double standard: usually, they were not promoted as quickly or as fairly as men were; they were not paid the same rate for the same work that men were performing; and they were discouraged or prohibited from holding certain positions or undertaking certain kinds of work. In addition, they were discriminated against in a great number of other ways.

At this early stage—during the middle 1960s—most attention was focused on the question of woman's right to hold a job fitted to her interests and abilities and to be paid and promoted fairly. The other side of this particular coin was the attack on myths about "femininity," myths such as those that chanted the incessant male doxology that "a woman's place is in the home."

Very rapidly, interest in this inchoate "movement" spread to women from other parts of the social spectrum—particularly to college women—and the probe cut deeper and more intensely into the extent and causes of the oppression of women. In a short time, the issue was refined into the basic question of role definition. This question included such matters as the meaning of "femininity" and "masculinity"; the socialization of children into "male" and "female" roles; the expectations of women regarding their futures and their self-image in general; social mores and mannerisms; the personality structures of males and females; the "sexuality" of males and females and the subsequent reappraisal of homosexuality and bisexuality; the reappraisal of motherhood and family life; the treatment of women in literature, the media, and advertising; and a host of other matters.

From these concerns many were led further to analyze the socio-economic system in which "sexism" flourished and to immerse themselves in intense political activity. Women involved in politics began to see that even in many of the political groups dedicated to the struggle against mistreatment of other groups in society, women had a lowly status and were relegated to the mundane rather than to the responsible tasks—to "support" work such as typing, filing, or making coffee. Or they believed that the woman's issue was being given short shrift by these movements. In response to these feelings and for other reasons, they came to demand that the "woman's issue" be transformed into the Woman's Liberation Movement—a movement in its own right.

Thus, in the short time between publication of *The Feminine Mystique*[1] in 1963—the first American book addressing the subject

---

[1] Betty Friedan, *The Feminine Mystique* (New York: Dell, 1970). Simone de Beauvoir's book, *The Second Sex* (New York: Bantam, 1961) was first published in French in 1949 and subsequently in English in 1953. This was considered a landmark book, but although it was highly acclaimed in intellectual circles, it did not capture the attention of a larger public in the way that Friedan's book did.

—and the late 1960s, the "woman's issue" had developed into a movement that was conscious of itself as representing a group or class, was learning its forgotten history, identifying its heroines, developing programs, elaborating world views, and striving for recognition and power. This movement contains within itself a whole range of world views, goals, values, and strategies for social change. It is not yet a unified, coherent ideology, if indeed it ever will be. In this chapter, we shall present what we perceive to be the two extremes and the middle position within the movement.

At the one extreme are those groups that fully accept the basic outlines of the social system; they are organized around the realization of certain limited and essentially legalistic goals within that system; they employ traditional and "politics-as-usual" strategies for achieving their goals; and they do not question the most fundamental mores of family and sexual life.

At the other extreme are those groups that believe a fundamental restructuring of the social system is necessary (for example, socialism), that their goals cannot be realized without such a restructuring, that extralegal strategies for change are necessary, and that existing family and sexual mores must be abandoned completely.

The middle position consists of those groups that can correctly be identified with reform liberalism in their orientation toward politics and change. These groups are not quite as legalistic as the conservatives are, their goals are not as limited, and they are not as satisfied with existing sexual mores and roles. Furthermore, whereas the conservatives of the women's movement tend to limit themselves to specified "women's" issues, the reformists tend to align themselves with a variety of reform liberal causes such as antiwar activity, minority rights, or ecology causes. On the other hand, they do not identify themselves with socialism and are comfortable with traditional strategies and tactics for change, endorsing such tactics as electoral politics, demonstration marches, and coalitional politics.

The Conservatives

The National Organization for Women (NOW) was the outgrowth of Betty Friedan's book *The Feminine Mystique*. "The feminine mystique," according to Friedan, is the mystique that has for centuries shrouded a certain model of "femininity." This model of femininity is based on the idea that all women's misery is the result of their envy and imitation of men, from whom they are by nature different. According to the feminine mystique, femininity revolves around sexual passivity, male domination, and a nurturing maternal love. The feminine mystique assumes its modern form in the role of housewife-mother, a role that becomes the pattern all women must follow or suffer the loss of their "femininity."

The membership of NOW originally included many of the women who were subsequently to break off and become leaders in rival groups. For example, Ti-Grace Atkinson, a leader of the Feminists, one of the most radical groups within the women's liberation movement, originally was a member of NOW. Most members of NOW are middle-class, college-educated women in the 30 to 50 year old age group. A great many of them are business and professional women, and this has led many to equate NOW with the many business and professional women's clubs that have existed for several decades.

NOW has centered around the basic concern of encouraging women to fulfill themselves outside the home, usually by developing a career, taking on a paying job, or engaging in some sort of meaningful community work. This does not by any means entail giving up their roles as mothers or wives. As Friedan expresses it, "she must create, out of her own needs and abilities, a new life plan, fitting in the love and children and home that have defined femininity in the past with the work toward a greater purpose that shapes the future." [2]

NOW addresses itself, then, to all of the issues that impinge on this basic concern. First of all, the woman must be able to relieve herself of any household or family responsibilities that might keep her from entering professional life or securing a job. To accomplish these goals, NOW recommends that household tasks should be shared within the family or outside help hired; it supports state-provided child care facilities; and it supports family planning and repeal of anti-abortion laws. Second, NOW insists on equality in the work place. This means equal pay for equal work, opening up traditionally male pursuits and positions to women, implementing a nondis-

---

[2] Friedan, *op. cit.*, p. 326.

criminatory hiring policy, and making promotions according to desert and qualification.

Perhaps NOW's attachment to the dominant capitalism-liberalism ideology and its diagnosis of the cause of the repression of women based on that ideology determines the character of its program. In her book, Friedan repeatedly refers to herself as a "reporter," and much of the book consists of informal conversations with the women she was "interviewing." The book is concerned less with discovering the origins or basis of "the feminine mystique" than with exposing the widespread extent of its existence.[3] The conviction that women can pull themselves up by their bootstraps underlies the book. This view does not reflect a condescending or censorious attitude toward the unfulfilled woman. Rather, it reflects the confidence that once the myth or "mystique" is exposed and rejected, women can achieve what they want and need within the present socio-politico-economic system. Thus, for example, rather than viewing media advertising (what she calls the "sexual sell") as an explanation behind or cause of the feminine mystique, she argues that if women reject the feminine mystique, the sexual sell will not succeed. Sexual sellers simply are aware of the conditions of women's lives, they do not help to create them, according to Friedan.[4]

Because Friedan conceived the problem in this way, her political analysis does not confront what is behind the sexual sell or what must be done about it. Rather, her political program consists of legislation that will remove tangible barriers to a woman's career advancement once she has divested herself of the feminine mystique—something she can do only by listening "to her own inner voice." [5] NOW basically is satisfied with the family-centered way of life and with the politico-economic system as it is. In fact, NOW frequently is referred to as the NAACP of the women's movement to indicate its essentially conservative character. The political posture of NOW

---

[3] It is interesting to note in this connection a comment by de Beauvoir that "We are still too preoccupied with clearly seeing the facts to try to penetrate the shadows beyond that illuminated circle. 'Women never go beyond appearances,' said a writer to me. It is true enough. Still amazed at being allowed to explore the phenomena of this world, they take inventory without trying to discover meanings." de Beauvoir, *op. cit.*, p. 668.

[4] Friedan, *op. cit.*, p. 199.

[5] *Ibid.*, p. 326.

calls for enactment of legislation to ensure equal rights for women and for greater participation by women in the political process as it is. It is expected that such legislation will be achieved in much the same way that legislation of any other kind is achieved: by lobbying, by gaining the attention of the media, and by attempting to win over public opinion. No restructuring of society, remolding of women, or reconstruction of family or sexual life is required. This vision is well illustrated in this passage from *The Feminine Mystique*:

> She must learn to compete then, not as a woman, but as a human being. Not until a great many women move out of the fringes into the mainstream will society itself provide the arrangements for their new life plan. But every girl who manages to stick it out through law school or medical school, who finishes her M.A. or Ph.D. and goes on to use it, helps others to move on. . . .
>
> When enough women make life plans geared to their real abilities, and speak out for maternity leaves or even maternity sabbaticals, professionally run nurseries, and the other changes in the rules that may be necessary, they will not have to sacrifice the right to honorable competition and contribution any more than they will have to sacrifice marriage and motherhood.[6]

What is basic to NOW and all other conservative groups within the women's liberation movement is their belief that realization of their particular limited goals will create a desirable life for all; that these goals can be achieved by traditional political processes; and they are compatible with the basic family and sexual mores of society and with the fundamental principles of capitalism-liberalism.

The Radicals

The radical position is composed of two essential factions. One faction believes that women's liberation is linked to socialism—that socialism is a necessary *and* sufficient condition for the liberation of women. The second faction believes that the oppression of women

---

[6] *Ibid.*, p. 361.

goes *deeper* than the economic class system to a class system all its
own—a system based on the biological functions of sex—and that
socialism is a necessary condition of the liberation of women, but it
is not a cure in itself. This second, more radical aspect of women's
liberation is represented by Shulamith Firestone's book *The Dialectic
of Sex,*[7] and this is the position presented here.

Firestone argues that beneath economic class structure "there
is a whole sexual substratum of the historical dialectic that Engels at
times dimly perceives, but because he can see sexuality only through
an economic filter, reducing everything to that, he is unable to evalu-
ate it in its own right." [8] Continuing her argument, she speaks of the
"untried alternative. . . . We can attempt to develop a materialist
view of history based on sex itself." [9] Such a materialist dialectic
posits that biology—procreation—is at the origin of the sexual class
dualism. Thus, "the natural reproductive difference between the
sexes led directly to the first division of labor at the origins of class,
as well as furnishing the paradigm of caste (discrimination based on
biological characteristics)." [10]

This conceptualization of the problem obviously is far more
fundamental, systematic, and analytical than Friedan's conceptualization is. It leads Firestone to regard the social system suspect in its
broadest sense: the social system reflects the power relationships and
attendant ideology of this biologically based class system. The cultural and economic superstructure is thus traced "not just back to
(economic) class, but all the way back to sex." [11] While this sexual
class system was at one time necessary for the perpetuation of the
species, it has developed into "a system consolidated over thousands
of years, lending the archetypal male and female roles an undeserved

---

[7] Shulamith Firestone, *The Dialectic of Sex* (New York: Bantam
Books, 1970). Simone de Beauvoir took the first position—that is, that
socialism would provide for feminism—in *The Second Sex*. In the early 1970s,
however, she abandoned that position for the second, declaring that socialist
countries were not, in fact, creating equality for women and that the woman's
condition could not await the remedies of socialism. See Alice Schwartzer,
"The Radicalization of Simone de Beauvoir," *MS.,* July, 1972, p. 60.

[8] Firestone, *op. cit.,* p. 4.

[9] *Ibid.,* p. 5.

[10] *Ibid.,* p. 9.

[11] *Ibid.,* p. 12.

legitimacy and seeming permanence." [12] Firestone rejects this "permanence" on the basis of the fact that "we are no longer just animals" and "the Kingdom of Nature does not reign absolute." Therefore, "we can no longer justify the maintenance of a discriminatory sex class system on grounds of its origins in Nature." [13] Even though the biological conditions on which this class system are based no longer exist, the power relationships on which the system originally was based have ensured its continued existence. "We shall need a sexual revolution much larger than—inclusive of—a socialist one to truly eradicate all class systems." [14]

Firestone believes that women cannot achieve their goals without a socialist revolution; at the same time, she says that the feminist revolution is best qualified to bring about the socialist revolution because women represent an oppressed *majority* class. They are the first and most successful group to have linked their personal experience with politics, to attempt to reconcile the personal with the public; and thus they are uniquely capable of avoiding the destructive results of "power psychology" in their movement in that they eschew factionalism, hierarchy and personality cults.

According to Firestone, two major requirements must be met if women's liberation is to be accomplished. First, women must be freed from the "tyranny of their reproductive biology by every means available [by extra-uterine pregnancy] and the diffusion of the childbearing and childrearing role to the society as a whole, men as well as women." [15] Second, "the full self-determination, including economic independence, of both women and children [must be achieved by] fundamental changes in our social and economic structure. This is why we must talk about a feminist socialism." [16]

Clearly, Firestone is contemptuous of the proposals of the more moderate feminist groups and other social movements that claim to embrace the women's cause. She regards these groups as "apolitical," as having "no solid historical analysis," and as "foundering in disunity." She considers their proposals "timid if not entirely worthless" even as a transition. For example, day care centers "buy women off"

---

[12] *Ibid.*, p. 15.
[13] *Ibid.*, pp. 9–10.
[14] *Ibid.*, p. 12.
[15] *Ibid.*, p. 206.
[16] *Ibid.*, p. 207.

and "ease the immediate pressure without asking why that pressure is on *women*." Nevertheless, she fails to provide an elaborate, consistent, or entirely clear picture of the means of change. Her blueprint consists almost entirely of replacing marriage and the family with other more flexible and liberated life styles such as "living together," "group living," and communal child-rearing. First she says that such changes ("the revolt against the biological family") "could bring on the first successful revolution or 'Messianic Age,' " [17] then she says that "we would first have to have, to be entirely successful in our goals, socialism within a cybernated state." [18] Thus, the ideology that regards feminism and socialism as separate but equally necessary struggles has yet to work out the relationship between the two and the means of their achievement in a satisfactory manner.

The Reformers

The reformers of the women's liberation movement have not restricted themselves to particular, limited legislative goals as have the conservatives, nor have they committed themselves to the elimination of capitalism-liberalism, as have the radicals. Rather, they advance broader objectives than the conservatives do and identify themselves with various reform liberal causes such as ecology and minority rights, but they do not call for a transformation of the politico-economic system. The reformist group is thus a rather amorphous one, and although leaders such as Bella Abzug and Gloria Steinem are highly publicized because of their intense involvement in political and public life, it is difficult to identify either its followers or a coherent program of change.

This group shares almost all the values of reform liberalism and seeks to add its special concerns to those of reform liberalism. It is concerned about poverty, war, racism, and ecology and favors more positive government activity in these areas, but it does not reject individualism, civil liberty values, the political process itself (if reformed to be "more representative" or "fairer"), and the attempt to achieve equality within the established property framework. It regards women's special concerns as free abortion on demand, paid

---

[17] *Ibid.*, p. 242.
[18] *Ibid.*, p. 235.

maternity leaves, state-provided child care, remuneration for household duties, equal rights for women legislation, greater participation
by women in the political process, and the repeal of all laws aimed
at regulating private sexual practice or reproductive life. In addition
to these "political goals," the reformers criticize the socialization of
children into traditional sexual roles, discrimination against homo-
sexuals, degrading images of women in advertising, and the barriers
—tangible and intangible—to the full participation of women in the
social, economic and political life of the country.

Like conservatives, it regards the solutions of women's problems as possible within the capitalism-liberalism framework, but it is
distinct from the conservatives in its belief that the problem is
broader and more fundamental in scope than mere legalistic reform
and career opportunity. It regards "sexism" on a par with racism—a
discrimination that appears *throughout* family, social, political, and
economic life and in subtle, tacit as well as more overt forms. Therefore, power is at least as important as persuasion is in the battle for
equality if not more so, and no aspect in the life of society should be
overlooked in the search for traces of "sexism." But while reformers
look for causes beyond a mere inventory of abuses, their analysis
does not find that the causes lie within the framework of capitalism-
liberalism itself. Sexism pervades the institutions of our society, but
it can be rooted out by intense and agile political and public relations activity rather than by a wholesale transformation of these institutions.

A good example of the reformist outlook in the women's liberation movement can be found in Kirsten Amundsen's book, *The
Silenced Majority*.[19] After documenting the pervasiveness of what
she terms "institutional sexism," Amundsen argues that a liberated
society demands "a variety of institutional innovations and a complete reordering of economic priorities." [20] But "it is clear that the
capitalist system need not be totally transformed in order to intro-
duce the reforms in question." [21] As to means, "political pressures
will have to be applied at all points; confrontation politics in many
instances will gradually have to be combined with the thrust of
organized groups of women and their allies." She enumerates such

---

[19] Kirsten Amundsen, *The Silenced Majority* (Englewood Cliffs, N.J.:
Prentice-Hall, 1971).
[20] *Ibid.*, p. 160.
[21] *Ibid.*, p. 161.

"out-group weapons" as newsworthy agitation, sit-ins, consumer boycotts, slow-down strikes, civil disobedience, electioneering, coalition
politics, public harassment, and financial injury.[22] Amundsen characterizes her politics as "nonrevolutionary," but not always "nonviolent." Thus, although "politics-as-usual" is not likely to redress
the grievances of women's liberation, reformers believe that "politics"
of a more dramatic kind ultimately can succeed.

Annotated Bibliography

Amundsen, Kirsten. *The Silenced Majority*. Englewood Cliffs, N.J.:
Prentice-Hall, 1971. Analyzes "institutional sexism" and sets out
a program for change. Reflects the reformist point of view.

de Beauvoir, Simone. *The Second Sex*. New York: Bantam Books, 1961.
This is the seminal work in the women's liberation movement. It
is comprehensive and highly literate and argues that woman's independence will come only with socialism.

Cudlipp, Edythe. *Understanding Woman's Liberation*. New York: Paperback Library, 1971. Identifies the various groups and leaders
within the women's liberation movement and provides a list of
organizations and publications.

Firestone, Shulamith. *The Dialectic of Sex*. New York: Morrow, 1970.
A radical analysis that posits a sexual class system based on bio-
logical-reproductive functions as more fundamental than the
Marxist class analysis.

Friedan, Betty. *The Feminine Mystique*. New York: Dell, 1970. The
landmark book in America. Emphasizes the need for the housewife
and mother to reject the "feminine mystique" and fulfill themselves in meaningful work outside the home. Focuses on equal
rights legislation that will enable women to engage in such work.

Greer, Germaine. *The Female Eunuch*. New York: McGraw-Hill, 1971.
A colorful attack on sexual mores and conventions arguing that
liberated sexuality cannot be achieved without a transformation
of present customs, myths, and relationships, but that women's
liberation should no reject sexuality itself.

Millett, Kate. *Sexual Politics*. New York: New American Library, 1969.
Concerns the treatment of women in literature.

Morgan, Robin, ed. *Sisterhood Is Powerful*. New York: Vintage Books,
1970. A collection of essays on all aspects of the women's movement.

---

[22] *Ibid.*, p. 162.

8

The New Left

Evolution of the New Left

The "new left" is not any one thing; most of all, it is not a coherent ideology. Probably, it is best understood as a convenient label attached to certain left-oriented moods, actions, and people of the period beginning in 1960. The term was first used as a means of distinguishing the beliefs and activities of this period from the more familiar principles and movements of the 1950s and earlier, which came to be known as the "old left." For this purpose, the term still is useful: clearly, there has been a break from previous left politics—at the very least, a revival in form. The shared sources, attitudes, and practices that developed among the groups after 1960 make the label something more than just a historical reference. But no single or coherent set of beliefs or doctrine can systematically characterize the new left. This is so particularly in light of the crises that have fragmented its various components into the splinters we see today.

The ideology of the new left is vague; nevertheless, it can be distinguished from reform liberalism easily. Adherents of the new left tend to place greater emphasis on equality and less on property than do reform liberals; they have less confidence in the electoral process, no particular faith in the law, and they tend to emphasize extra-legal strategies and tactics for change; and they accept neither the desirability nor the inevitability of the current capitalist economy. In short, the new left is radical where reform liberals are liberal, but it has not developed a socialist analysis. In fact, the new left has not really developed an *analysis* at all.

We see the new left as a transitory stage, essentially coterminous with the decade of the 1960s, but still existing in certain forms in which rapid ideological evolution occurred. Action was taken in response to some key issues—for example, civil rights, poverty, student power, and the war in Vietnam; some basic analyses appeared or were adopted to help the public to understand these issues and some essentially reform liberal goals were announced; and many college and university young people became radicalized by the conditions of their world. But no single or coherent ideology was involved—only shared reactions to these conditions and democratic-egalitarian aspirations. Explanations of injustice were not fully developed or shared; goals were not well considered or related to theoretical underpinnings; and actions were taken with little strategy or sense as to how change could be brought about. Nevertheless, this was a vital and creative stage, for it spawned many separate ideologies, some of which have now become more coherent and emerged as major factors in their own right. Minority liberation, women's liberation, and socialism were all born or reborn out of the ferment of this period. Some fragments of the new left remain in much less developed form. Whether they are permanent or not is yet to be seen.

We shall approach this body of beliefs and reactions in combined historical and analytical terms, as befits the crucible of modern ideological conflict. Two analysts provided much of the early perspectives of the new left: Herbert Marcuse and C. Wright Mills. In part, these ready-made interpretations were adopted because the new left had no time or interest for developing its own position; in part, they were not adopted at all, but merely used as window dressing for actions that were felt to be right in their own terms. Next, we shall follow part of the trail that was followed by so many within the new left—by tracing the character and evolution of the values, goals, and social actions of Students for a Democratic Society (SDS), the central organized force within the new left from 1962 to 1969. In effect, we shall see the limited ideology and ultimate fragmentation of the larger movement through this single organization. It should be clear that this ultimate fragmentation always was implicit in the *lack* of a coherent ideology. Finally, we shall examine several of the fragments remaining within the loose and general umbrella of the new left, among them, the workers' movement and the community control movement, anarchism, counterculture, the Jesus People, and other identifiable splinters. Much of the new left remains a mood and reaction without analysis or program, including most of the above movements. As such, it has little political significance. Nevertheless, because anyone may develop coherence and emerge as well-formed as are minority liberation, women's liberation, or socialism, all of them deserve analysis.

Precursors of the New Left: Herbert Marcuse and C. Wright Mills

HERBERT MARCUSE

Herbert Marcuse's critique of American society is subsumed under a more general analysis of the present historical epoch. Basically, Marcuse sees the contemporary era as dominated by highly industrialized, bureaucratized societies in which human nature is twisted and destroyed by the structures it encounters. He sees the United States, with its capitalist ethos, as the leading example of the prevailing mode, but considers his analysis almost equally applicable to socialist nations such as the Soviet Union. Marcuse is concerned with the general quality of man's life and spirit, and he sees advanced technological society as presently organized as destructive. Man is shaped by the needs of the technology he has created, instead of the reverse.

In Marcuse's analysis, the present destruction of human life has an ironic quality because, for the first time in man's history, he possesses the opportunity to fulfill himself in completely new dimensions. The technological base has been established and developed to the point where the legitimate material aspirations of all men could be satisfied, the battle with scarcity and deprivation ended, and a free and full life established. Marcuse points out that the present level of technology could support a greatly reduced workweek, progressively liberating time for leisure and creative living. On this basis, the potential for a complete qualitative change in life amounts to a change in human nature itself. For the first time in history, Marcuse believes, man is free to develop in a truly human way.

This formulation of the gap between potentiality and actuality in American society rests upon Marcuse's understanding of the psychological and social nature of man. Historically, human beings have been violent and competitive, lacking attitudes of human solidarity and cooperation. But this is a quality induced by the necessity for the struggle for survival rather than intrinsic to the nature of man. The struggle against scarcity having ended, the truly human qualities in man are free to emerge. Because such a liberated life cannot truly be known by the unfree man in present-day society, Marcuse only hints at the form a liberated life would take. In one passage where he does attempt a positive formulation, he writes:

> The Form of Freedom is not merely self-determination and self-realization, but rather the determination and realization of goals which enhance, protect and unite life on earth. And this autonomy would find expression not only in the mode of production and productive relations but also in the individual relations among men, in their language and in their silence, and their gestures and their looks, in their sensitivity, in their love and hate. The beautiful would be an essential quality of their freedom.[1]

As we shall see, this sense of the discrepancy between the potential and the actual, in a sense not only material, but also psychological or spiritual, is also found in a variety of forms among new left thinkers.

Marcuse explains the failure of societies and humans to transform themselves in terms of a number of factors. Most basic is the desire of a vaguely defined ruling group to maintain power and thus necessarily the established social relations. Although the establishment uses coercion and violence, its primary method is cultural manipulation. The communication and other cultural media are used to instill the materialist and competitive values that keep men slaves. In industrial society, man constantly is bombarded with messages designed to sell him commodities and gadgets connected with acquisitive and violent life styles. The media also manipulate

---

[1] Herbert Marcuse, *An Essay on Liberation* (Boston: Beacon Press, 1968), p. 46.

political judgments. For example, alternative ideologies such as socialism are presented as impracticable or un-American. The accumu-
lative effect of training and media manipulation is so great that it
not only affects attitudes, but structures the physical needs of men.
"The people recognize themselves in their commodities, they find
their soul in their automobile, hi-fi set, split-level home, kitchen
equipment." [2] Man has been transformed into "one dimensional
man" in whom "the inner dimension of the mind in which opposition to the status quo can take root is whittled down," in whom the
power of critical thinking is absent.[3]

Thus, for Marcuse, the full realization of a bureaucratic welfare state, or even a socialist society in which one receives goods
according to his needs, is insufficient as a goal because needs themselves are the (suspect) product of manipulation. The problem of
social change is monumental because the repressive mechanisms
of society have thoroughly distorted human nature. As we shall see,
new left thinking parallels much of Marcuse's thought without accepting these pessimistic conclusions regarding change.

C. WRIGHT MILLS

C. Wright Mills presents a view of society that generally resembles the concepts of Marcuse. His work, however, focuses more
specifically and in more detail upon social institutions and is more
explicitly political. This is particularly true of his analysis of the
power elite and the middle and working classes, which we will
consider in some detail.

Mills saw the United States in the process of transformation into
what he termed a "mass society," one in which masses of individuals
are manipulated by remote rulers and lose any potential for democratic direction of important societal institutions. The underlying
tendency is toward bureaucratization and centralization of all institutions and a related trend toward stark disparity between the
few who are powerful and the great mass of those who are power-

---

[2] Herbert Marcuse, *One Dimensional Man* (Boston: Beacon Press,
1969), p. 9.
[3] *Ibid.,* p. 10.

less. Mills explicitly criticized the liberal notion of a pluralistic political and social structure in which competing groups exercise power. He argued that the United States was, in fact, governed by a power elite composed of corporate leaders, political leaders, and military men or "war lords." He asserts that the traditional pluralist institutions such as voluntary associations and political parties are hollow shells capable of no meaningful exercise of power on the national level.

Mills identified two trends of great importance. First is the centralization and bureaucratization of the political, business, and military institutions, which we have mentioned already. Second is the increasing interdependence and interpenetration of these institutions. "There is no longer," he writes, "on the one hand, an economy, and, on the other, a political order, containing a military establishment unimportant to politics, and to moneymaking. There is a political economy numerously linked with military order and decision." [4] This centralization and interlocking, combined with technological development, created power of an unprecedented nature in the hands of a small circle of men, whom he termed "the power elite." [5]

Mills criticized not only the centralized and exclusive nature of the structure of power, but also the substance of the policies pursued or allowed to emerge by the power elite. He was critical primarily of the power elite-constructed policy of "cold war," feeling that foreign policy decision-makers disregarded rationality and common sense and pursued policies that increased the chances of a deadly world war. The permanent threat of the cold war period created a situation in which a military definition of reality dictated political and economic judgments. The domestic consequence was the creation of a permanent war establishment. In Mills' view, the power elite was motivated in these decisions by both economic and ideological considerations fearing the loss of U.S. capitalism's position as the primary world power from both perspectives.

---

[4] C. Wright Mills, as quoted in Irving L. Horowitz, ed., *Power, Politics and People: The Collected Essays of C. Wright Mills* (New York: Ballantine Books, 1965), p. 27.
[5] Mills' description of the power elite referred specifically to national power. He felt that the pluralistic model of multiple groups was a more realistic description of what he termed the middle ranges of power.

Mills also criticized the power elite for its failure to properly control and guide technological development. Rather than becoming an instrument of man's advancement, development becomes a social fetish devoted to frivolous or harmful ends. Technological gadgets accumulate, but they produce a decline rather than an improvement in the quality of human life. In part, this results because the power elite must use technology as an instrument of manipulation and control. In Mills' view, the rulers of the United States were not only powerful, but also commensurately irresponsible.

Mills' analysis of other strata of society extended and supported his thesis of the power elite. Mills identified the middle class as critical to the political power descriptions of liberal theorists and viewed it as increasingly impotent with regard to national decision-making. He pointed out that farmers and small businessmen, who historically possessed power, had declined drastically in numbers. The new middle class of white-collar workers and professionals, including the professional and technical workers who Galbraith and others make much of, had failed to develop their power potential. Mills acknowledged the growing importance of expertise and technical skill in U.S. society, but felt that power emerged from conscious exercise and political organization rather than as an automatic accrual to functional importance. He found no such consciousness among the disorganized, disoriented, and ideologically subservient professional classes.

Mills saw the working class as similarly reduced to powerlessness. As a class, it was declining as a proportion of the population and being replaced in importance by a steadily expanding white-collar class. Unions that once had the potential to share in power had sunk to the middle ranges. Like other institutions, they had become bureaucracies that contained the demands of the workers rather than pressed for them. Thus, both the middle class and the working class are part of the mass. Denied any participation in meaningful decision-making, they devote themselves to material acquisition and the pursuit of status.

Like Marcuse, Mills identified the media of communication as important instruments of mass subservience. Controlled by the elite, the media confuse and trivialize issues. Other nominally independent institutions, such as the churches and particularly the universities, were equally culpable. Thus, the institutions of pluralism are not working, and the power elite is effectively unchallenged in its management of the masses.

Mills, like Marcuse, viewed the problem of social change pessimistically, seeing little if any chance of breaking into the cycle of rule and manipulation. Both Marcuse and Mills concentrated on explication of the scope and nature of problems and of the depth of their roots in the fundamental values and institutions of American society. In places, both appear to have assumed that some individuals would be able to free first themselves, and then others, but neither described the process. This is where the new left takes over, both expanding and refining their analysis and developing the prescriptions for change.

The World View of the New Left

Much of new left analysis is developed in the context of critiques of particular societal institutions or practices, and little in abstract theorizing. Nevertheless, a number of general beliefs about American society are broadly shared. We shall explore three central themes: technocracy and materialism, bureaucracy and unresponsiveness, and alienation. The Port Huron Statement (the founding document of SDS, named for the Michigan town in which the convention of 1962 was held) is a seminal document that may serve as a principal source. Although it is dated with regard to emphasis and some specifics, it is an excellent summary of the new left world view.

TECHNOCRACY AND MATERIALISM

Perhaps the most pervasive concern of new left thinkers is the heavily technological and industrialized character of the United States. New left ideology does not celebrate or even accept the inevitability of industrialization as do the dominant ideologies. At best, technology is seen as a mixed blessing, carrying with it the potential for both the enhancement or the destruction of human life. Machines that can create leisure alternately are sources of unemployment or destructive weaponry. New left writing is somewhat ambivalent as to whether technology per se or the uses to which it has been put are the core of the problem. The latter position probably is endorsed by most. Technology is susceptible to abuse and, in the opinion of new left thinkers, it has been cruelly abused in capitalist American society.

The Port Huron Statement points to the creation of a permanent war economy, frivolous materialism, and superconsumption as perversions of technological promise. In the United States, it claims, technological skill and industrial fruits are channeled into wasteful production rather than into the solution of pressing human problems such as poverty and discrimination. In American society, "the potentiality for abundance" becomes "a curse and a cruel irony." [6] This irrational establishment of priorities is attributed to the existence of the "military-industrial complex," which is in turn related to another major theme of the new left—the decline of democracy caused by bureaucratization and centralization of power.

BUREAUCRACY AND UNRESPONSIVENESS

In opposition to liberal notions of an open, flexible, and competitive society, the new left offers the image of a bureaucratized and increasingly stagnant society. For new left thinkers, bureaucracy is equated not with productivity, efficiency and rationality, but with irrationality, waste, and the destruction of human potential.

With regard to the political system, new left thinkers reject the democratic model accepted by liberals and reform liberals. The Port Huron Statement characterized the major national political institutions as antiquated and calcified. The major political parties, assumed by the dominant ideologies to outline differences and organize conflict, were characterized as homogenous and lacking in issue orientation. Congress was seen as reduced to meaninglessness by virtue of the domination of the conservative committee system. Institutions that are capable of action, such as the executive, were seen as dominated by business and military interests.

The power potential of the economic institutions is seen as equally inaccessible and irresponsible. The wealth of the country is

---

[6] Students for a Democratic Society, *The Port Huron Statement* (Chicago: Students for a Democratic Society, 1966), p. 20.

concentrated, rather than diffused. Large corporations, monopolies, and conglomerates dominate the economy and prevent the competition that is supposed to result in diversity and consumer welfare. Economic decisions have dramatic impact upon society as a whole, in every area from domestic welfare to foreign affairs, but there is neither responsiveness nor public control of its functioning. Contrary to the beliefs of reform liberals like Galbraith, the new left thinkers assert that profitability rather than humanistic values remains the criterion of decision-making in the economy.

These notions of the bureaucratization and unresponsiveness of political and economic institutions come together for the new left in the concept of the military-industrial complex. In terms reminiscent of C. Wright Mills, the Port Huron Statement refers to "the powerful congruence of interest and structure among military and business elites which affects so much of our development and destiny." [7] According to new left thinkers, elites in these two fields combine to create and foster the war economy described earlier. From positions of power, they direct societal resources to create a domestic warfare state and a foreign policy that is adventuristic and imperialistic. These decisions are made not on the basis of necessity or for the public good, but, as noted before, on the basis of what is beneficial for private enterprise—particularly, what is profitable for the giant corporations. The new left asserts that much of defense spending is motivated by orientation to profit rather than reaction to threats of external aggression from Russia or China.

ALIENATION

The new left's analysis of the distribution of meaningful power and control compels the conclusion that alienation and deprivation exists at all levels of American society. Blacks and poor whites suffer most because they are subject to economic deprivation and political powerlessness. But the relatively affluent worker and the middle class also are deprived because they are equally isolated from the decisions that affect their lives. This powerlessness is most obvious with regard to the most critical of all decisions, to make war, and

---

[7] *Ibid.*, p. 17.

other closely related decisions such as the relative levels of government spending for defense as opposed to welfare.

But this powerlessness also affects the individual's life in other less obvious ways. In their employment, men are lost in massive hierarchical institutions in which they function as easily replaced cogs. The blue-collar worker takes part in a mechanized production process that he does not understand and is unable to control. The working conditions of the middle-class individual are somewhat more pleasant but almost equally mechanical. In addition, all are subjected to the constant barrage of media propaganda that shapes their activities and desires even (or particularly) in connection with their leisure time.

This aspect of the new left's world view—deprivation of the affluent—is based upon the perception of the gap between the actual and the potential in human development that Marcuse noted. It means that the new left thinker conceives of himself as not concerned solely with the need for freedom of less fortunate individuals such as the poor, but as concerned with his own freedom, which is equally threatened by the American social system. This vital theme of the new left is expressed incisively by Greg Calvert in the course of distinguishing the radical and the liberal:

> The liberal reformist is always engaged in fighting "someone else's battles."
>
> He does not sense himself to be unfree.
>
> Radical or revolutionary consciousness perceives contradictions in a totally different fashion. The gap is not between oneself and the underprivileged but is the gap between "what one could be" and the existing conditions for self realization. It is the perception of oneself as unfree, as oppressed—and finally it is the discovery of oneself as *one of the oppressed* who must unite to transform the objective conditions of their existence in order to resolve the contradictions between potentiality and actuality.[8]

---

[8] Gregory Calvert, "In White America: Radical Consciousness and Social Change," in Teodori, ed., *The New Left: A Documentary History* (Indianapolis: Bobbs-Merrill, 1969), pp. 414–415.

The Values and Goals of the New Left

The Port Huron Statement indicates the nature and general direction of new left values: "We regard *men* as infinitely precious and possessed of unfulfilled capacities." For all new left thinkers, the emphasis is upon the essentially good, capable, and cooperative nature of man. New left thinkers see themselves as consciously setting this view of human nature against a dominant one that emphasizes the limitations of man and therefore his need to be controlled and manipulated—to be reduced, in the terminology of the Port Huron Statement, "to the status of things" [9]—for the sake of efficiency and the smooth functioning of the society. The value premises of new left ideology and its concept of human nature replace elitist conceptions of human development and progress with an affirmation of the innate capabilities of all men. In the words of Tom Hayden, "Above all, I reject the claim that only a privileged few can be independent, the view that creativity is necessarily the function of culture-preserving elites. I believe that independence can be a fact about ordinary people." [10]

In the new left scheme, property all but ceases to exist as a value. Certain material necessities are seen as the basis of an independent life, but emphasis is on the human qualities of freedom, creativity, and spontaneity that reasonable material security can foster. The value that liberal thinkers place upon the accumulation of property and competition is seen not as a source of progress, but as one cause of the alienation of men from their true humanity.

Similarly, the value liberals place on technological and industrial progress is subordinated to human values. In the words of the Port Huron Statement, "The personal capacity to cope with life has been reduced everywhere by the introduction of technology that only minorities of men (barely) understand." [11] The writers go on to suggest the need to control, and even to reverse in some cases, the trend toward increased mechanization and bureaucratization. Decentralization is offered as an important means by which institu-

---

[9] Students for a Democratic Society, *op. cit.*, p. 6.

[10] Tom Hayden, "Student Social Action: From Liberation to Community," in Cohen and Hale, eds., *op. cit.*, p. 293.

[11] Students for a Democratic Society, *op. cit.*, p. 50.

tions can be reduced to manageable size and man can recapture the sense of mastery over his environment. The Port Huron document asserts further that "The transfer of certain mechanized tasks back into manual form, allowing men to make whole, not partial, products, is not unimaginable." [12] The argument made by the new left is not in behalf of a complete return to the virtues of an agrarian society. It is simply that in pursuing technological innovation, the criteria of human needs and preferences must always be applied. These somewhat negative goals, emphasizing the need to reverse trends and break down institutions, are related to a major positive goal of the new left—the desire to create a community.

COMMUNITY

By community, the new left means the creation of a society in which the principles of organization are no longer competition and struggle but cooperation and brotherhood. "Human brotherhood," the Port Huron Statement asserts, "must be willed . . . as the most appropriate form of social relation." [13] A truly human society will be created only "when a love of man overcomes the idolatrous worship of things." [14] Society, then, must be organized not primarily to foster technological and material progress but to foster the development of human independence and freedom. Individual freedom is conceptualized as complementary rather than contradictory to the concept of community since it is believed that freedom is expressed in solidarity with other men rather than in competition with them. For new left thinkers, the goal of community is seen not as a distant Utopia growing out of abstract notions, but as something that can be created and experienced in the present.

PARTICIPATORY DEMOCRACY

The basic meaning of the term participatory democracy is the return of the institutions of society to the control of the people. The

---

[12] *Ibid.*
[13] *Ibid.*, p. 7.
[14] *Ibid.*

bureaucratization and centralization of institutions that prevent masses of people from exercising power and allow elites to monopolize decision-making must be eliminated. Real substantive democracy must replace the formal rhetorical democracy that prevails in American society.

The new left's goal of participatory democracy has several implications for political institutions. It seems doubtful that the new left thinkers would find pluralism acceptable even if they saw it as an accurate description of reality. The new left's emphasis on the need for solidarity and brotherhood in the relationships among men contrasts with the emphasis on bargaining, compromise, and accommodated conflict that are components of pluralist politics. The new left notion of participatory democracy emphasizes the things that unite men rather than the differences among them. It appears to be conceptualized as a process in which face to face discussions in small groups produce consensus on issues and generate solutions to common problems.

Participatory democracy is not seen merely as a way for individuals to register their preferences and attain their desires, but as a process in which the lives of individuals are qualitatively transformed. Men move from alienation, isolation and powerlessness to participation, control and solidarity. "Politics," in the words of the Port Huron Statement, "has the function of bringing people out of isolation and into community, this being a necessary though not sufficient means of finding meaning in personal life." [15]

Given this idea of its importance, the notion of participatory democracy applies not only to the instructions of the political system but extends to other societal institutions. In the words of Richard Flacks, "It means, too, the development of a concept of citizenship which extends beyond the conventional political sphere to all institutions of the society—the workplace, the school, the corporation, the neighborhoods, the welfare bureaucracies. The idea that men are citizens with respect to all exercise of authority, that each has responsibility for the actions of the institutions in which he is embedded." [16]

---

[15] *Ibid.,* p. 8.
[16] Richard Flacks, "Is the Great Society Just a Barbeque?" in Teodori, ed., *op. cit.,* p. 195.

The new left's insistence on participatory democracy provides the basis of its rejection of the welfare state that reform liberals champion. In order to receive the social services that welfare bureaucracies provide, the individual seeking help must accept a definition and evaluation of himself applied by a middle-class professional. The operation is a "top-down" one in which the individual may receive some financial aid, but in which his essential condition of powerlessness remains unchanged. Again, Tom Hayden makes the point incisively:

> Our suspicion begins with the belief that welfare-state reforms, conducted within the private, selfish control of the economy, are ineffective because they are not conceived by the poor people they are designed for. Instead they mangle and manipulate the poor while relaxing most of the middle class into the comfortable sense that everything is being managed well.[17]

It is clear, then, that new left thinkers go beyond liberals and reform liberals in their vision of the necessary changes in the economic system. However, the character of their more positive prescriptions in this area remains rather vague and general. In line with the commitments to participatory democracy and community, the Port Huron Statement declares the need to reverse the centralization of wealth and recapture the decision-making power it confers. The statement goes on to offer two basic principles for the economic sphere. First, "the economic experience is so personally decisive that the individual must share in its full determination." [18] Second, "the economy itself is of such social importance that its major resources and means of production should be open to democratic participation and subject to democratic social regulation." [19]

Statements like the preceding raise the question of the extent to which the goals of the new left can be described as socialist. This question becomes more pressing in view of the trend in the most

---

[17] Tom Hayden, "Up from Irrelevance," in Jacobs and Landau, eds., *The New Radicals* (New York: Vintage Books, 1966), p. 271.

[18] Students for a Democratic Society, *op. cit.,* p. 8.

[19] *Ibid.*

contemporary new left literature to use terms such as "ownership of the means of production" and "monopoly capital," terms that clearly originate in the socialist traditions. There is also a tendency to emphasize the possibility of economic dislocations as the catalyst of revolution and, as we shall see, a new interest in the American working class as an actor in a revolutionary movement. The inference drawn by some commentators is that the new left is becoming increasingly socialist and therefore less original in its thinking.

To some extent, the problem depends upon one's definition of "socialist" and "new left." We believe, however, that a distinction can be made on the basis of the fact that the new left's approach to the economic system evolves from the emphasis on creating community and participatory democracy in all institutions, rather than more specifically Marxian analysis that identifies the economic institutions as uniquely important. In new left thinking, economic institutions are among the many institutions in need of modification in the direction of decentralization and popular control.

Social Change and Tactics

Like the most militant black leaders, the new left has opted for revolutionary change but has not yet articulated a comprehensive theory of social change. In this area too, the new left's approach has been consciously experimental and eclectic, as suits an evolving ideology.

Many different processes of social change appear to have revolutionary results; these range from the elitist coup d'etat to a mass-based participatory movement. In general, the thinkers and activists of the new left appear to be committed to a mass-based popular revolution as both the most desirable and practical in a post-industrial society. They are inclined to view participatory democracy as a means as well as a goal and to conceptualize the revolutionary process as the swelling up of change from the grass roots. As they put it, they have attempted to build a movement in which everybody is a leader. There appears also to be consensus that any revolution in the United States must occur as part of the worldwide revolutionary movement led by the nations of the Third World. The movement must be both anticapitalist and anti-imperialist. But even with these general orienting principles established, a number of questions remain unanswered.

On a more specific level, the new left has had to face many of the same tactical issues as have the writers and activists of minority liberation. They have had to consider with whom, and under what conditions, to form coalitions. They have discussed both the justifiability and the efficacy of violent as opposed to nonviolent tactics. And they have argued the merits of slow and patient organizing techniques as opposed to dramatic direct action techniques. But, again as in the black movement, no decision or broadly shared answers have as yet emerged.

In addition, the new left has had to face a problem that does not arise in the same form for black militants: the question of what group to organize. Much new left thinking about social change is devoted to the search for what is often labeled the "historical agency of change." In simplest terms, this means seeking the group or groups within the society that are capable of acting to fundamentally change the social order.

The new left's understanding of oppression encourages eclecticism and experimentation along this dimension of social change, as it does on the question of means. Because (in terms of new left analysis) almost all groups in the society belong to the oppressed, almost all groups are potentially organizable. The problem for the new left is not so much in identifying oppression as in identifying the conditions under which people can be brought to *perceive* themselves as deprived and oppressed. This brings up the question of which of the large number of issues, ranging from the Vietnam war to the character of welfare and the existence of unemployment, can trigger perceptions of oppression. Again, no decisive answer has been forthcoming.

In practice, new left groups have focused their organizing activities around a variety of groups in the society and attempted to organize them with various means and issues. Often, these disparate attempts have led to bitter and damaging disputes within the ranks of new left activists. For instance, there has been a constant tension between new leftists who focused on the college campuses and tended to use dramatic action techniques and community organizers who identified the poor as the primary target and attempted to use the slower community organizing techniques. A second example occurred in 1969, when SDS, the largest national new left organization, split into three groups because its members could not agree on such questions as the role of blacks in the movement, the organizational potential of the working class, and the efficacy of violence.

It would be impossible in this short chapter to reproduce all of the debates concerning social change and tactics that have engaged new left thinkers. We have chosen instead to focus on the question of the historical agency both because it has given rise to much thoughtful new left writing and because many of the other arguments are similar to those discussed in the chapter on minority liberation. In the discussion that follows, we describe the major groups identified by new left thinkers as potential agents of change and the rationale for the choices. We also indicate the methods used by new left activists in approaching each group. We hope, thereby, to provide some notion of the scope of new left tactical thinking and the disputes to which it has given rise.

THE POOR

The poor have been a major target for new left organizing efforts. Initially, new left efforts were directed at both blacks and whites, but with the development of the black power movement in 1965, the focus shifted to poor whites, particularly in urban areas. New left thinkers identified the poor as a potential agency of change for several reasons. First, and most obvious, they are a clearly powerless and materially deprived segment of the society. Having little stake in the status quo, they might be expected to welcome opportunities to mobilize and act for change. In Todd Gitlin's words, "The poor know they are poor and don't like it; hence they can be organized to demand an end to poverty and the construction of a decent social order." [20]

A second rationale emphasizes not what the poor lack, but what they have. New left analysis hypothesized that since they were excluded from the mainstream of society, the poor were less steeped

---

[20] Todd Gitlin, "The Battlefields and the War," in Mitchell Cohen and Dennis Hale, eds., *The New Student Left* (Boston: Beacon Press, 1966), p. 126.

in its dominant values, the individualism, materialism, and competitiveness that are viewed as pervading middle-class America. The poor were thought to possess communal and cooperative values and goals. Thus, the activists hoped to find in the poor a set of values and beliefs that would guide the revolutionary movement. As Staughton Lynd expresses it, "There is an unstated assumption that the poor, when they find voice, will produce a truer, sounder radicalism than any which alienated intellectuals might prescribe." [21]

New left activists believed that slow, patient community organizing techniques were most appropriate in attempting to organize the poor. This meant that organizers should move into the community and, as far as possible, share the life of the people. There were attempts to form neighborhood groups around relevant issues such as unemployment, welfare, urban renewal, and the police behavior. The groups raised demands concerning these problems on the level of local administration and city government. Occasionally, direct action techniques such as sit-ins and rent strikes were employed.

Organizers, while beginning with local issues, constantly kept in mind the need for raising local reform issues to more far-reaching structural demands. In Todd Gitlin's words, "The special quality of *radical* issue-organizing is the intertwining of two different kinds of demands: demands for tangible concessions which can be granted by existing institutions, and demands for control and substantial restructuring of these institutions." [22] The move toward more radical demands on the part of the poor was expected to grow naturally out of confrontations on the local level, which would make clear that more far-reaching change was necessary. For example, it was expected that an issue such as the size of welfare payments would evolve into an issue over grass-roots control of the welfare bureaucracy, leading to an analysis of the causes and necessities of welfare, the overall structure of the economy, and so forth. In this manner, the poor would begin to connect the conditions of their own lives with the questions of participatory democracy and community organization that the new left thinkers felt were essential.

---

[21] Staughton Lynd, "The New Radical and 'Participatory Democracy,'" in Teodori, ed., *op. cit.*, p. 229.

[22] Todd Gitlin, "The Radical Potential of the Poor," in Teodori, ed., *op. cit.*, p. 139.

These issues were also expected to arise through the participation of the poor in the day-by-day activities of the community organization they had founded. The organizers were determined to establish participatory democracy not only as a goal, but also as a means, which meant building participatory democracy into the grassroots movement from the start. Therefore, in the community organizations, formal structure was kept to a minimum, with decisions made on the basis of full discussion and consensus. When formal structure was found to be necessary, offices were to be elective and frequently rotated. As soon as was feasible, initial new left organizers were expected to abdicate, rather than maintain control of organizational power. Although this method of organizing was conceded to be somewhat inefficient, it was thought to have the virtue of allowing many to share in a real decision-making process, thereby eliminating feelings of inadequacy, incompetency, and powerlessness that the poor might harbor. In the words of Staughton Lynd, it was expected to result in "the building of a brotherly way of life in the jaws of Leviathan." [23]

Some writers raised questions as to the effectiveness of organizing only the deprived. The poor, although a large segment of the society, are far from a majority. The need for allies arose, creating problems such as the advisability of cooperating with liberals and reform liberals. Further, the poor, particularly poor whites, were difficult to locate in a geographic community. Unlike blacks, poor whites were diffused throughout the city in a series of small concentrations. Also, there were splits within the poor that prevented them from acting as a unified force. Most obvious and often discussed was the split between blacks and whites. The new left confronted, first, white racism and, then, black power as formidable obstacles to an effective interracial movement of the poor. There were also, however, differences of age, ethnic identification and employment status among whites, which gave rise to problems in organizing whites alone. In short, many new left thinkers felt that they had overestimated the extent to which the problems of the poor were common problems; perhaps it is more accurate to say that they had underestimated the difficulty of revealing the common root of these problems.

---

[23] Staughton Lynd, quoted by Todd Gitlin, *ibid.,* p. 139.

The second major challenged assumption was the ability of the poor to generate counter-values. Organizers found that resentment toward the system existed side-by-side with a feeling that poor people, because of laziness or lack of competence, had only themselves to blame for their problems. It was more difficult than originally anticipated to bring people to see problems as structurally caused and collectively shared. In addition to racism, there was often a vehement anti-Communism reaction that made the discussion of socialist-like alternatives difficult. The poor were found to share to a considerable extent the values of materialism and competitiveness that the new left was seeking to destroy. The organizers found themselves in the position of having to distinguish "real" and "manipulated" needs, a distinction clouded by elitist counter-democratic implications.

This type of problem led some activists to experiment with new approaches to organizing the poor. Some turned to other groups as potentially more fruitful for initial organizing efforts. The debate within the new left over "the radical potential of the poor" continues, as do various attempts to organize them.

THE "NEW WORKING CLASS"

As we have seen, the new left considers the middle class as deprived and powerless. Some new left thinkers have argued that this group could be a vehicle of social change, identifying it as the "new working class." The notion of the "new working class" as an agent of change probably originated with the observation that, in fact, it was the middle-class students on the college campuses who were originating demands for change. Indeed, it was from this group that the ranks of the new left were drawn. Despite this origin the "new working class" analysis emphasizes the structural position rather than the age composition of this group.

The rationale underlying the choice of this group as an agency of social change is as follows. The fastest growing and functionally most significant occupational category in the economy consists of technological experts, management, and other "mind workers" such as teachers and social workers. Although absolutely necessary to the working of the corporate machine and compensated at a rate that categorizes them as middle class, they are subjected to many of the same structural strains described in the discussion of the university student. In spite of the fact that they are highly educated, as specialized cogs in large bureaucracies, they are allowed little independence of thought or action. In fact, they lack the freedom that was a characteristic of middle-class life when this class was composed of small businessmen, independent farmers, and professionals. Potentially, therefore, they can be brought to recognize their lack of freedom and to act to recreate it.

Although, as noted, the concept of new working class refers to an occupational rather than an age category, actual attempts at organization have tended to take place in the universities. This focus makes sense in view of the new left's belief that "students are 'trainees' for the new working class and the factory-like multiversities are the institutions which prepare them for their slots in the bureaucratic machinery of corporate capitalism." [24] Similarly, many campus confrontation tactics are seen as valuable not only for what they may immediately achieve, but for their radicalizing effect on the future "new working class."

Campus organizational efforts, in contrast to the community organizing style, tend to lead very rapidly to direct confrontations such as sit-ins and, less frequently to destruction and violence. A number of arguments underlie the use of such tactics. To some extent, they are motivated by a moral imperative to "put your body on the line" in protest of the present societal structure. But more pragmatic reasons can be found to justify their use. Concrete concessions often are won from university administrations in response to such tactics. Armed forces and corporation recruiters have been forced off campuses, and ROTC programs and war-oriented research operations have been eliminated. In addition, sit-ins and similar tactics have the effect of dramatizing issues that might be ignored by both the college community and the public. During demonstrations, university classes tend to lose their character of irrelevance and become forums in which issues are hotly debated. Wide television coverage of the more dramatic elements of a protest brings the issue before large audiences, although in somewhat distorted form. This is in line with the new left's emphasis upon the media as an important manipulative force. Through dramatic direct-action

[24] Gregory Calvert, in Teodori, ed., *op. cit.*, p. 417.

techniques, new left activists have found themselves able to raise issues of public policy that the media would otherwise ignore or cover only in passing.

While much of the organization of the new working class focuses on the colleges and universities and follows the patterns outlined above, there are other areas of activity and methods in which new left activists have engaged in attempts to organize this group. This extension of organization of groups of the new working class beyond the college campuses is still a tentative but nonetheless significant area of new left organizing attempts.

YOUTH

New left thinkers also have explored the possibility that youth, as a group in itself, is a potential agent of social change. New left thinkers point out that in post-industrial society, adolescence is prolonged because the economy is unable to employ the large number of individuals available. This has led to the formulation of a separate youth culture with its own values and goals, often focused around drugs, rock music, and communal living. The new left attitude toward youth culture, particularly the hippie variation, is somewhat ambivalent. While welcoming it as a partial rejection of capitalist morality and a strong expression of the drive for community, new left thinkers consider questionable its ability to create significant change without the interjection of more consciously political analyses and goals. Organizing activities of the new left are designed to nurture this political consciousness.

The new left has employed a number of tactics in its attempt to organize youth. The relevance of campus organizing drives is clear. There have also been attempts to engage non-student youth, particularly young people of draft age, by establishing draft counseling centers and picketing and leafleting induction centers. Groups in high schools have been organized around a variety of issues. Perhaps the most significant attempts being made are those to organize armed forces personnel on active duty, both through the establishment of GI coffee houses near army bases and the organization of GI rights groups within the services.

THE WORKING CLASS

New left theory, in its search for an agency of change, originally tended to ignore the working class (manual workers) except to the extent of including its members in other categories such as the poor or youth. This tendency can be attributed to the fact that the new left identified this class as the old left's traditional agency of social change—a group which, in the opinion of some new left commentators, had been "bought off" by capitalist materialism and a corrupt union bureaucracy. As a result of the new left's growing concern with classical Marxist theory and the events that shook France in the Spring of 1968, a reappraisal of the revolutionary potential of the working class appears to be under way. The French working class, catalyzed by a strike within the universities, conducted a general strike that came close to toppling the government.

A case for the working class as an agent of social change can easily be constructed from standard new left concepts. The general new left notion of oppression and powerlessness clearly applies to this group. Furthermore, in spite of the fact that the working class is not increasing as a proportion of the population, it is the largest occupational group within the country and it will continue to be the largest for a long time. Any mass-based revolutionary movement would necessarily include members from these ranks. Finally, the increasing number of wildcat strikes in recent years attests to the growing restlessness and dissatisfaction of the working class with the compromise-oriented union bureaucracies.

New left activists have made initial attempts to organize this group, primarily through the establishment of worker-student alliances on the campus. These campus groups attempt to act as resource groups for workers both in normal and in strike situations. The 1970 wave of campus protests against GE recruiters was conceived both as a protest against the Vietnam war and as an act of solidarity with striking GE workers. There has also been a small movement for students to quit the campuses and work in factories in order to participate directly in the life and struggles of the working class. Although the focus on organization of the working class is in its beginning stages, this movement shows signs of growing into a major concern of new left thinkers.

EXTERNAL SOURCES

In concluding this discussion of social change and tactics, we must consider another line of new left reasoning that represents a real departure. In essence, it suggests that there are no potential agencies of social change within the contemporary United States in the sense described above. This argument, originally enunciated by a now defunct splinter group of SDS known as the "Weathermen," emphasizes the materialism and racism of *all* segments of white American society and the almost impossible task of wooing its members from these attitudes. Advocates point out that on a worldwide scale, the masses of white Americans of every class represent a tiny and privileged sector. They contend further that Third World social-ist nations such as China and Cuba are the only viable revolutionary force in the contemporary world. Within the United States, only blacks and other colored peoples (considered to be colonized Third World peoples) and a small number of young whites have any revolutionary potential. This argument expects the decisive defeat of capitalism by these forces within the present generation.

This analysis of the sources of change leads on a tactical level to an almost total identification with Third World revolutionary movements and to an insistence on the necessity of using violence. Advocates have organized for, and have engaged in, violence—primarily the destruction of property which they consider imperial-ist and racist. The rationale behind these activities is twofold. First, they concretely aid Third World liberation movements, such as the struggle of the Vietnamese, by forcing the U.S. government to de-ploy troops and expand forces to quash internal turmoil—thus hav-ing the effect of tying its hands in the international sphere. Second, advocates admit the possibility that some whites, particularly the young, can be brought to a realization of the futility of their ma-terialist and racist values. The technique that will succeed in mak-ing this point is not the community organizing or even direct action technique, but a confrontation with violence and fear. In the words of Shin'ya Ono with respect to the early Weathermen:

> What Weatherman is about is breaking through the racism
> and chauvinism at its core by forcing white people to grapple
> with the existence of a white fighting force that understands

that this imperialist mother country will come down, and
actually fights on the sides of blacks, yellows and browns, of
the world. If our action, struggle and words often put white
working class people (and movement people, too) up against
the wall forcing them to fight us, so be it.[25]

All of the new left approaches to social change outlined above
share the conclusion that the Third World revolutionary movements
are of vital importance. But the latter emphasis upon the intransigence of the masses of white Americans and the need to confront
them violently represents a real departure from new left conceptions of mass-based revolution and perhaps even from some of the
value and goal orientations that we have described as fundamental
elements of new left thought.

Will the New Left Survive?

The new left as a movement has undergone considerable fragmentation—a development that is not difficult to understand given
its lack of a coherent ideology. It has splintered off into a number
of other groups such as women's liberation, socialism, and minority liberation. Nevertheless, some groups have remained under the
new left umbrella—anarchist elements, community control, and the
counterculture. Many of the Jesus People came out of this latter
group and espouse apolitical solutions and sometimes even decidedly
conservative viewpoints.

The anarchists, those who call for decentralization or community control, and the counterculture continue to attack bigness, impersonality, unresponsiveness, militarism, inequality, consumer-
mania, alienation, and the like, but they remain new leftists precisely
because they have not formulated an ideology. Thus, they are lacking
all those things that an ideology provides: an analysis of the way
the society works, a theory of social change, and a set of strategies
and tactics appropriate to a view of the "is" and a vision of the
"ought to be." Further defection from and fragmentation of the new

---

[25] Shin'ya Ono, "You Need a Weatherman . . ." *Leviathan,* Dec.
1969, p. 17.

left thus seems inevitable, and it seems likely that the reform liberals, the socialists, and the conservatives will be the beneficiaries.

Annotated Bibliography

Berger, Peter, and Richard J. Neuhaus. *Movement and Revolution*. New York: Vintage Books, 1970. Perhaps the most perceptive work on the ethical issues involved in revolution, written from both conservative and radical perspectives—but with very little difference between the two conclusions.

Chomsky, Noam. *American Power and the New Mandarins*. New York: Random House, 1967. A powerful criticism of American involvement in the Vietnam war and in particular of the complicity of intellectuals.

Chomsky, Noam, et al. *Trials of the Resistance*. New York: New York Review of Books, 1970. A collection of articles concerning the trials of persons involved in the resistance movements of the 1960s. Provides a good insight into the new left's perspective on the law and the legal process.

Cohen, Mitchell, and Dennis Hale, eds. *The New Student Left*. Boston: Beacon Press, 1966. Somewhat dated, but still a valuable collection.

Gettleman, Marvin, and David Mermelstein. *The Failure of American Liberalism: After the Great Society*. New York: Random House, 1967. A collection of essays proclaiming the weaknesses and failure of liberalism and addressing the major problems of American society from a radical perspective.

Goodman, Paul. *New Reformation: Notes of a Neolithic Conservative*. New York: Random House, 1969. An anarchist who resents bureaucratic impersonality, oppressive government interference, government sponsored brutality and violence, business hegemony, and the traditional classroom. But he is also critical of left systematizers and collectivists. Has a wide following among the counterculture.

Harris, David. *Goliath*. New York: Richard Baron, 1970. Criticizes bureaucracy, inequality, materialism, war, poverty and sees the system as a "goliath," which can be overturned by enough little people joined together. Emphasizes nonviolence.

Hayden, Tom. "The Trial." *Ramparts,* 9, no. 1, July 1970. Most recent work by the prolific and insightful founding member of SDS, viewing the Chicago Trial in the context of a pending revolutionary situation.

Hoffman, Abbie. *Steal This Book*. New York: Grove, 1971. The early counterculture, with all its strengths and weaknesses.

Keniston, Kenneth. *Young Radicals*. New York: Harcourt, Brace & World, 1968. Compares the committed young radicals with the uncommitted. A study of the family and social background, experiences in the new left, and psychological development of the young radicals.

Kotler, Milton. *Neighborhood Government*. Indianapolis: Bobbs-Merrill, 1969. A study of the prospects and form of "community control." Criticizes reform liberal and conservative notions of "community control" as symbolic rather than substantive programs.

Levin, Murray B. *Political Hysteria in America*. New York: Basic Books, 1971. A historical study which argues that American radical movements have been defeated repeatedly by the invocation of a paranoid anti-Communist, antisubversion hysteria at each point that radical movements threatened to succeed or win a following.

Mailer, Norman. *Armies of the Night*. New York: New American Library, 1968. A personal account of the March on the Pentagon by one of the more colorful figures in the new left.

Marcuse, Herbert. *An Essay on Liberation*. Boston: Beacon Press, 1968. A short, direct statement summarizing his major arguments and projecting them toward programs of action.

————. *Counterrevolution and Revolt*. Boston: Beacon Press, 1972. Analyzes the prospects and strategies of the new left in terms of the development of advanced capitalism.

————. *One Dimensional Man*. Boston: Beacon Press, 1964. The classic statement of contemporary unfreedom—a book with important impact on the left.

Mills, C. Wright. *The Power Elite*. New York: Oxford University Press, 1956. A full-scale analysis of the concentration of power in the United States.

Newfield, Jack. *The Prophetic Minority*. New York: New American Library, 1966. A sympathetic study of the issues and people who initiated the new left as a political movement.

Reich, Charles A. *The Greening of America*. New York: Random House, 1970. Highly controversial book argues that revolution will originate with the individual and with culture, rather than with a class or with political change. Representative of counterculture analysis.

Roszak, Theodore. *The Making of a Counter Culture*. New York: Doubleday Anchor, 1969. A good introduction to some of the cultural aspects of new left thinking not emphasized in our analysis.

————. *Where the Wasteland Ends*. Garden City, New York: Doubleday, 1972.

Schwartz, Edward. *Will the Revolution Succeed?* London: Criterion Books, 1972. Former president of the National Student Association (NSA) says everything must be measured against the standard of justice and calls for the formation of alliances between community organizers, developers of counter-institutions, and radical professionals. A good example of the new left's failure to delineate an analysis and an ideology.

Students for a Democratic Society. *The Port Huron Statement*. Chicago: Students for a Democratic Society, 1966. The seminal document.

Teodori, Massimo, ed. *The New Left: A Documentary History*. Indianapolis, Ind.: Bobbs-Merrill, 1969. Certainly the most comprehensive and reasonably current collection of new left writings.

9

Marxism and Socialism

The 1970s have seen a substantial growth in interest in both Marxism and socialism. In part, this interest is the result of a combination of events and circumstances: the rhetoric and achievements of Third World leaders have inspired American minority leaders; the fragmentation of the new left created a void of leadership and ideology; and the economy appeared to be declining. But in a larger sense, intellectual interest stimulated a renewal of attention to these ideologies. Marxism offers a comprehensive interpretation of the relationship between economics, social structure, and politics—and an explanation of why and how capitalist societies must act in both domestic and foreign affairs. Socialism presents an equally comprehensive alternative, offering to replace capitalism-liberalism in every aspect of life, from basic values of structure, procedure, and policies to the very character and quality of life itself. And Marxism leads provocatively toward that elusive necessity, a theory that will explain how change might lead to realization of the socialist goal in spite of the many obvious obstacles that appear to bar the way to socialism within the United States today.

Marxism is a comprehensive system of thought in which socialism is included as one necessary but preliminary goal. Not all "socialists" are Marxists: some are merely utopian, and others are limited to very simple societies (in some cases, single communes) and/or employ no analytical or theoretical framework at all. Neither are all "Marxists" visibly socialists. Some merely apply Marxian analytical concepts in part or whole to existing capitalist societies without discussing the socialist alternative or the process of change

at all. We shall include the latter within our review because much
important analysis is produced by such self-styled Marxists. For our
purposes, Marxists are those Americans who identify themselves as
such, and who (1) see the character of economic organization as the
basic factor in shaping a society's value system, social class structure,
and political institutions and practices; (2) see a capitalist economy
as creating profit-oriented, materialist values and a class structure in
which wealthy owners constitute a ruling class that uses the power of
the state, both at home and abroad, in exploitative and selfish ways;
and (3) believe that such a social system is unjust, unnecessary, and
inconsistent with man's potential under a more rational socialist system that should be instituted, peacefully if possible, but by force if
necessary.

This is a very broad definition, far looser than most Marxist
scholars would accept. To be more precise and to do justice to the
careful work of such scholars and theoreticians would require a disproportionate (and here unjustifiable) investment of time and space.
In addition, we would have to choose among the many distinctive and
competing groups and organizations that claim to be the true followers of Marx or of Marx and Lenin. The understanding of Marxian
principles held by various Marxist groups and organizations differs
greatly, as do the interpretations and applications of Marx to present
conditions that guide their strategy and tactics.

The great diversity in understanding and application of Marxist
principles among contemporary American Marxists is one of the distinctive features of Marxism. It requires some effort at explanation
and at the same time offers a certain insight into Marxism itself. One
major reason for this diversity concerns motivation: many people use
Marxism merely as a symbol, perhaps as a shorthand way of saying
that they reject the established system completely, but they have little
understanding of Marxism. They are not serious about the intellectual
or theoretical basis of their revolutionary posture, and they use any
argument they can find to support positions taken opportunistically
or on other grounds. A study of Marx's complex system of thought
demands an intensive and self-disciplined dedication, and only isolated scraps can be picked up without such application. Nevertheless,
the drawing power and symbolic appeal of Karl Marx is so strong
that many people with widely differing viewpoints insist on identifying themselves as Marxists.

Another reason for the diversity in interpretation of Marx applies to those who sincerely undertake to understand and apply Marxism. For one thing, the many volumes of Marx's writings cover decades of scholarship and reflection. Some have only recently been published, and some are available only in German. In addition, Marx's analyses appear to many to have been written for one age and to require more or less extensive modification in order to be applicable to our present circumstances. In both cases, of course, there are infinite opportunities for differences in emphasis or interpretation.

Perhaps the most serious obstacle comes from differences between the intellectual frame of reference and the socially produced consciousness within which Marx wrote, and those within which most Americans read his work today. Marx wrote in the tradition and with the concepts, concerns, and style of thinking of eighteenth and nineteenth century German critical philosophy. Thus, he set the problem of the nature of true knowledge at the forefront and evolved a comprehensive set of tools and methods for using his solution to that problem to understand both present and potential social systems. Americans read him from the perspective of capitalist-liberal orthodoxy and with only the language and tools of thinking that are consistent with their contemporary capitalist-liberal society. Thus, most Americans can see only parts of Marx—those parts that sound similar to approaches or concepts that are familiar to capitalist-liberal thinking, parts that seem to follow the kind of logic and empirical nature of evidence with which we are conversant. As a result, most of what he is saying either is missed entirely or understood only dimly.

In this situation, American Marxism is bound to display a wide range of strongly held and frequently conflicting positions. We shall present only an overview of what actually exists under the label of Marxism. We shall not try to resolve any of the issues over which group or organization is closer to the original or to a "proper" application of the Marxian method today. However, the diversity will be recognized in two broad categories. After a brief survey focusing chiefly on the world view evident in the analyses of several prominent Marxists, we shall expand the values and goals and tactics of change sections by means of two extended illustrations. The first will be representative of those Marxists, many of them old left or academics, who believe that socialism can and should evolve gradually out of the welfare state. These will be presented under the label of democratic socialism. The second will reflect the views of one of the several Marxist organizations which believe that only revolutionary action can achieve socialism. The contrast between these two goes much deeper and is much more comprehensive than the question of evolutionary versus revolutionary transformation to socialism, as we shall see, but the breadth of these categories will permit us to survey the subject more comprehensively.

World View

Marxism challenges nearly all of the fundamental assumptions and premises of capitalism. It sees that combined economic and social system as creating a false ideology and a self-limiting consciousness that leads people to become satisfied with individualistic, materialistic, exploitative, self-gratifying attitudes and behavior. In economic terms, capitalism perverts production and the capabilities of the people. It diverts production away from a variety of socially necessary and desirable uses to those forms that produce maximum profits: it diverts production from the needs of working people to the self-gratification of the owning (and ruling) oligarchy. The resulting sharp conflicts between classes and continued need for exploitation generate instability and raise the probability of war. In simple empirical terms, where capitalism sees affluence, harmony, and stable progress, Marxism sees human misery, class conflict, deliberate waste, and unstable stagnation. Of the many components of the Marxist critique of capitalism, we shall focus on four major points: the nature of monopoly capitalism, imperialism, the role of government, and the character and prospects of the current economy.

MONOPOLY CAPITALISM

Capitalism and, to an even greater extent, reform liberalism have begun to acknowledge the concentration of economic power and its effects on the free market. Marxism, however, puts this insight at the center of its analysis of the contemporary economic and social systems, terming it "monopoly capitalism," and draws several distinctive implications from it.[1] Monopoly capitalism is a system in which huge corporations dominate entire sectors of the market, rendering the economy bureaucratized, hierarchical, and totally controlled. More important, unprecedented levels of profit are generated and a constantly increasing economic surplus (the excess of money and products above what can be absorbed in investment or consumed) is created by its domination of the market.[2] One major analysis, *Monopoly Capital* by Baran and Sweezy, describes the new situation in these terms:

> While competitive capitalism also generated economic surplus in substantial proportions, monopoly capital has produced it at an unprecedented level, both absolutely and as a share of total output.[3]

Moreover, under monopoly capitalism, surplus is generated at such a rate that "normal" outlets such as capital replacement, consumption by wealthy elites, and even technological innovation are insufficient to absorb it.

The presence of this unabsorbable surplus is the key fact of contemporary American economic and political life, in the eyes of these Marxists, and the main reason for the current pattern of governmental policies. In order to maximize profits, corporations continually strive to cut their costs, control markets more effectively, and reduce competition. Thus, the surplus continues to rise, but under capitalist principles, only a few things legitimately can be done with it. In itself, the tendency of the economic surplus to rise might be looked on as an indication of the essential well-being and richness

---

[1] There are a number of formulations of the monopoly capital concept in current Marxist thinking. Here we draw primarily upon the one advanced by Paul A. Baran and Paul M. Sweezy in *Monopoly Capital* (New York: Modern Reader Paperbacks, 1968).

[2] This analysis is supported by a wealth of theoretical argument and the presentation of considerable evidence in several Marxist works, among them that of Baran and Sweezy drawn on here. But it is impossible to do justice to these complex and technical analyses, and we have been forced to telescope and summarize them briefly.

[3] Baran and Sweezy, *op. cit.,* p. 79.

of the economy. As Baran and Sweezy suggest, "the size of the surplus is an index of productivity and wealth, of how much freedom a society has to accomplish whatever goals it may set for itself." [4] Instead, it is argued, capitalism cannot absorb this surplus because it will not direct the surplus toward social goals or toward the masses of workers. However, these attempts to absorb the surplus must somehow be made or the capitalist engine will slow down to a stop. The problem of disposing of the surplus thus becomes both the principal dynamic and the major contradiction of modern capitalism. The irony of this situation is that capitalism's ability to produce such a surplus ultimately will be the cause of its stagnation and collapse. In Marxist analysis, the self-imposed standards of monopoly capitalism lead to a scarcity of acceptable means of absorbing this surplus and an abundance of those that cannot be allowed.

(a) *Forbidden channels: social uses.* Marxist thinkers see immense social needs in the United States for which the surplus might be used. Under a rational economic system oriented to serving human needs, demonstrable requirements for public housing, public transportation, health and educational facilities, and the like would prescribe the direction of surplus use. Under monopoly capitalism, the level of government expenditure for such purposes remains severely limited. This is so because government is responsive to the preferences of the corporations, groups and individuals that comprise monopoly capitalism's ruling oligarchy, and their interests are not served by such government activity. They do not want government competition with private enterprise's opportunities in these areas, nor do they wish either to create expectations or undermine the present distribution of power in the society. Broader support for education, for example, might threaten the permanence of the existing class structure, make it difficult to obtain low-wage menial employees, and even create new political awareness among the lower classes. For these reasons, Baran and Sweezy argue, national support for education is kept unconscionably low and such government financing as is undertaken is channeled disproportionately to elite private schools and colleges.

---

[4] *Ibid.,* p. 9.

(b) *Approved channels: defense, imperialism, and the "sales effort."* Marxism is quick to point out that the corporate oligarchy is not opposed to government spending as such. Government spending of a particular kind is a vital means of surplus disposal. Private enterprise can only gain from military contracts, and a strong military serves the further purpose of protecting the overseas involvement of monopoly capitalism—its markets, investments, and sources of raw materials. For Marxists, defense expenditures are doubly irrational. They are not only a wasteful disposal of the economic surplus; they contribute to the essentially destructive impact of overseas corporate expansion, protect it against the justified wrath of exploited Third World peoples, and bolster immoral and fruitless efforts to oppose socialism in other nations. A less dangerous but equally irrational means of absorbing the surplus is the "sales effort" —the unprecedented advertising and promotional efforts by which monopoly capitalism seeks to promote demand for its products. Marxist critics agree with others' distaste for such manipulative efforts to create artificial and unnatural "needs" and for the cultural debasement which results. But they add that the sales effort promotes unnecessary materialism and wasteful emphasis on consumer goods because it is a structural necessity of monopoly capitalism.

In summary, two major points regarding monopoly capitalism may be made. Marxism holds first that the capitalist economic system operates in such a way that only destructive and dehumanizing directions are possible for it. Waste is the typical mode of surplus use. Second, capitalist society is so structured that its operations automatically create the forces that ultimately will destroy it. The channels chosen for absorbing the surplus are both inadequate and dangerous. Foreign investment leads to conflict, and military armament increases the risk. Inevitably, capitalism must undergo a crisis of surplus absorption, and the depression, stagnation, and social conflict that result may lead to a complete restructuring of the society along more rational lines. This basic framework of analysis and expectation is the major building block of the American Marxist world view, from which flow all other images and interpretations. The remaining components of the Marxist world view are selected from among the many corollaries of the basic propositions of monopolistic capitalism on the grounds that they are among the more important and distinguishing features of the larger Marxist ideology.

IMPERIALISM

Probably no characteristic attributed to the American economic system is as much discussed by contemporary Marxists as imperialism. It is a fundamental tenet of Marxist ideology that capitalism is a world system rather than a system confined to national boundaries. The Marxist image of the United States as a major imperialist power contrasts sharply with the traditional ideologies' view of the self-sufficiency and insularity of the American economy. Marxism sees the economy and, therefore, the social structure of the United States as linked to, and dependent upon, its foreign operations. It holds that understanding of these links is vital to understanding the past growth and present state of our capitalist economy.

Marxists argue that exploitation of foreign nations, particularly those of the Third World, historically has been of major importance to capitalist development. Andre Gunder Frank and Paul Baran both argue that the rapid growth of the United States was aided by drawing capital and raw materials from undeveloped nations, particularly Latin America.[5] The result was destruction of local agriculture and other industries and conversion of such nations into dependent markets. Gunder Frank declares that it is fundamentally incorrect to view the development of advanced capitalist countries and the underdevelopment of nations as two distinct processes. The capitalist system must be seen as developing as a whole, as a world system, rather than as developing in a particular nation. Thus, the achievements of the advanced capitalist nations were realized at the cost of the Third World, not because of the intrinsic superiority, capacity, or ingenuity of domestic capitalists. Marxist analysis is similar to that of the black liberation thinkers who call attention to the importance of the institution of slavery in the economic and social development of the United States. Both challenge the traditional image of an economic system based upon freedom and independently generating great wealth and plenty.

Marxism takes direct aim at the claim that American involvement in the affairs of other nations is attributable primarily to philo-

---

[5] Paul Baran, *The Political Economy of Growth* (New York: Modern Reader Paperbacks, 1968); Andre Gunder Frank, "The Development of Underdevelopment," *Monthly Review*, Sept. 1966.

sophical or political motivations. It is often said, for example, that economic motivations are not important because American foreign trade represents a very small proportion of total gross national product. In *The Age of Imperialism,* Harry Magdoff argues that when the cumulative, rather than yearly, amount of foreign investment is considered and when its strategic, rather than gross, significance is examined, the American economic interest abroad is substantial.[6] Overseas investment is a major outlet for the surplus, according to both Victor Perlo and Paul Baran.[7] Others have noted the need to acquire raw materials, strategic materials, cheap labor, and assured markets.

Magdoff presents what probably is the most sophisticated argument regarding motivations. He asserts that large corporations have a general need to assure themselves of as controlled an environment as possible. This need encompasses all the specific motivations that might or might not be operative at a given time and in a particular situation. In his words,

> The urge to dominate is integral to business. Risks abound in the business world. Internal and external competition, rapid technological changes, depression, to name but a few, threaten not only the rate of profit but the capital investment itself. Business therefore is always on the lookout for ways of controlling its environment, to eliminate as much risk as possible.[8]

One implication drawn by Magdoff from this analysis is that it is incorrect to look for a specific economic explanation for every act of U.S. foreign policy. The need to expand and protect economic interests and the sanctity of the profit motive is a general guiding principle. Resources and markets must be protected for their future and potential value as much as for their present use. For instance, areas such as Vietnam are critical not because of their direct and specific economic importance, but because the general principle is threatened by the attempt of a Third World people to establish in-

---

[6] Harry Magdoff, *The Age of Imperialism* (New York: Modern Reader Paperbacks, 1969).

[7] Baran, *op. cit.;* and Victor Perlo, "Relevance of Marxist Economics to U.S. Conditions," *Political Affairs,* Feb. 1969.

[8] Magdoff, *op. cit.,* p. 35.

dependence, especially when accompanied by a socialist economic perspective. Thus, Magdoff sees a general U.S. scheme of domination in which even economically marginal countries are of importance.[9]

Marxists do not claim that political and philosophical motives play no part in American foreign policy. In a sense, some Marxists would assert, freedom is a goal of overseas policies. Historian William A. Williams declares, that

> certain freedoms and liberties are essential to capitalists, even though capitalism is not essential to freedom and liberty. There is no discrepancy, therefore, in going to war for a free marketplace and going to war to defend, secure, and even extend the political freedoms and liberties associated with such a marketplace political economy.[10]

Freedom then may be considered a goal of U.S. foreign policy if the term is understood in a limited and culturally specific way. Political freedom can mean only the Western style of democracy, and economic freedom means only a capitalist market economy. These are encouraged because they complement rather than contradict the basic interests of the corporations in profitable foreign relations. Other freedoms, such as freedom to create a truly planned economy, freedom to control the country's economic resources internally, and freedom to make a socialist revolution, are a danger to U.S. corporate domination and cannot be tolerated.

Marxism denies that Third World nations develop significantly from American investments and, instead, asserts that capital is withdrawn, one-crop economies established, and the rate of growth slowed by American involvement. Considerable attention has been paid by Marxist economists to developing evidence about the impact of American involvement, particularly in Latin America. Three points make up this argument: first, isolation from the advanced capitalist nations appears to promote economic progress; second, those nations subject to capitalist intervention developed faster during periods when ties were temporarily weakened; and third, Cuba

---

[9] *Ibid.*
[10] William Applemau Williams, *The Great Evasion* (Chicago: Quadrangle Paperbacks, 1968), p. 46.

has progressed far more rapidly alone than have those nations that remain within the American orbit.[11]

Marxists concede that some industry has been built and some workers employed at improved wages. But they see this development as superficial. Capital is still extracted, because the high profits generated are returned to the United States and/or the raw materials devoted to American use. Between such extractive operations and the insistence upon one-crop economies for the benefit of American interests, the underdeveloped nation may end up worse off than it would have been without any contact with the advanced American economy. Gunder Frank comments about formerly prosperous regions of Latin America:

> These regions' participation in the development of the world capitalist market gave them, already in their golden age, the typical structure of underdevelopment of a capitalist export economy. When the market for their sugar or the wealth of their mines disappeared and the metropolis abandoned them to their own devices, the already existing economic, political, and social structure of these regions prohibited autonomous generation of economic development, and left them no alternative but to turn in upon themselves and to degenerate into the ultra-underdevelopment we find there today.[12]

Furthermore, when the growth of non-extractive local industry *has* been fostered, it is constructed in the image of the monopoly capitalism of the advanced countries and therefore fails to generate sustained growth in other areas of economic activity. Paul Baran declares:

> In most undeveloped countries capitalism had a peculiarly twisted career; it never experienced the vigor and exuberance of youth, and began displaying at an early age all the grievous features of senility and decadence. To the dead weight of

---

[11] For the first two points, see Andre Gunder Frank, *op. cit.* For the last, see Leo Huberman and Paul M. Sweezy, *Socialism in Cuba* (New York: Monthly Review Press, 1969).

[12] Frank, *op. cit.*, p. 28.

stagnation characteristic of pre-industrial society was added
the entire restrictive impact of monopoly capital.[13]

Thus, Marxism argues that in its monopoly stage, capitalism
inherently is incapable of generating true economic development, i.e.,
economic development that ultimately sustains itself. The major need
of Third World nations to develop viable, balanced, and ultimately
independent economies contradicts the need of capitalist countries
to control and dominate. Monopoly capitalism dictates a process in
which the world metropolis continues to develop and the backward
areas sink deeper into underdevelopment. In harsher terms, the rich
get richer and the poor get poorer. The only remedy lies in development outside the monopoly capital processes.

THE ROLE OF GOVERNMENT

We have seen that capitalism has come to accept certain supportive state functions and that reform liberalism has evolved to the
point of viewing government as an effective manager of economic
stability and growth. Both of these ideologies, however, assume that
the natural relationship between economy and state is one of private
initiative supplemented by government action in situations where the
economy or individuals subject to it need help. Marxism, on the
other hand, holds that the state has always been and still remains
the agent of the corporate ruling class. Often, but not always, this
implies positive direct intervention on the part of the state in the
service of that class. Under conditions of competitive capitalism, for
instance, corporate interests were in fact served by minimal governmental activity, and the relationship between government and business approximated that of the capitalist image. But the powerful
forces that shaped the development of monopoly capital also transformed the relationship between the state and the corporate economy, making the former into the willing agent of the latter.

The positive use of the state by the corporate oligarchy is seen
by most Marxists as predating the Depression of the 1930s by a half
century. The research of several Marxist historians suggests that since

---

[13] Baran, *op. cit.,* p. 177.

the late nineteenth century, the ruling class used the state to regulate the damaging and anarchistic behavior of the corporations themselves and the relationship between capital and labor. The United States government, in this view, has never been a neutral arbiter between classes but has always been the instrument of the wealthy oligarchy.[14]

Since the Second World War and the immense expansion of the federal government, the symbiotic relationship between state and corporation has taken on even greater importance.[15] This relationship goes well beyond anything contemplated in Keynesian economics under monopoly capitalism. The state becomes a major channel through which economic activities are carried out and profits obtained. One Marxist analysis holds that the national budget has been transformed into a powerful instrument of national economic planning in accordance with the needs of national capital.[16] Moreover, the state supports the defense establishment which, in turn, serves both as a source of profits and as protection for overseas ventures. Government subsidies for research and development, as well as for highways, shipping, and other transportation facilities developed by private enterprise, also serve the needs of the ruling class.

One of the primary consequences, and indeed aims, of this increasingly active role of the state is that the costs of profit making are increasingly socialized. That is, they are supported by general tax revenues—while profits, of course, remain private. As William A. Williams characterizes it,

> the private use of public money has been and continues to be a central element in the success of American capitalism, which nevertheless attributes its achievements to the creative powers of private property and individual enterprise.[17]

---

[14] For a summary of this research, see James O'Connor, "The Fiscal Crises of the State, Part I," *Socialist Revolution*, Jan.–Feb. 1970.

[15] Some Marxist thinkers, like James O'Connor, suggest that the contemporary relationship between state and capital represents a qualitative as well as quantitative break with the past, *ibid*. Others, like Baran and Sweezy, view it as a significant intensification of an established trend.

[16] O'Connor, *op. cit.*

[17] Williams, *op. cit.*, p. 75.

THE CHARACTER AND PROSPECTS
OF THE CURRENT ECONOMY

In the course of its continuing challenge to the basic assumptions of capitalism, Marxism also denies that the present economic situation in the United States can fairly be termed affluence. It argues further that the true nature of the American system is unstable and crisis-prone, so that future prospects are by no means good.

(a) *Affluence versus inequality*. Marxism denies that the existing economic system produces steadily increasing affluence for the average man, challenging both the perspective from which such claims are made and definitions of affluence that are restricted to materialist dimensions. Claims that credit capitalism with creating affluence are, in Marxist eyes, narrow-minded chauvinism; growth rates in the Third World are declining, and in world terms, the capitalist economies are generating not affluence, but poverty. Within the proper frame of reference, therefore, capitalism is *not* generating affluence. The orthodox claim is on sounder grounds when it is applied exclusively to the United States, but even in this context, it is subject to challenge. Workers' real wages have increased over the long term, but the pattern of distribution has remained constant. Workers are neither "affluent" nor "middle class." Like other social critics, Marxists point to the large segment of the population that lives below the poverty level, in absolute deprivation and misery. Some Marxist thinkers claim that even for the average employed individual, affluence and even moderate comfort are not always attainable. Victor Perlo draws on official government figures to point out that:

> The wages of American workers fall far below the U.S. labor department estimates of what is needed for a "moderate" living standard; 65 percent of workers—including white collar and blue collar, white as well as black—are able to consume much less than the so-called affluent American standard of living.[18]

---

[18] Perlo, *op. cit.*, p. 43.

Finally, Marxist thinkers argue, the material progress that has been made by workers under capitalism constantly is threatened. Inflation has destabilized the economy and led to government policies that raise the level of unemployment. Even if the application of Keynesian policies prevents a recession, workers will continue to slip backwards for some time. The prospect of a depression is always present in a capitalist economy and could wipe out the gains of decades in a very brief period.

A second strand of Marxist ideology disputes the claims to affluence by suggesting that any viable definition of the term must include noneconomic dimensions. If affluence be held to include such nonmaterial aspects as the capacity to live a fully human and creative life (or, in the words of William A. Williams, "to establish an environment which supports human beings in their search for integration and wholeness" [19]), a great gap between true affluence and the capitalist performance is revealed. The nature of the profit-oriented capitalist workplace, in Marxist eyes, makes for alienation, subjection to machines, and meaninglessness. To the lack of control over conditions and products of work and the hardships of speedups and automation is added the lack of choice as a political man, as consumer, and as leisure man. In terms of all of these dimensions, Marxists assert, monopoly capital is destructive. To cite Williams again,

> the essential meaning of wealth has to do with an individual's participation and influence within his society. The great majority of Americans do not possess or exercise that kind of share or stake in contemporary society.[20]

(b) *Instability and crisis.* As we have seen, the dominant ideologies and even reform liberalism present a picture of capitalism as an economic system immunized against severe crisis. The picture is one of steady growth and expanding affluence. This is attributed to the efficiency and rationality of market processes, supplemented by the steadying hand of government's new Keynesian tool. From

---

[19] Williams, *op. cit.*, p. 108.
[20] *Ibid.*, p. 24.

the Marxist perspective, however, the picture looks quite different. Marxists see instead a hesitant and uncertain mechanism maintained only by constant patchwork. They contend that when studied empirically, the economic history of the United States is one of constantly threatening recession and depression coupled with general underutilization of industrial capacity. In particular, the depression of the 1930s and 1940s is of considerable interest to Marxists because it is thought to have been curbed by the new Keynesian tools of government management. Marxists contend that the crisis was resolved not by the success of deliberate manipulation of the economy by government but by the entry of the United States into World War II. This war and the boom that followed did create a period of prosperity, but Marxists point out that prosperity was dependent on the use of surplus to rebuild Europe and pursue the cold war. This prosperity has been accompanied by steadily increasing inflation, which undercuts the world trade position of the United States, increases the domestic cost of living, and reduces real wages.

Furthermore, Keynesian policies do not offer any possibility of basically restructuring the economy. They serve only to bolster an economy that is based upon the continued military spending, the maintenance of an overseas empire, and (as a last resort) war. Williams alleges,

> American capitalism has never since 1861 functioned effectively enough to decrease economic misery over any significant period of time, save as it has been stimulated by war or cold war.[21]

Thus, Marxist ideology contends that the notion of crises as an exceptional rather than a typical state of the capitalist economy is fundamentally incorrect. As Baran and Sweezy contend:

> The Great Depression is not the Great Exception but is the normal outcome of the workings of the American economic system. . . . Here for the first time we get a crystal clear view of the system operating with minimum external stimuli

---

[21] *Ibid.*, p. 83.

for an extended period of time, laying bare what Marx called its "law of motion" for all to see.[22]

Mature capitalism naturally tends toward stagnation, depression, and, therefore, crises; military spending, imperialism, and war can counter this tendency, but ultimately produce crises of the same dimensions. Marxism raises questions as to whether the capitalist economy can continue to function, even as badly as it does, for an indefinite period. The nearly unanimous answer is, of course, negative. The only point of dispute is the way in which this self-destruction will be accomplished.

Values and Goals

Capitalist and liberal ideologies assume a complementary relationship between man's nature and the processes of the capitalist economy. The competition of the market is seen as mirroring the competitive nature of man. The institution of private property follows from and supports his individualistic quest for freedom. Marxists stress man's potential cooperative and social aspects, his search for fulfillment in relationships with others, his propensity for communal and cooperative efforts, and his ability to perform work as art or as a good in itself. Thus capitalism is seen as a perversion rather than an expression of man's real and essential nature.

Marxism focuses on the cooperative nature of the work that produces most goods in an advanced industrial society, pointing particularly to the contrast between the social nature of the productive processes and the private appropriation of the goods and profits as a major contradiction in capitalist society. It seeks to create a society in which this contradiction is resolved and production, ownership, and distribution of goods are social processes. Such an economic system is termed "communist" or "socialist." [23] These terms take on specialized meanings when used by different Marxist thinkers but, at minimum, they refer to a society in which private

---

[22] Baran and Sweezy, *op. cit.,* p. 24.

[23] While a distinction that describes socialism as a phase in the development of communism is sometimes made, it is unnecessary, for our purposes here, to distinguish the two.

ownership of the means of production is abolished and replaced by social ownership[24] and equal distribution of goods. That is, the entire wage system and the most fundamental structural relations underlying capitalism are eliminated. This change establishes the basis for the fundamental social and political changes that reorient human life entirely. While this change from private to social ownership may be identified as the most basic component of the transition to socialism, there is general agreement among Marxists on additional characteristics of a socialist society.

Under socialism, the unplanned and anarchic character of the capitalist production process is replaced by some system of planned economy. In some way, socialist societies must make a collective decision on general economic and social goals and organize the society to implement them. In such a system, Marxists argue, waste and irrationality would be eliminated and resources used to maximum advantage. The instability and cyclical crises that are characteristic of capitalism would disappear. Of equal importance to Marxists is the goal of reorienting the productive processes of the society from production for profit to production for use. In a socialist state, under conditions of abundance, production would be freed from the limiting criteria of profitability and would be directed instead by the needs and opportunities for human use. Capitalist economic "needs," such as the need to destroy food and keep land out of production, would be eliminated. Technological innovations that are restrained or abandoned because they are profitable could be introduced. Resources could be directed into "unprofitable" projects such as parks, education, and cultural activities. Finally, in a socialist society, the need for productivity would be balanced against the need for creative work opportunities and for abundant and well used leisure.

In addition to these characteristics of the socialist economic goal, Marxist thinkers see it as making possible a truly democratic political system. Mass participation in various forms would enable people to share in the crucial decisions over matters of economic

---

[24] It should be noted that we are using the term *social* ownership rather than *state* ownership. Although, in practice, the countries usually referred to as "socialist" are characterized by state ownership of the means of production, Marxist theory speaks in general terms of communal or social ownership. State ownership may or may not operate as social ownership.

planning and to help resolve other issues concerning fundamental direction of the society. Marxists do not see such goals as utopian in the pejorative sense. They contend that capitalism has already created the material preconditions for the existence of socialist societies in the advanced industrial nations. Their present productivity is huge, and it need only be redirected away from waste and inequality. But Marxists acknowledge that the political and social obstacles are formidable. Even assuming a socialist revolution, the process of building a true community would take decades, according to Paul Baran, "decades in which a new generation of human beings will be educated as members of a socialist society, rather than as competitive wolves in the jungle of the capitalist market." [25]

Marxism also acknowledges the additional difficulties of establishing socialism in the underdeveloped nations where the industrial base and abundance does not exist. They argue, however, that the establishment of socialism in the United States would have profound effects upon the development of the Third World. The elimination of capitalism and the profit motive would remove the structural pressures for imperialism, freeing nations to engage in real cooperation and perhaps move toward elimination of nationalism.

In regard to such a general level of values and goals, Marxists concur. But their solid front begins to crumble when more specific details of the future socialist society are discussed. It is of great importance to contemporary Marxist ideology that there are several nations in the world (the Soviet Union, China, Cuba, and the Eastern European countries, among others) that claim to be socialist or, at least, on the road to socialism. The legitimacy of these claims is a matter of intense dispute. Some recognize only China and Albania as worthy of the socialist designation and denounce the Soviet Union and other Eastern European nations as "revisionist." The Communist Party of the United States contends that the Soviet Union remains the first and most advanced socialist state. To other Marxist organizations, Cuba seems the most firmly established and promising model of genuine socialism.

Underlying these disagreements are complicated questions concerning the nature of socialism and the proper means of establishing it, many with roots in the Russian revolution of 1917. Many of

---

[25] Baran, *op. cit.,* p. 296.

these questions focus around the internal development of nations attempting to establish socialism. Marxist thinkers disagree over the extent to which bureaucratization, undemocratic practices, and even repression must be tolerated in the initial stages of socialist development. There is also disagreement concerning the legitimacy and necessity of maintaining or reintroducing certain capitalist economic structures such as the market and the use of monetary rather than moral incentives.

Social Change and Tactics

Marxism calls for far-reaching change in the American social system; as we have seen, its goals contrast almost completely with those of capitalism and liberalism. Marxism's image of the scope of change required is more far-reaching than any of the change-oriented ideologies we have examined, and its theory of how change may come about is the most comprehensive. When black liberation thinkers dispute questions of social change, usually they are concerned primarily with questions of tactics. Similarly, new left thinkers tend to focus on very concrete and specific issues. In contrast, Marxism attempts to set up general principles about the dynamics of change in any society and to apply them to the contemporary United States. Although we can do little more than present the bare outlines of this theory, it should be enough to show its comparative depth and comprehensiveness.

At the basis of the Marxist theory of change is the principle that capitalism, like all economic systems before it, is developing toward its own destruction because of unsolvable strains and contradictions from within. Analysis reveals dynamic processes that are inherent in the system and create the conditions that inevitably will lead to socialism. More specifically, groups in the society are constantly led by their own self-interest to oppose the policies of the ruling class and ultimately to stand in opposition to capitalism itself. Monopoly capitalism is not just powerful and static, but steadily generates internal strains and develops class conflict.

The strains and contradictions exist at many levels of the society. The American monopoly capital system generates tremendous productivity and creates great wealth but must waste and destroy that wealth. Poverty and deprivation exist side by side with waste and frivolous consumption; the misery-ending and work-saving potential of automation, for example, is experienced as actual or threatened unemployment. Imperialism is an imperative, but its effect is to unite the Third World and a portion of the domestic population against the United States. Vast increases in the national budget socialize the costs and risks of production, but the profits are still privately appropriated; meanwhile, revenue demands provoke taxpayer revolts and general political unrest. In these and other ways, monopoly capitalism inevitably generates conflict and paves the way for its own transformation.

Marxists argue that while contradictions themselves will not establish socialism, they give rise to social conflict between classes in the society that eventually can culminate in the socialist revolution. The traditional revolutionary class of Marxist analysis is the working class or proletariat who do not own the means of production and can exist only by selling their labor. But contemporary Marxists see the question of the revolutionary class as more problematic. They are confronted by the seeming indifference of the American working class to socialist ideology. Their varying response to this problem constitutes another dimension of difference among them. Some, such as Baran and Sweezy, have come close to abandoning the concept of the working class as an agent of revolutionary change. They see the working class under monopoly capitalism as oriented toward middle-class materialism and divided by racism. They argue that the major forces in opposition to capitalism are the Third World liberation movements. Sweezy says, "I believe that it is this revolutionary movement in the Third World, with its roots in centuries of exploitation and bitterness, which is the primary engine of change in the world today." [26] In this view, though the principle of internal contradictions is not abandoned, the primary instrument of the destruction of U.S. capitalism is external.

A second position, and the one endorsed by what is probably a majority of Marxist thinkers, is considerably more optimistic concerning the revolutionary potential of the American working class. The worker's alienating circumstances and his inability to share in the returns from productivity remain unchanged or are height-

---

[26] Paul Sweezy, *Monthly Review,* October 1968, p. 47.

ened under monopoly capitalism. Further, the conditions of work of some groups not usually thought of as part of the traditional working class (semi-professionals, white-collar workers, agricultural workers) are coming to resemble those of the other workers. Monopoly capitalism operates to increasingly "proletarianize" masses of people. Thus, the working class remains a major target of Marxist organizing efforts which focus on the factory and other workplaces.

Marxists disagree substantially about the specifics of the process of change as well as about the specific characteristics of the future socialist society, as our earlier examination showed. Not surprisingly, these differences in goals and tactics are linked to differences in analysis of contemporary American economic and social conditions. The following two illustrations indicate the breadth and character of such differences more effectively than any descriptive catalogue could.

Democratic Socialism

The term "evolutionary socialism" might be more appropriate for this set of ideas. Almost all forms of socialism are democratic in some sense of the word, and the American version's civil libertarian, peaceful, evolutionary approach to change is distinctive. But common usage has operated to label these views as democratic socialism, and we shall follow that precedent.

What we shall see here under this label is little more than a modest extension of reform liberalism. In all major respects, democratic socialism accepts the same limitations that reform liberalism does, and it experiences exactly the same contradictions and dilemmas. It accepts the contemporary welfare state as a point of departure for gradual progress toward full popular control of the economy. It places its highest priority on equality and the established civil liberties and rejects all tactics not consistent with liberalism's democratic procedures, visualizing the American political process as offering ample opportunity for persuasion and successful change through electoral means.

Democratic socialism sees the United States of the late twentieth century as characterized by ferment, conflict, innovation, violence, a measure of madness—but nevertheless at a point where significant gains are possible. A welfare state of sorts has been accomplished, and some milestones of individual liberty and material well-being can be identified. According to Irving Howe, editor of the journal *Dissent,* this is partly the product of previous struggles between classes:

> The welfare state is importantly the result of social struggle on the part of the labor movement. If the working class has not fulfilled the "historic tasks" assigned to it by Marxism and if it shows, at least in the advanced industrial countries, no sign of revolutionary initiative, it has nevertheless significantly modified the nature and softened the cruelties of capitalist society.[27]

According to democratic socialists, the achievements of the welfare state have been brought about by knowledgeable action on the part of coalitions of groups, each in turn pressing for its fair share of economic rewards available through the American system. The kind of political process envisioned is the familiar pluralist one, but the democratic socialists see no reason why such a process need be passive or static. There is danger that dominant elites will be able to deflect thrusts from below, but such a result is far from certain. Democratic socialists deny that mass needs or wants have been satisfied and insist that the established framework can still be pressed to yield great additional returns for many people. Pressing for more through the system need not result in blunting or co-opting (buying off through appearing to accept) such demands. The proper coalition, animated by the appropriate moral urgency, can achieve new waves of progress if people will be "realistic" about the means of getting from here to some desirable future point.

This opportunity is partly attributable to some internal contradictions in the current character of the welfare state. Rapid transformations and dislocations now characterize the American economy as it shifts to a technological and automated basis. At present, the transformation of the economy (and hence the society) is proceeding in an unplanned, arbitrary, and chaotic fashion—with dis-

---

[27] Irving Howe, "Notes on the Welfare State," in Jeremy Larner and Irving Howe, eds., *Poverty: Views from the Left* (New York: Morrow, 1965), p. 293.

astrous results for all but the few whose wealth enables them to protect themselves. New forms of large-scale organization are inevitable, and unimagined accumulations of economic power are being built. But this inevitable thrust toward change is also inherent in the character of the promises made by the welfare state. Commitments to eradicate poverty, for example, carry certain promises about the future and contribute to expectations about what that future will be like. Because the political processes are essentially open, a demand thus raised will become a major factor in the ensuing political dynamic.

VALUES AND GOALS

The major operative value of democratic socialism is the preservation and enhancement of democratic civil liberties. There is a unity between democracy, understood in terms of such civil liberties, and socialism. In the modern sense, socialism involves popular control over the economy, and there are various means by which such control might be institutionalized. The achievement of socialism has nothing to do with totalitarianism or authoritarianism, but is rather the natural extension of the reality of democracy to all spheres of life. According to Irving Howe:

> To preserve democracy as a political mode without extending it into every crevice of social and economic life is to allow it to become increasingly sterile, formal, ceremonial. To nationalize an economy without enlarging democratic freedoms is to create a new kind of social exploitation. Radicals and liberals may properly and fraternally disagree about many things; but upon this single axiom concerning the value of democracy, this conviction wrung from the tragedy of our age, politics must rest.[28]

Observance of the civil liberties is thus the primary commitment of democratic socialism; these rights are the key to social change be-

---

[28] Irving Howe, "New Styles in 'Leftism,'" in *Steady Work: Essays in the Politics of Democratic Radicalism, 1953–1966* (New York: Harcourt, Brace & World, 1966), p. 78.

cause they are the means by which individuals may hope to secure their ends. Within this framework, the secondary goal of popular control over the economy may be realistically anticipated.

Democratic socialists do not strongly emphasize the goal of nationalization of the economy. This is so not because they do not hold such a goal as primary, but because in the American context, there are better ways to phrase the goal and because they perceive a certain inevitability about arriving at nationalization or its equivalent if the commitments of the welfare state are seriously pursued. Democratic socialists see uncontrolled power flowing from aggregations of economic resources, with serious consequences of actions within the private economy. Thus, the impulse to assert popular control through government may be seen as merely another application of democratic principles of participation and control over sources of power that threaten individual freedom. Furthermore, the end result of the promises implicit (and explicit) in the nature of the welfare state inevitably must involve such popular control over the economy. Anything short of such a relationship will amount to a denial of welfare state promises.

The process of change envisioned by democratic socialism is a natural and evolutionary one. Democratic socialists believe that when the inherent or implicit dynamic of the welfare state's promises is combined with popular perception of the limitations and consequences of capitalism, an irresistible force for change will be generated. Thus, the crucial task of democratic socialists is to link the acknowledged problems of the society to the imperatives and characteristics of capitalism, pointing out how different procedures and policies could lead to better results for most people. Any serious effort to eradicate poverty, for example, eventually would have to confront the reality of the poor's lack of skills in a technological economy. The amount of economic growth that would have to be promoted in order to create enough prosperity to assure jobs for the poor would require a fundamental change in the relationship of government and economy; if it were successful, the number of newly employed poor might spur a new effort to organize and give new impetus to a left-wing political coalition. As things stand, government efforts to stimulate growth are beneficial chiefly to the middle-class contractor or entrepreneur. Keynesianism, to democratic socialists, is increasingly conservative in character, actually creating a kind of social-industrial complex. But liberalism's patchwork efforts may readily be exposed as the illusory "solutions" they are.

The inevitability of popular recognition of the failures of capitalism is a central component of democratic socialist images of change. The future of political democracy itself is involved in the choice of how (or if) the new aggregates are to be controlled: the only future for democracy, according to Michael Harrington, lies in creating means whereby the people can manage the economy.

> From the very beginning, the socialists knew that modern technology could not be made just by dividing it up into tiny parcels of individual ownership. It is of the very nature of that technology to be concentrated and collective. Therefore, the socialists assigned a new and radical meaning to democracy. The people's title to the social means of production would be guaranteed . . . through votes. The basic economic decisions would be made democratically.
>
> In this context, the nationalization of industry is a technique of socialism, not its definition. It is one extremely important way of abolishing the political and social power that results from concentrated economic ownership. It also facilitates directing economic resources to the satisfaction of human needs. . . .
>
> The one set and undeviating aspect of socialism is its commitment to making the democratic and free choice of citizens the principle of social and economic life.[29]

Democratic socialism thus holds an optimistic view of the capacity of unsatisfied groups to press the welfare state for delivery of its promises, ending ultimately with the transformation of that welfare state into socialism, defined as a truly integrated politico-economic democracy. But it does not fail to recognize that there are many obstacles, although it maintains that these are frequently exaggerated. It rejects the claim that the material benefits provided by the welfare state have so trapped people in acquiescence and material tranquility that there is no longer any serious popular desire for fundamental change. Individualism and humanism are too strong to succumb to such conclusions on the grounds of "technology" or

---

[29] Michael Harrington, *The Accidental Century* (New York: Macmillan, 1965), pp. 278–279.

mass society; instead, democratic socialism argues that such theories are antihistorical and assume that, somehow, the movement of history has been arrested at this particular stage. To act in accordance with such a view, furthermore, is to impose self-limitations and create a self-fulfilling prophecy. The end of social transformation has not been reached, and the sincere radical must commit himself to the long-range task of creating a social structure that will promote and support humane values.

In spite of some early intimations that socialist intellectuals should carry the burden of bringing understanding to the public and generating change in that manner, democratic socialists promptly came to the conclusion that the need for action was so pressing that socialists should form coalitions with other like-minded groups and get about the business of extending the welfare state as far as its flexibility would permit. In *The Accidental Century,* for example, Michael Harrington was not optimistic about finding political support among the poor or labor; instead, he envisioned a constructive minority of educated middle-class students and intellectuals—perhaps the core of a new political party. Three years later, however, in *Toward a Democratic Left,*[30] Harrington talked less of specifically socialist solutions and more of the need and opportunity to build a new, broadly based major party of the Left. To the core previously envisioned, he would add labor, the poor, and members of civil rights movements to construct a large coalition mobilized around the issue of controlling corporate power and ultimately questioning the myths of free enterprise. He anticipates that liberalism's inability to provide real solutions to the visible and pressing problems of the day will become increasingly obvious. He warns that the far left is equally unable to provide solutions: "A hazy apocalypse is no substitute for an inadequate liberalism." [31] The new majority coalition is both possible and necessary to see that the use of government to which we have reluctantly become accustomed is not diverted to the mere maintenance of the status quo or to the advantage of corporate enterprise. In particular, central public planning and widespread citizen participation at various stages of policymaking and imple-

---

[30] Michael Harrington, *Toward a Democratic Left* (New York: Macmillan, 1968).
[31] *Ibid.,* p. 17.

mentation are proposed. Public choices about the rate and direction of economic development would be facilitated by a series of reports on current conditions in America and the alternative prospects for the future. It seems clear that these are beginning routes to the ultimate restructuring of basic values to supplant materialist and acquisitive motivations by concern for the human and spiritual qualities of individuals—routes to socialism. These goals can be effectuated by exerting mass-based political pressure through a revitalized majority party. The basic strategy remains one of forcing the welfare state to makes its promises good.

Though we have sought to avoid repetition by emphasizing only the distinctive aspects of democratic socialism, it should be clear that it sees many of the same problems and adheres to the same values as do the other reform liberal ideologies. It is somewhat more explicit in assigning capitalism the blame for many current social problems, and similarly about the need to bring the economy under popular control. The envisioned process of change appears to rest more firmly on mass-based action. But, like the other reform liberal ideologies, democratic socialism's complaints are limited to the charge of failure to live up to sound values and goals, and it perceives the established political process as essentially open and capable of delivering the new goals it seeks. The traditional civil liberties lie at the core of the good political process, and if they are scrupulously followed (as, for the most part, they are today), desired changes can be achieved. Thus, even though its goals include radical transformation of the economic system itself—as fundamental a change as may be contemplated in social life—democratic socialism envisions attaining such ends through the existing political framework. With such principles, it belongs squarely within the reform liberalism category, sharing both the strengths and the problems of those ideologies.

Revolutionary Socialism

Revolutionary socialism earns its label because of its conviction that evolutionary transformation to socialism is impossible in the United States and that only revolutionary action can bring it about. Some revolutionary socialists see the peaceful achievement of socialism as impossible because of the inevitable use of massive centralized power by a threatened American ruling class. Others have reached the same conclusion because of the stranglehold that liberal ideology and/or capitalist consciousness has maintained on nearly all Americans. Many see both these and other obstacles. Nevertheless, at least rhetorically, all revolutionary socialists place their faith in an ultimate revolution involving large numbers of people.

Revolutionary socialist groups and parties have existed since Marx's ideas first gained impact in the United States in the late nineteenth century. Foremost among them is the Communist Party of the United States. Although it was severely damaged, first by the series of rapid policy shifts dictated by the Soviet Union in the 1930s and 1940s and then by cold war-inspired repression in the 1940s and 1950s, the Communist Party is still the largest organization in the United States officially committed to revolutionary socialism. Whether it is now so aged, rigid, bureaucratized, and tied to both Soviet and domestic capitalist interests as to be essentially a hollow shell empty of all serious potential is a question much debated among non-Communist Party Marxists. The Socialist Workers Party is another party of relatively long standing. It originated in the Trotskyist split-off from the Stalin-dominated Communist Party. The activities of the Socialist Workers Party are principally electoral, middle-class, and issue-oriented. Nonetheless, its rhetoric includes the image of a revolution of some undefined character at some time in the future.

Most of the upsurge in Marxism during the post-1960 period, however, occurred in the form of the founding and/or growth of newer (and still relatively small) revolutionary socialist organizations. Some have their origins in earlier factional splits within the older parties, but all have developed in the wake of the fragmentation of SDS and the new left generally. Students for a Democratic Society still exists, although its numbers are drastically reduced and there is considerable overlap with the Progressive Labor Party. Among other of the newer groups are the International Socialists, the Spartacist League (Revolutionary Communist Youth), the National Caucus of Labor Committees, and a number of local organizations. Most of these groups would reject our prior characterization of Marxism as tame, liberal, and flat. They have a much greater sense of urgency and moral necessity than is revealed in the works of established Marxist scholars; they want the revolution now, as soon as possible, and they devote themselves to organizing the working class in one or another form to attain that end.

The differences among them as to all key issues as well as in regard to other characteristics are vast. Some are local, limited to one city or region; others are national in scope. Some take their Marxist scholarship and the role of theory very seriously; others use Marx in essentially symbolic ways. Some see their proper role as factory workers and organizers of militant trade union caucuses, while others view themselves as the Leninist vanguard party. Still others, less tied to the 1917 model, see themselves as the necessary intellectual cadre preparing the working class and themselves for the coming opportunity to seize state power and reconstruct the society.

Of these groups, we shall illustrate revolutionary socialism by briefly describing some of the major positions of the National Caucus of Labor Committees. Although this group is relatively small, it is a national organization and it has been growing steadily. It also has a theoretical approach that probably is the most comprehensive and precisely stated of all of these groups, evidenced in several significant publications.

The Labor Committee takes its Marxist scholarship very seriously, insisting that one must approach Marx only through study of the work of his key predecessors, Kant, Hegel, and Feuerbach. In this way, one sees both the concerns against which Marx was writing and the great scope of what he sought to accomplish. The Marxism that emerges is a totally integrated and comprehensive interpretation of man and societies and their relation to nature, a joining of epistemology, philosophy, and the social and natural sciences. It is all one whole, emphatically not subject to the categorizing fetishes of American academia, such as an early versus a late Marx, the philosophical Marx versus the empiricist Marx or the economic determinist. (Nor, it follows, would Marx properly be subject to the world view, values and goals, social change and tactics approach of our analytical framework.) According to the Labor Committee, to treat Marx in any such compartmentalized fashion is to rob his work of its distinguishing integrated and wholistic character.

Nor can Marx be understood properly by looking at him from the capitalist-liberal perspective. He is not just another Western historical figure whose words and thoughts, though sometimes obscure, foreign, and now archaic, must nevertheless be tested and understood through our standard criteria of meaning, logic, and intelligibility. Marx was writing in another consciousness, with a totally different style of thinking, another type of logic, in which concepts unknown to capitalism-liberalism play vital roles. To understand him, the Labor Committee maintains, one must cross the threshold from capitalism-liberalism to Marx's world. One must pick up new tools of thinking, new concepts and language to express them, and seek to rise to Marx's level and quality of approach. One can neither vacillate between capitalist-liberal thinking and true Marxism nor exist simultaneously in both worlds because both are all-encompassing, all-pervading, essentially *self*-defining. Once one *does* cross the threshold to awareness of the true Marxist consciousness, things suddenly fit together, perhaps for the first time—psychology, ecology, anthropology, philosophy, politics, economics, personal identity, social systems, alienation, and concepts of natural science. This unity and understanding comes as such a revelation and opens up such potential that one is unlikely to be willing to return to the impoverished, compartmentalized, narrow world of capitalist-liberal thinking.

The Labor Committee thus makes of Marxism a method, a way of thinking in which the present society can be understood in terms of its potential to become the future socialist society. What is real is what has meaning in the light of that future possibility, not necessarily what capitalist-liberal society happens to recognize or value today. Real value in Labor Committee Marxist terms is something that can be used for the maintenance and development of socially necessary production and the maintenance of workers. For example, the "paper titles" of capitalist private property such as bonds, mortgages, and other certificates of indebtedness are not of real value. Labor Committee Marxism is not non-empirical in the sense of rejecting all tangible evidence about what is happening in the world today. It is empirical, but in a different way. It rejects the notion that one can understand or act properly merely by assembling all the "facts" within the context of present assumptions, expectations, and projections from the existing system. These are fixed by the style of thinking that is associated with the capitalist-liberal social order. Instead, the Labor Committee selects those "facts" differently, orders them differently, and thus extracts wholly different implications because the facts now have meaning only in terms of potential social chaos, revolution, and socialist reconstruction.

Perhaps the central factor in Labor Committee analysis is the concept of consciousness. Consciousness includes both the concepts, language, and other tools and manner of thinking and the premises, assumptions, and expectations that are characteristic of people in a given society. Consciousness is not self-generated; rather, it is produced in people by the social institutions and organizations and practices of their society. In turn, such social formations necessarily are extensions of the particular economic and social system that produced and sustains them—in this case, American capitalism-liberalism. *Everything* of long standing in a given social order is coherent; that is, consistent with each other and serving mutually sustaining functions. Thus, the existing consciousness reflects and serves the needs of the capitalist social order (and thus ultimately the capitalist ruling class) just as do all accepted intellectual criteria of judgment, interpretations of social and natural phenomena, and approaches to knowledge itself. Ideologies that rationalize and justify the capitalist social order not only are generated out of this consciousness but also help to sustain it. Even such contending ideologies as populism and radicalism are so rooted in and shaped by this capitalist-liberal consciousness that they generate attitudes and behavior that ultimately is supportive of that same social order. The key to understanding present-day attitudes and behavior of Americans as well as to future change lies in the nature of this consciousness, its social origin, and the way in which it can and may be changed—first for the intellectual cadre, and then for the masses.

Labor Committee analysis ranks its conception of the nature and current state of capitalism next in importance. Capitalism is seen as a wholly interdependent world system, delicately coordinated through the monetary manipulations of American and European central bankers. Because of the bifurcation between real value and the paper titles and profit maximizing of capitalist owners, capitalism has an inherent and imperative need to absorb more and more real value from somewhere in order to forestall its own collapse. In the Labor Committee's eyes, this is a matter not of disposing of a surplus, but of continuously finding ways to narrow the gap between the real value produced within the system and the fictitious value represented by indebtedness, speculation, and the "value" grounded in ownership of technologically outmoded means of production. The real value needed by the capitalist system is secured through exploitation of the Third World (frequently via usurious loans and other monetary manipulation), deliberately managed inflation, and/or severe restriction on the wages of workers. This looting and/or wage gouging is spurred by the pressures on national currencies generated within the world monetary system, which is the register that reflects the widening gap between real and fictitious value and other instabilities in national capitalist economies. In effect, it translates these economic problems into forms that have worldwide impact. The various capitalist ruling classes are forced to act to protect the future value of their own holdings in the integrated world system in ways that constantly threaten to become either anarchic and mutually destructive competition or eventually self-destructive extraction of real value from suppression of the real wages of their own domestic working classes.

The Labor Committee believes that world capitalism is in a state of imminent collapse. Deep tremors have run through the world monetary system at least twice in the recent decade, reflecting a serious imbalance in actual production of real value and the weight of pyramided paper titles in several key capitalist economies. One of these tremors occurred in August 1971, when a series of desperate maneuvers to patch up the system and delay its downfall was begun. Key among these was the imposition of wage controls on the American working class, which together with deliberately staged inflation provided a new injection of real value for the support of capitalist titles in the United States and corresponding aid to the value of the American dollar in world markets. The monetary reforms and currency revaluations that followed are seen as incapable of really remedying such other U.S. and world problems and instabilities as are reflected in our balance of payments deficits, inflation, unemployment, and general economic stagnation. Any apparent "recovery" is just that—illusory and short term only—because of these deeper currents as analyzed under the Labor Committee's interpretation of Marx's law of value.

The Labor Committee thus foresees economic collapse, severe depression, and resulting social chaos in the United States in the near future. In this context, the key to change lies in fundamental consciousness change—not just of a few items of belief or in terms of shifting priorities, but of the whole manner of thinking and the entire set of premises and assumptions that constitute capitalist-liberal consciousness. Who are the people who can achieve such a transformation? How will it be accomplished? And how will this new force be able to seize state power? The Labor Committee's answer consists of several steps, all drawn from their understanding of Marx as applied to the special conditions of the United States today.

First, the agency of change can be only the historical working class. This is true for both theoretical and practical reasons: theoretical because only the productive workers have the capacity to shape the future society appropriately—to reproduce themselves under conditions that promise a higher material and spiritual life for all humanity in a manner consistent with man's continued links to nature and practical because only the working class has the potential for socialist consciousness now, its role in the economic system is crucial, and its numbers and potential power are sufficient, when mobilized, to seize power.

The Labor Committee's concept of class is one of its major distinguishing features. Drawing on Marx's use of (and reaction to) certain aspects of Feuerbach and Hegel, the Labor Committee emphasizes the distinction between a "class-in-itself" and a "class-for-itself." A class-in-itself is a class (in the objective sense) that subjectively is divided into separate segments that pursue what they believe to be their interests in essentially individualistic, mutually conflicting ways. They are imbued with enough elements of capitalist consciousness that they seek only self-interested goals, and they never perceive the much deeper and more fundamental interests that they share with all other members of the objective working class. However militant, their separatism and self-interestedness can be only an obstacle to the ultimate overthrow of capitalism.

A class-for-itself, on the other hand, is a class that has become *self*-conscious; it is aware of the complete identity of needs and purposes shared among all its members and prepared to act cohesively to assert their (socialist) goals for the society as a whole. Self-interest has been subordinated to the larger needs and purposes of the class as a whole. The focus has shifted, and previously parochial and potentially conflicting interests have been understood as either low priority or capable of being truly realized only through incorporation into the far broader reconstruction of society to be achieved through the success of the class efforts.

This distinction is crucial to Labor Committee tactics. Only the class-for-itself can generate the new socialist consciousness and successfully make the revolution. Thus, the Labor Committee must act only in ways that promote such attitudes and practices and prepare the way for as many members of the working class to come to such orientation as possible. Separatist tendencies among militant trade unionists, racial and ethnic minorities, women's liberationists, and other localist or uniqueness-emphasizing groups must be fought. All of these self-oriented groups threaten to divide the working class, diffuse its energies, and hold its consciousness within the capitalist-liberal frame. Through propaganda, persuasion, and confrontation, the Labor Committee seeks to bring the vision of a united, cohesive, self-conscious, purposeful class-for-itself before all potential socialists. Because the only way to make a successful revolution is through the class-for-itself method, there can be no acceptance of the "every group do your own thing" approach. The Labor Committee believes it would be better to discredit or eliminate parochial and pseudo-socialist groups (if possible) than to permit them to engage in destructive activities that ultimately endanger the revolution itself.

Another tactical step in this process is the task of establishing hegemony on the left. The Labor Committee asserts that potential socialists and other people who are in the process of seeking competent left leadership (or who are just becoming aware of the failures of the capitalist-liberal social system) do not systematically review the theoretical underpinnings of every group on the left. Instead, they move toward the largest, the most visible, or the most active of the groups espousing the revolutionary position, and they tend to follow its leadership as their best alternative—learning its theory and practice in the process of struggle that ensues. The Labor Committee's goal, therefore, is to establish itself as such a leading force, to gain hegemony over all other left groups. It seeks to do so through challenging them to compare their theory and strategy with that of the Labor Committee. In the ensuing debate and confrontation, it is believed, the best and most viable elements of the other groups will be absorbed into the Labor Committee because of the clear superiority of its understanding and overall approach to the problem of establishing socialism.

Armed with the class-for-itself concept and moving to establish itself as the hegemonic left organization, the Labor Committee believes it will be situated so as to help inspire and to take full advantage of the spark that will bring about the revolution. In the context of depression and chaos, a mass strike will erupt at some point —a broad-based and essentially spontaneous strike by productive workers that will spread quickly to other industries and regions of the country. In this cataclysmic social process, years of alienation and gradual detachment from capitalist consciousness come to a head, and workers eagerly seek some new explanation, a vision of an alternative social system, and the leadership to achieve it. Into the void comes the cadre of knowledgeable socialists, the hegemonic organization recognized by the more advanced workers as the one whose foresight and theory has given it the potential revolutionary force capable of bringing about the new social order. Acting from their theory, the Labor Committee will be able to bring enough key workers to something approaching socialist consciousness. Chaotic mass strikes will be pointed increasingly toward political goals, and more and more supporters will be accumulated in a series of waves. As increasing numbers of workers develop the new consciousness amidst this struggle, elite fragmentation and arbitrary uses of power add support to the purposeful actions of the dominant leadership. Finally, state power either is handed over or is forcibly seized, perhaps in a struggle with fascist reactionaries.

Reconstruction of the social order then ensues. Labor Committee principles include the prompt development of the new consciousness by as many people in the society as possible. The underlying belief is that through the establishment of new social institutions predicated on a vision of the new society now so close to realization, people can become humans much different than they now are. There is nothing inevitable or inherent about competitiveness, selfishness, materialism, racism, or other "characteristics of human nature." All of these are products of capitalism and its social institutions and consciousness. Thus, people can in time generalize from the class-for-itself consciousness developed by many in the course of the revolutionary struggle and expand it into an overall identification with the needs of all humanity—including the many nonmaterial dimensions that the true concept of humanity implies.

In objective terms, socialism requires central planning to rationalize and organize production for the benefit of all. The Labor Committee does not envision a decentralized, locally controlled system. This is so because of its image of the world's economy and people as so intimately interdependent. The task of socialism is to enable the world population as a whole to reproduce and uplift itself through rational use of the resources of nature. Workers are to be democratically involved in determining priorities of production and other policies, once they have entered the new consciousness, through real participation in shaping national actions. In this way, worldwide order and mutuality will be established. Only within such a framework can personal fulfillment and cultural diversity be provided at the local level; subject to such broad national standards and policies, local self-determination can be practiced.

Although these Labor Committee principles are drawn from Marx, they are not shared by other self-identified Marxist groups. The question of whose understanding of Marx is correct is less important in practical terms than is the question of whose theory and practice is capable of generating a revolution in the United States of the 1970s. The issue is often fought, however, over the relative validity of each group's claim to be the true interpreter of Marx and thus the rightful possessor of the symbol of Marxism. Although non-Marxists may feel that such bitter conflict among the supposed heirs of Marx is self-defeating, in the latter's eyes, it is almost essential that it go on until one or another group emerges with clear hegemony. This is so because the slim chance of achieving a successful revolution requires that all resources be applied coherently in accordance with a single strategy. And each group is committed to a different strategy, which it believes to be the only correct one and which requires that that group be in a position to guide the revolution. In other words, a continuing problem of revolutionary socialism is the enduring conflict for hegemony; until one or another group establishes its views as controlling, energy will continue to be dissipated (or constructively applied, depending on one's viewpoint) in such intra-left battles.

Annotated Bibliography

Baran, Paul A. *The Political Economy of Growth*. New York: Modern Reader Paperbacks, 1968. A good statement of the Marxist argument concerning the cause of U.S. imperialist policy and its consequences for underdeveloped countries.

Baran, Paul A., and Paul M. Sweezy. *Monopoly Capital*. New York: Modern Reader Paperbacks, 1968. A detailed presentation of the theory of rising surplus under monopoly capital.

Frank, Andre Gunder. "The Development of Underdevelopment," *Monthly Review,* September 1966. Another analysis of the consequences of U.S. imperialism, with particular attention to Latin America.

Howe, Irving. *Steady Work: Essays in the Politics of Democratic Radicalism, 1953–1966*. New York: Harcourt, Brace & World, 1966.

Huberman, Leo, and Paul M. Sweezy. *Socialism in Cuba*. New York: Monthly Review Press, 1969. An appraisal of the socialist revolution in Cuba which touches on some of the points of contention among American Marxists.

Magdoff, Harry. *The Age of Imperialism*. New York: Modern Reader Paperbacks, 1968. An argument for the economic motivation analysis of U.S. foreign policy.

Mandel, Ernest. *An Introduction to Marxist Economic Theory*. New York: Merit, 1969. A brief introduction to the basic principles of Marx's economic thinking.

Mills, C. Wright. *The Marxists*. New York: Delta, 1962. A good overview of the historical development of Marxism. Contains both interpretive essays and documents.

O'Connor, James. "The Fiscal Crisis of the State, Part I," *Socialist Revolution,* February 1970. A discussion of the present role of the state in American capitalism.

Perlo, Victor. "Relevance of Marxist Economics to U.S. Conditions," *Political Affairs,* February 1969. An argument for the continued application of Marx to the United States.

Williams, William A. *The Great Evasion*. Chicago: Quadrangle Paperbacks, 1964. A discussion of the consequences for Americans of failing to come to grips with the Marxian notion of "community."

Zeitlin, Irving. *Capitalism and Imperialism: An Introduction to Neo-Marxian Concepts*. Chicago: Markham, 1973.

PART III

Implications and Prospects

10

Contrasting Ideologies and Their Implications

In this chapter, we shall first use our analytical framework to suggest some of the basic contrasts between the mainstream and the challenging ideologies—and occasionally some of the contrasts between ideologies within each category. Then we shall briefly examine some implications and prospects. For example, we shall return to one of the central questions with which this inquiry began: how significant are the differences between ideologies? How far do the "change-seekers" travel outside the dominant system of thought reflected in the mainstream ideologies? And we shall speculate about the meaning of all this—the implications that contemporary ideological conflicts have for the future of American politics.

Mainstream and Challengers: A Summary Analysis

(1) CONTRASTING IMAGES OF THE AMERICAN SYSTEM

Perhaps the most crucial difference between the various ideologies' world views lies in *the images they hold of where power is located* in the American system and *the nature of the political process* to which that pattern of power distribution gives rise. An important cause of these contrasting images is found in the concepts held by each ideology about the relationship between the economy and political power. We shall first sketch the conceptual alternatives before we turn specifically to the images to which they contribute.

One can view politics as if it were a separate, compartmentalized area of human activity. From this perspective, neither economic resources nor social settings are relevant to the power or purposes of individuals when they engage in political activity. Because of the division of labor in society and the specialization of knowledge within academic disciplines, businessmen, politicians, social scientists, and citizens alike may come to view economics and politics as distinct and unrelated fields. Or, in sharp contrast, one may view social life as an integrated whole in which people acquire political power and purposes directly from their economic and social situations. In this view, power flows from economic resources and social class structures as well as from the possession of legitimacy under established social and political traditions; the latter, of course, may be seen as little more than the residue of *past* economic and social realities. From this perspective, people who possess or control aggregates of power must use the machinery of government to defend their achieved status and to further their current goals. To understand such a world, one cannot treat political activities in isolation, as if the influence of every person were equal or the purposes of government neutral.

Capitalism and liberalism see economics and politics as quite separate areas. Economic life occupies primary status because it involves the individual's natural self-serving needs and aspirations; it thus generates the primary shaping forces in the society. Politics is secondary, but it is an independent and open process analogous to the market economy. Acting as equivalent consumer units, individuals select among products that compete for their support until majorities are developed.

Consistent with these premises, capitalism and liberalism see the American economic engine producing impressively, proof that the individuals involved are achieving their real goals. They see a distribution of wealth in which practically everyone enjoys some share of American abundance. Although some are very wealthy, as a result of their special capabilities, most Americans are at a reasonably comfortable middle-class level—with the highest standard of living the world has ever known. There *are* pockets of poverty that are the result of cultural deprivation and/or personal inadequacies, but the poor are steadily moving up into the middle class. Large corporations have recently created aggregates of economic resources, but these remain subject to the general control of the state and their managers are, in any event, sensitive and responsive to public preferences and needs.

Because each individual has one vote, the political process is also seen as working well. Power is distributed broadly. The organization of the population into interest groups both reflects social reality and provides further equalized representation. In short, the many benefits of pluralist democracy are being realized through American politics. And a variety of individual and social functions is being served, perhaps chief among which is the political system's service as the supportive agent of the economy. Capitalism sees the state increasingly as the agent for promotion of its growth and stability, and liberalism accepts responsibility for furthering the needs of the technological economy.

Reform liberalism has begun to see some connections between the economic and social order and the nature of the political process. For example, reform liberals diverge from the generally contented image held by capitalism and liberalism in certain ways, some of which are based on perceived links between economic status and political power. They see greater inequality between economic levels and a more permanent poverty status for some. Corporate concentrations appear to create a more serious problem and threaten technological domination of people's wants and opportunities. Political power may follow such accumulation of economic resources in the hands of the giant corporation and pose a threat to the real independence of the state. In addition, modern developments have placed far too much real power in the hands of the military and the oligarchs in Congress. The normal channels of political representation are not working adequately. As a result, disproportionate power resides in the hands of those with outdated or dangerous ideas.

Individualist conservatism operates with the same sort of compartmentalized approach as does capitalism-liberalism, reaching essentially the same conclusions. Organic conservatism, although often unheard, long has recognized the existence of close relationships between the character of economic organization, the social class structure, and political power and purposes. Seeing such linkages, organic conservatism seeks to guard the property and prerogatives of the upper class in order that their talents might be applied to governing. Both forms of conservatism concur, of course, that the United States currently is threatened by excessive and unjust leveling. Because personal incentives appear to be artificially low, people are not as unequal as their natural talents warrant, and progress is thus endangered. Political power either lies with, or is responsive to, the desires of masses of people. Consequently, government intervention in the economy is too frequent or unwise in some cases and not sufficiently firm in other matters.

With the exception of reform liberalism's modest sense of linkage and organic conservatism's nearly negligible voice, the dominant ideologies uniformly maintain a view of economics, society, and politics as separate spheres. By thus compartmentalizing, they go a long way towards assuring that those subject to their influence will not see power as concentrated in a relatively few hands. Where one looks at only one area at a time, any similarities among those at the top of *each* area will go unnoticed, and many centers of power will appear to exist at the middle ranges within each area. In short, compartmentalization fosters pluralist images of power and process.

To varying degrees, however, the other ideologies conceive social reality in more integrated terms. Some make the link between economics and politics in quite a direct fashion. They focus explicitly on the economic and social sources of political power. For example, Marxism rests on the basic postulate that the character of economic organization shapes the social class structure and strongly affects political power and purposes. The others show awareness of this unexceptional social fact only occasionally. Minorities and women readily identify the different dimensions of racism and sexism, and they forcefully point out that these matters are not economic, social, or moral issues unfit for political action. They see wealth either in the hands of whites or males generally, or at least as available to them. And they see this wealth denied to all but a few individual minorities or women and as a group. But they do not go beyond this group-based differentiation to analyze the distribution of wealth within white or male society except in a few instances; for the most part, they accept the capitalist-liberal image of middle-class distribution as correct. Political power is perceived in much the same way. While they recognize that power is not evenly distributed among whites or males, they think of white or male groups as being able to achieve their goals in accordance with the liberal image. But when it comes to seeking *their* special goals, all of white male society coalesces and, in effect, forms a unified power structure to oppose them.

The new left sees many illustrations of poverty, inequality, and racism and, unlike reform liberalism, finds them caused by basic structural features of the American system and the values that accompany it. Uncontrolled corporate concentrations are arrogantly shaping the social and political conditions of the United States as their profit-seeking needs require. Political power has been effectively removed from the people by bureaucratization and institutional imperviousness as well as by the determination of the establishment to effectuate its special version of economic and political necessity. The established political processes not only are not working, but they are essentially diversionary means of preventing people from gaining their desired ends.

Socialism sees even further class divisions arising from faulty structure, with an inevitable worsening of inequalities between rich and poor. Political power lies with the economically based ruling class, which uses the state exclusively for its selfish purposes.

It should be clear from this comparison of world views that there is a further distinction to be drawn concerning the approaches taken by the various ideologies. This is the *level of causation* or the *frame of reference* with which the ideology understands events and processes. Capitalism and liberalism, perhaps because of their compartmentalized approach and their focus on the individual, tend to find such explanations in the decisions of individuals. If certain corporations prosper, or particular policies are followed by the government, the causes lie in the decisions made by a few people, or by many people together. Analysis of their interests, personalities, and interaction would probably explain why they acted that way.

Reform liberalism is somewhat more sensitive to regular patterns in such decisions, patterns that recur over time regardless of the people who make them. It therefore looks for characteristics shared by such people or aspects of the institutions in which the decisions are made that might explain their consistent actions. It finds such explanations in the ideology held by key individuals or the circumstances in which they operate, including the tendency of subordinates to report what superiors want to hear, the difficulty of getting accurate information to the President, the President's dependence on military advisers, the impotency of Congress, and the apathy of the people.

The other ideologies move even farther from an individual focus toward a still deeper, more structural analysis. They do not believe that mistakes, faulty information, or inefficient institutional arrangements are the causes of today's deplorable situation. They look for explanations in the basic values of the society or in the imperatives of the economic system because they see the political system as functioning entirely in accord with those fundamental forces. Regardless of the individuals or institutions involved, policies and practices would be essentially the same. They disagree as to whether the economic system is the first cause (socialism) or whether self-perpetuating cultural values are an independent factor (minority liberation and the early new left). But they share the conviction that one cannot explain the American system and its actions by looking at the behavior of individuals abstracted from the broad total context in which they act. By implication, neither would it be possible to correct the ills of the society without reaching to such basic causes.

(2) CONTENDING VALUES

In earlier chapters, we made much of the tension within the dominant ideologies over definitions of equality and the relative priorities assigned to several natural rights, including property rights and civil rights, and particularly to equality. This property-equality tension often is seen as the principal dynamic of American political development. Clearly, it is a source of divergence today between reform liberalism, liberalism, capitalism, and conservatism.

Capitalism and conservatism would define equality principally in terms of formal opportunities such as the availability of university education for qualified and motivated youths. It would place property at the top of its priorities, but it would acknowledge its obligation to contribute to the support of those who were less successful. Liberalism defines equality in a broader scope, extending it to cover more of the reality of opportunity. For example, it would recognize that there are cultural, social, *and* financial obstacles to providing university education for large proportions of the population on a truly universal basis. In spite of its commitment to property rights, it would try to serve the needs of equality wherever practical.

Reform liberalism, operating with a broader and more contextual sensitivity to problems, might define equality in this case in terms of the actual mixture of students attending universities. A disproportionate representation of the wealthier strata would demonstrate the inequality of opportunity. To the extent that equality can be provided under established procedures (defined as equality of condition or "human rights"), it should be given coequal status with the still valid principle of property rights.

By contrast, minorities and, to some extent, women would accept no other claim as legitimate if it prevented realization of the long delayed goals of racial and sexual equality. The new left and Marxism would deny the possibility of actually realizing either racial equality or their communitarian, humanistic versions of equality as long as individualism and property rights continued as major contending values. These two ideologies as well as some minority ideologies deliberately pose the ideal of community against the traditional commitment to individualism. They insist that people have goals that are higher than and ethically superior to mere material satisfaction and infinite self-aggrandizement. Among these goals are aesthetic enjoyment, creative use of leisure time, awakening to new dimensions of interpersonal relationships, and the fulfillment that comes from sharing and helping others. With pressures removed, the human personality might develop new emotional and creative capacity and ultimately reach new levels of social achievement. In short, life could be converted from a struggle to serenity.

Clearly, some sharp differences in assumptions concerning the nature of man lie behind this basic contrast of values and goals. Are people, by nature, egoistic, competitive, and aggressive, as nearly all of these ideologies assume? Or are they by nature cooperative and rendered competitive only by the teachings of a capitalist value system and its artificial scarcities, as some of the new left, some minorities, and socialists assume? In either case, could their circumstances be so modified and their growth so encouraged as to develop a truly fraternal community where freedom, justice, and equality might be realized? The revival of a sense of utopianism in the latter ideologies has challenged the "realism" of the dominant ideologies, asserting that their pessimistic view of the nature of man is no more than a component of their ideology, one intended to justify the economic system and political constraints that they favor. The rise of this challenge explains the recent convergence between libertarian individualists (and some individualist-conservatives) and anarchist factions of the new left. Both deny the validity of centralization, bureaucratization, and greater power in the corporate state, arguing that man's true nature can be realized only when external restraints and pressures are lifted from him. The fewer the rules, the more human and cooperative man will become.

Related to this divergence is a less visible question about the nature of rulership in modern society. Is man inevitably to be ruled by some elite, either because of societal complexity, the need for expertise, or the sheer problem of scale? If this is unavoidable, as most capitalists, liberals, organic conservatives, and reform liberals would say, then the question becomes one of which elite is best under all the circumstances. A number of fairly technical and familiar issues arise, and much institutional tinkering ensues. But if genuine mass-based democracy is possible, as some minorities, the new left, and socialism argue it is, a whole new range of questions is opened. What are the conditions, the size, and the character of organizations, the protections against elite dominance, and so forth that make this possible? Even more crucial: how can masses be persuaded of this possibility, then enabled to achieve it? In the eyes of most change-oriented ideologies, masses are now managed by elites and are subject to their ideological and physical dominance. What tactics are justified in order to make possible a genuine mass-based democracy? Specifically, should (must) masses be "forced to be free" by some vanguard group in view of their inability to realize real freedom from their currently deprived and repressed conditions? If so, can such an action be honestly distinguished from the masses' prior captivity by some other elite? The issue of whether a believer in mass-based democracy can justify elite-accomplished change to such a system is of course one of the enduring dilemmas of politics. Much evil has been done in the name of laudable ends, and most are alert to this danger. Much evil is done under present conditions, they note, and the calculus as to which route would be better for the mass of the population may be very close.

(3) CHANGE: HOW MUCH, AND HOW?

Many conflicting prescriptions for the kind of change required and the manner in which it should be brought about are embodied in these ideologies. At first, it might seem that the more drastic the change sought, the more radical the measures that would be endorsed to do so. But this does not necessarily follow in all cases. Some ideologies may have internal inconsistencies, their world views may tell them that the conditions are not yet right for transformation of the society, or their values may prevent them from taking steps that might seem logically implied in their world views and goals. As a means of exploring the complexity of prescriptions concerning change, we will first return to our distinction between reform and revolution and then employ other means of contrast and evaluation.

Reform involves modest extensions or adjustments of the basic values of the society and is carried out within the general political framework and without substantially altering established patterns of wealth, status, and power. Revolution implies major alteration or outright replacement of basic values and fundamental change in economic, social and political structures. Such sweeping changes may occur more or less peacefully, but often they require sustained violent upheaval; the timing of such upheaval, however, may be a matter of disagreement among revolutionaries. Thus, reform and revolution are distinguished not only by the scope of change sought, but also by the kind of process through which it is sought.

These two dimensions of difference serve to point up some of the crucial distinctions of change-seeking ideologies. Including reform liberalism for purposes of comparison, we find some sharp contrasts between them. The new left and socialism not only redefine and reorder priorities among familiar values, but also give humanitarian and communitarian values first priority and drop such standbys as property rights, individualism, and materialism. The steps they would take to expunge racism also imply severe reconstruction of values. The class structure, too, would be sharply altered in the direction of egalitarianism. The consequences of all changes for the character of the capitalist economic system are clear: it is to be replaced by some form of socialism.

Minority and women's liberation ideologies differ over what

should be the scope of change and for whom. The integrationists and some others focus chiefly on racism and sexism and on the social and economic conditions of minorities and women in the context of the existing economy. While the value change involved for white males presumably would be the elimination of racism and sexism, this change would be less drastic for men than for minorities and women, whose entire life situation is affected by racism and/or sexism. In this sense, the integrationists seek revolutionary change for minorities and women, but something less than that for whites and males. Some minorities, and a minority of women, by contrast, call for changes in *everybody's* values. They ask not for the extension of the good things of white male society to minorities and women, but for a radically reconstituted society. In many respects, they seek the same changes endorsed by the new left and socialism. Reform liberalism, on the other hand, justifies our characterization by seeking the solution to problems through implementing familiar values within the existing economic, social, and political systems. Neither reform liberalism nor integrationists can be called revolutionary.

Much the same pattern of distinction applies to the strategies of change endorsed by these ideologies, although in this regard, there is greater diversity within each general category. Some components of the new left, some black groups, and some socialists believe that violent upheaval will be necessary to accomplish their goals. But they disagree sharply as to the timing, the nature of alliances required, and the method of accomplishing the upheaval. For some, immediate efforts are essential to incite repression, destroy complacency, and build support. Others, probably a majority, insist that a period of organizing among students, workers, blacks, and other deprived groups must precede any serious effort to seize power. Some elements of each still hold to an image of a relatively peaceful (but protest- and riot-studded) process of change, either through the drastic transformation of values or the collapse of capitalism because of its inherent problems. On the other hand, all reform liberals and integrationists and some socialists believe that full-scale violent upheaval is unjustifiable, impossible, or ultimately self-defeating. They cling to the established procedures and a number of pressure-maximizing embellishments with varying degrees of reluctance. Once again, the distinction between reform and revolution is clear, although in some cases, it separates individuals within ideologies. Revolutionaries are those who have reached the point of believing that peaceful, within-the-system methods of change cannot achieve their essential goals. Therefore, they accept the necessity of whatever level of force is required.

The point of this analysis is not to show that there are inconsistencies among individuals or divisions within ideologies—or even that only some qualify for the label of "revolutionary" in both its dimensions—but to illustrate the normally close link between the level at which an ideology explains the nature of the political world, the character of its central value commitments, and its strategy of change. Inconsistencies among these components carry implications for the viability of the ideology itself. For example, the attractiveness of reform liberalism is reduced for some (and paradoxically increased for others) by the fact that it accompanies a near-fundamental critique of American problems, practices, and values with a quite orthodox, self-limiting set of within-the-system prescriptions. One may feel justified in logically concluding that either the problems are not as bad as reform liberalism describes them or the remedies urged are incapable of solving them.

(4) THE ROLE OF VIOLENCE IN THE PROCESS OF CHANGE

As we suggested earlier, violence is often a focusing agent for ideologies' value reactions. Dominant ideologies tend to view non-official violence, whatever the provocation or justification, as inherently wrong and always punishable. Change-seeking ideologies are more likely to see violence as justifiable counter-violence, a response to continuing official violence (in recent years, the Vietnam war, racism, or police repression). We have noted that dispassionate analysis and value judgment about the *propriety* of violence should be contextual rather than automatic. For example, value judgments about violence should consider the contending ideological perspectives from which participants view it, the human costs that violence carries with it, the current balance of equities (power, wealth, deprivation, and so forth) between the parties, and the prospects that violence will render that balance any more justifiable afterwards. In this way, at least some greater rationality—and less ideological triggering—will be brought to bear on the judgment.

But in this section, our question is pragmatic and not value-oriented. We are concerned about the *utility* of violence, and about how ideologies resolve the question of whether (and if so, where and when) violence may be productive of desired results. Clearly, change is not likely to occur without *some* violence. Our history teaches that lesson well, from the Revolution and the Civil War to the labor and civil rights movements. Nevertheless, each ideology understands the utility of violence distinctively, some transcending it and others embracing it. Reform liberalism, for example, denies its utility under all circumstances. Perhaps this is the result of reform liberalism's strong commitment to the established procedures, but it also reflects the view that great danger lies in the powerful reaction from the right that violence is sure to provoke. This reaction is seen as inevitable, very powerful, and probably destructive of the many good qualities of the existing system; in short, the veneer of civilization is very thin and easily removed.

Minority liberation and the new left have a more ambivalent view of violence. One of the advantages of nonviolence as a direct action technique lies in the way in which it plays on the prospect of provoking violence. If other citizens employ or seem about to employ violence, local authorities may be forced to aid protestors and perhaps even grant their demands in order to avoid bloodshed. If the authorities themselves resort to violence, nationwide public reaction to the spectacle could be an incalculable aid to the cause. In recent years, protests and demonstrations that carry the clear possibility of erupting to violence have seemed to be a means of both mobilizing support and of persuading policy-makers that they must grant demands. Unplanned ghetto riots have been used after the fact to bolster the force of black demands. For most minorities, the threat of violence is a major tool for loosening white society's hold on them.

The actual use of deliberate violence is seen by only a few elements of the new left and by minority ideologies as a productive tactic in the current context. Where there are no other effective ways to make opposition known or to apply pressure, violence may be the only means available to attract public attention to existing evils. It may serve as a vehicle for radicalizing individual participants (few see the American system in the same way as they saw it before a police clubbing or a night in jail), for revealing the "true nature" of the (repressive) system, or for attracting wider support from liberals who react against excessive police actions. It may simply harass and soften officials or other elites, who may then be willing to change nonessential policies in order to prevent further conflict and/or social disintegration.

In each of these cases, there is an attempt at rational calculation of the odds in which the risks of repression, backlash, and misunderstanding are weighed against potential returns. (Often, of course, what is planned as a peaceful demonstration is converted into violence by a single provocative act or by the rigidity of officials. We are speaking here only of *deliberate* uses of violence.) But, in the process of calculating the utility of deliberate violence, the lack of alternatives is an important factor. Where competing in elections seems futile and there is no hope of creating a favorable image through the mass media, there is no sense in considering the impact of violence except on the target populations—sometimes public officials but more often potential allies in the path to revolution. Workers or other minorities, the most likely allies, are the groups whose reactions are most important, and violence counter to their interests or understanding usually is avoided except under provocation.

Revolutionary socialists are more likely to embrace violence in the indefinite future than in current practice. Most envision a period of violence at some point in the future, either when capitalism collapses in chaos or when the cohesive revolutionary movement succeeds in overthrowing it. In the first case, there will be a period when right-wing groups contend for power and must be thrust aside; in the latter, a more sustained period of revolutionary effort will be required to achieve control of the entire nation. But these occasions are not yet near, and for the moment, the task is to organize workers and other deprived groups and to prepare for the future struggle. Violence now, under current conditions of weakness, usually is seen as counter-productive in that it calls down severe repression, makes organizing more difficult, and creates unnecessary hysteria.

Some socialists and most of the women's and minority liberation movements reject violence completely. They view it much as do reform liberals: either as unjustifiable in the presence of civil liberties or inevitably counter-productive.

In seeking to understand the utility of violence in concrete situations, ideologies must estimate its consequences at various levels. Violence has obvious physical consequences in which people are killed or injured and property is destroyed. It has deeper effects as well, because death and destruction shift the world views, values, and political loyalties of people—perhaps moving the range of possibility sharply one way or the other. Over time, repeated violence may lead officials to far greater degrees of change than they otherwise would have considered or to the defensive surveillance, preventive detention, and harassment equivalent to a police state. In the latter case, it is often argued on the left, more people come to see the need for revolution; by that time, of course, their prospective leaders may all be dead, in jail, or underground.

Note that the change-seeking ideologies develop a calculus or balance of costs and benefits of any act of deliberate violence by weighing it objectively *from the perspective of a theory of revolution,* not in terms of probable success under the standards of orthodox American political practices. The revolutionary left rejects the established procedures and knows that its goals are not attainable within the American system as presently constituted. In its eyes, it is building a process of revolution that may take some time to reach fruition but that *will* happen at some future point. The only relevant questions to be asked under such conditions are whether new allies have been gained or made more open to persuasion; whether the resolve of existing members has been heightened; whether officials have lost confidence in their capacity to control events; and whether the general public has come to see a wider range of possibilities for the future—including, of course, sheer chaos. For the new left, it would be well worth converting two apathetic supporters into equally apathetic opponents if one strongly committed new recruit could be gained in the process.

The risks of building deliberate violence into the political process are, of course, very great. Many can take part in that type of politics, and throughout American history, they have—usually against those who sought change. The modern society is highly vulnerable to bombings, attacks on municipal facilities, assassinations, kidnappings, and other violent acts. Such acts appear to justify the surveillance and repression that fearful officials employ in response. Although repression probably does build consciousness of the need for change, in the ordinary course of events, it is more likely to eventuate in entrenched fascism than in the change desired. Thus, the stakes in the use of violence are high, and one may well come full circle back to reform liberalism's recognition of the purposes served by the established civil liberties and other procedures.

(5) THE RELATIVE PARTS PLAYED BY ELITES AND MASSES

Neither ideologies nor movements spring fully formed from the minds of millions; at some point, they are always initiated by a small number of thinkers and activists. It is not the original source or the number of current advocates that characterizes an ideology as elite or mass based, but rather the substance of the ideology itself—the roles it allocates for elites and masses in various ways. Sometimes, the commitments are clear in the category of values and goals. The participatory democracy commitment of the new left is a clear illustration of a mass-oriented goal. In sharp contrast to, for example, conservatism, forms of participation from the grass roots play a major part in new left thinking. At other times, these commitments may become clear from the process of change that an ideology prescribes. Some images of the process of change are clearly more mass-based than others. Again, the new left component that sees change emerging from the broad dissemination of the values of the young "counter-culture," for example, is readily distinguishable from Galbraith's allocation of responsibility for change to the scientific and technological experts.

In general, change-oriented ideologies are forced to become more mass-based than those that are dominant. This occurs for communitarians and democrats partly by definition: the reason why change is needed is that there are unfulfilled needs, recognized or unrecognized, on the part of numbers of people. It also rests on pragmatism: because the machinery of the state is controlled by *some* elite, which wants to retain its power and status, an opposing ideology is induced to turn to the masses as a means of mobilizing an alternative source of power. Dominant ideologies, firmly entrenched in power, may be primarily concerned with justifying their acts. Though they may do so on the grounds that such policies serve mass needs or preferences, they are likely to insist that their acts are correct or necessary in the absolute sense, and regardless of the masses' views.

But even granting this practical pressure to assert a mass

basis, some ideologies are clearly more oriented toward mass decision-making and control than others are. There are substantial
differences in the respective roles assigned to elites and masses, both
in the system of government that is their goal and in the process of
change by which it is to be reached. In regard to the ultimate form
of governing sought, for example, reform liberalism does not raise
fundamental questions about the present relatively elite-centered
system. The elaborate checks, balances, institutional independence,
and hierarchical structure of American politics effectively insulates
decision-makers from much popular pressure and removes real
power from masses to a relatively small set of elites. Reform liberalism either accepts this as inevitable or views it as desirable; essentially, its prescriptions call for better actions—wiser policies—on the
part of responsible elites. Minority and women's liberation move toward a more important role for mass preferences, at least as far as
they are concerned. But essentially, they call for active participation
on an equal basis with whites and males—that all should be fairly
represented in the familiar and ongoing American governmental
structure. Both the new left and socialism, on the other hand, assert
their commitment to a much broader role for masses in the ultimate
economic, social, and political order to be created. Decentralization
and popular control in both the workplace and the polity are fundamental elements of these ideologies.

In regard to the process of change by which such goals are to
be attained, the distinctions become more particularized. Reform
liberalism sees a crucial role for the nation's universities. Either
through the quality of social analysis and prescription offered policy-
makers by academics or through the values communicated by them
to the rising managerial elite, new policies will be generated and,
in time, the political preferences of the mass public will be reshaped
toward better goals. Beginning with a relatively small elite focus,
in other words, reform liberalism sees an ever-widening set of consequences emerging from the progressive values and goals generated
by educators. Although it probably reaches this position more from
a lack of alternatives than from any demonstrable basis for optimism
in the present character of the American university, reform liberalism
does thereby present a consistent image of elite-generated, mass-
supported change. Minority liberation, again, has a larger immediate
role for (minority) masses, who are to act in solidarity with their

leaders in ways that will force the larger system's policy-makers and ultimately, the entire white society to grant them fully equal status.

For the new left and socialism, the role of the masses in accomplishing change is more problematical. Although nearly all subideologies agree that masses are to play a major role in the system of government ultimately erected, they disagree on the extent to which change should be mass-based, and even more over the timing of mass participation. The concept of "mass" itself, it should be noted, presents opportunities for differences. Clearly, it need not mean majorities, but distinguishing mass participation from that of a moderately large elite may amount essentially to a value judgment. Some components of both ideologies hold that no major efforts to acquire power can or should be made until the movement is strong enough to have a real chance for success, by which presumably is meant a substantial and strategically located mass base. Few advocates of either ideology adhere to coup d'etat theories of change or to seizure of power by any small group, except as an incitement to further action by many others. But there are many and bitter disagreements over the precise number and character of supporters necessary to begin the revolution and over the best means of organizing them for that purpose. Furthermore, what begins as action by a minuscule elite may mushroom into a mass action under the right conditions—as nearly happened (in the eyes of these ideologies) in France in 1968. Again, most subideologies in these two categories believe that conditions are not yet right for such actions in the United States, but there is no consensus on what the necessary conditions are, when they will be reached, or how.

The change-seeking ideologies are thus faced with a very large and difficult problem: what route toward change (a) offers real chance of achieving essential goals, (b) is possible under contemporary conditions, *and* (c) is consistent with the ideology's value commitments? The dilemma can be cruel, and the temptation to suspend one or another value commitment *or* much-desired goal may become very strong. We may note, at least, that the definition of what is possible under contemporary conditions is a question that continually is subject to shifting answers. What looks impossible at one moment may seem routinely attainable the next; in many respects, the range of the possible is a product of one's imagination and intensity of desire to make something happen. The limits of the possible are not found exclusively in objective conditions, but also in the hopes—and fears—of people.

Ideological Conflict: Are the Differences Significant?

Earlier, we raised the question of whether there really were significant differences between the change-seeking and the dominant ideologies and whether the change-seekers were outside the dominant system of thought or consciousness. Why is this such an important question? To begin with, it provides a productive intellectual framework and perspective to understand and compare the basic elements of ideologies and their frameworks. Most important in practical terms for our present purposes, it is central to the issue of the actual scope and level of change that are sought by various nominally change-seeking ideologies. Ideologies that appear to be in direct opposition to capitalism-liberalism, but turn out to be made up of the same ingredients and/or contained within the same system of thought under a careful analysis are not likely in the long run to contribute to significant social change. Let us try to answer the second part of our question before we undertake the first.

By "the dominant system of thought" we mean capitalism-liberalism extended and deepened, expanded comprehensively to incorporate the language, concepts, logic, premises, assumptions, and other tools of thinking generally available to people in the society. Ideologies that accepted the basic outlines of the existing capitalist economic system as enduring or assumed that the social structure essentially would not change would be totally within the dominant capitalist-liberal system of thought. But so would ideologies that adopted the same key values of individualism, competitiveness, materialism, and so forth, seeking only marginal alterations in such priority rankings as the relationship of property and equality. And ideologies that sought to make capitalism-liberalism live up to its ideals, those that sought *inclusion within the existing social order* and *improved distribution of its benefits,* rather than a new social order based on different values also would be included. Finally, ideologies that employed the conceptual tools, logic, and language of capitalism-liberalism also would be within the dominant system because they would be trapped by such usage within their confines (and, of course, ultimately led back to capitalism-liberalism, no matter how hard they tried to frame new goals, for that very reason).

What would it take to go beyond the system of thought that is so completely suffused by capitalism-liberalism and reigns so completely in the United States? In simple terms, it would require not a reordering of values, but the complete rejection of many traditional values and the inclusion of new and unfamiliar values in their place. It would require not the assumption of continuity of the existing economic and social systems or even the projection of a future based on extending the outlines of those present systems, but the vision of a totally different economic and social order with a wholly new structure, purposes, and procedures. In more complex terms, it would require a new manner of thinking, new concepts, new language in some respects, a new capacity to imagine the future; in short, it would require new intellectual paradigms, criteria, premises and expectations. Probably it would require new social organizations of like-minded people, deliberately forcing themselves to develop and maintain such a new system of thought despite the powerful effects of the existing system with which they are fully surrounded.

Where amongst our contending ideologies do we find indications of such characteristics? We have noted again and again that reform liberalism is just that—liberalism; it offers only the most modest variation from the existing social order and belief system. Most representatives of minority liberation and women's liberation ideologies seek only inclusion within the existing systems on an equal footing with whites and males, in effect the realization of the traditional values and ideals for all. Democratic socialists also work from premises broadly shared within the society, and they try to speed up what they see as an ongoing process of expanding distribution of welfare state benefits. Most new left "radicals" also appear to carry forward many familiar values, assumptions, and approaches. The anarchist and counter-culture variants emphasize individualism, localism, and laissez faire; they mount little or no challenge to the existing economic and social systems.

It is evident that there are very few strains within the contemporary American ideological spectrum that show signs of having or developing a really new and different consciousness. Some elements within the minority liberation category such as certain black nationalists, some Chicanos, and the American Indians do have distinctively different value systems and thought patterns. Nevertheless, for just this reason, they appear to be turned inward at present, to be engaged primarily in trying to preserve their ways against the pressures mounted by capitalism-liberalism. Even slimmer strains within the women's liberation movement are seeking to build on wholly different premises and to envision a completely reconstructed society in which sexual roles would be drastically changed. For the most part, however, they do so with the current capitalist-liberal logic, assumptions, and thought processes. With the exception of the single dimension of sex, their consciousness is much closer to the dominant one than are the minorities just mentioned. Within revolutionary socialism, there are signs of deliberate efforts to develop and sustain a new consciousness, one that would permit broad-scale transcendence of the limits of capitalism-liberalism. But these groups remain small and at least at present isolated; moreover, their very distinctiveness makes it difficult for others to understand what they are saying.

Thus, we must conclude that contemporary ideological conflicts are taking place for the most part among contenders that employ essentially the same tools. Capitalism-liberalism is being attacked by its own first cousins, using its own premises and values and challenging it to live up to its promises as a social order. Very few voices are being raised from perspectives that would promise a significantly different social order or fundamentally altered purposes and quality of life.

This conclusion again emphasizes the powerful grip of orthodox ideologies in the United States. It also suggests that these orthodoxies are grounded deeply in unconscious thought patterns and habits, and that the latter are so much a part of the way in which Americans view the world that they are almost unable (under ordinary circumstances) even to imagine really different alternatives. The urge to "be realistic" or "practical" about the kinds of change that can be accomplished follows this point directly: if we always begin from our present understanding of the "is" and insist on only those changes that appear attainable based on that image, we shall probably always remain within the range of contemporary capitalism-liberalism. Thus, ideological conflict in the United States takes place within a relatively narrow band of the possible (or, to the rest of the world, real) spectrum of political alternatives. Our arguments are between the slightly left version of capitalism-liberalism and the slightly right version of capitalism-liberalism.

But this does not mean that the conflicts generated are less bitter, less dangerous, or less likely to provoke disruption of the society. Just because normally we are not confronted by ideas that are really different, we may be more shocked and react more drastically when we are. Or vast stakes may be involved in the contests between the left and right variants of capitalism-liberalism, and some may be ready to do whatever is necessary to defend their presumed rights against any change, however minimal in real terms. Moreover, very deep-seated social problems that exist in the United States show no signs of either going away or being solved. We really do not need the many writings of sociologists and anthropologists to tell us that we are experiencing continuing social fragmentation or deepening strains in the basic social fabric. This conflict seems likely to grow more and more serious as the 1970s wear on.

Nor is this necessarily an undesirable result. There is little we can do now to change the fact that we have real problems and on-going social fragmentation. Ideological conflict at least provides some representation for people who sense these problems and do not accept the soothing reassurances of the dominant ideologies. It forces confrontations with alternative ways of doing things, and permits choices of sorts. If there were no such ideological conflict, if people generally sought to avoid ideological involvement, the result would be continued triumph of orthodox capitalism-liberalism. Those who insist on avoiding ideological positions are in practical terms opting for whatever "solutions" would otherwise be provided by capitalism-liberalism. There is no such thing as nonideological thinking or decision-making: *all* thinking or decision-making reflects *some* ideological premises and goals, particularly in the United States where capitalism-liberalism is so completely dominant that it has become the unconscious "natural" way of thinking for so many people. To avoid ideology in this context simply is to avoid alternatives to capitalism-liberalism.

What can ordinary people do? It would be easy to say, as so many textbooks do, that they should become involved in political participation in some way. Most books add, if only implicitly:

within the capitalist-liberal system. We are at this point too sensitive to the ideological quality of any such exhortation to end on such a note. We urge only that people use their experience in the analysis of ideologies to free themselves from whatever intellectual constraints they are now under, long enough to become independent— to see the limits of vision to which they are subject, and then to think and act for themselves as they see fit. It is crucial that each person develop an independent and autonomous mind capable of understanding, choosing, and acting. But it is easy to devote too much time to that cause and thereby to avoid confrontation with the realities of life in a time of crisis. And there is very little time. We hope it will be well used.

Annotated Bibliography

Brink, William, and Louis Harris. *Black and White*. New York: Simon and Schuster, 1968. Opinion studies of blacks and whites, showing stark differences.

Cantril, Albert H., and Charles W. Roll, Jr. *Hopes and Fears of the American People*. New York: Universe Books, 1971. A brief but current and provocative report on the attitudes of Americans as gleaned from a special public opinion survey.

Domhoff, William. *Who Rules America?* Englewood Cliffs, N.J.: Prentice-Hall, 1967. A brief analysis concluding that the United States is governed by a permanent upper class.

Free, Lloyd A., and Hadley Cantril. *The Political Beliefs of Americans*. New York: Simon and Schuster, 1968. Full-length analysis, though at a relatively superficial level, of the political attitudes of the general population.

Graham, Hugh Davis, and Ted Robert Gurr. *Violence in America*. New York: Signet Books, 1969. Historical and comparative perspectives on violence in the United States, showing its continuing role.

Kolko, Gabriel. *Wealth and Power in America*. New York: Praeger, 1968. Empirical study showing degree of inequality and permanence of this pattern in the U.S.

Lane, Robert E. *Political Ideology: Why the Common Man Believes What He Does*. Glencoe, Ill.: Free Press, 1962. Depth study of fifteen working men, arguing that there is a "fear of equality" among ordinary people.

Lasch, Christopher. *The Agony of the American Left.* New York: Vintage Books, 1969. Excellent analysis, not unsympathetic, of the intellectual and other problems facing the radical in the United States.

Lens, Sidney. *Radicalism in America.* New York: Crowell, 1966. Good basic history.

Mitchell, William C. *Why Vote?* Chicago: Markham, 1971. A brief and optimistic argument for participation in electoral politics.

Terkel, Studs. *Hard Times.* New York: Avon Books, 1971. An excellent oral history, spoken by people who passed through the depression of the 1930s, about what that period was like and how they reacted politically.

Young, Alfred F., ed. *Dissent: The History of Radicalism in America.* DeKalb, Ill.: Northern Illinois University Press, 1962. Useful collection of articles and lectures about various radical movements and their problems in gaining their goals.